Moon
in the
Darkness

100 Reflections on the Kingdom of God

Doug Tweed

WESTBOW
PRESS®
A DIVISION OF THOMAS NELSON
& ZONDERVAN

Unless otherwise indicated, all Scripture quotations are from the ESV Bible (*The Holy Bible, English Standard Version*), copyright © 2001 by Crossway, a publishing ministry of Good News Publishers. Used by permission. All rights reserved.

Scripture quotations marked (AB) are taken from *The Amplified Bible*, copyright © 1954, 1958, 1962, 1964, 1965, 1987 by The Lockman Foundation. Used by permission (www.Lockman.org).

Scripture quotations marked (NASB) are taken from the *New American Standard Bible*, copyright © 1960, 1962, 1968, 1971, 1972, 1973, 1975, 1977, 1995 by The Lockman Foundation. Used by permission (www.Lockman.org).

Scripture quotations marked (NIV) are from the *Holy Bible, New International Version®*, copyright © 1973, 1978, 1984 by International Bible Society. Used by permission of Zondervan. All rights reserved worldwide.

Scripture quotations marked (NKJV) are taken from the New King James Version. Copyright © 1982 by Thomas Nelson. Used by permission. All rights reserved.

Scripture quotations marked (NLT) are taken from the *Holy Bible, New Living Translation*, copyright © 1996, 2004, 2007, 2013 by Tyndale House Foundation. Used by permission of Tyndale House Publishers, Inc., Carol Stream, IL 60188. All rights reserved.

Scripture quotations marked (NRSV) are from the New Revised Standard Version Bible, copyright © 1989, National Council of the Churches of Christ in the United States of America. Used by permission. All rights reserved.

WestBow Press books may be ordered through booksellers or by contacting:

WestBow Press
A Division of Thomas Nelson & Zondervan
1663 Liberty Drive
Bloomington, IN 47403
www.westbowpress.com
1 (866) 928-1240

ISBN: 978-1-4908-8278-9 (sc)
ISBN: 978-1-4908-8279-6 (hc)
ISBN: 978-1-4908-8277-2 (e)
Library of Congress Control Number: 2015908851

Print information available on the last page.

WestBow Press rev. date: 06/29/2015

Contents

Introduction... xv

Reflections on Being a Disciple of Jesus 1
    Jesus Has Many "Believers" but Few Disciples 5
    We Need the Full Message of the New Life 8
    Be with Jesus, Be like Jesus, Be for Jesus 11
    Dive into The Deep End Of God 13
    Repentance May Be Your Missing Ingredient 16
    We Need Both the Blood and the Cross..............................19
    It Is Time to Evaluate Ourselves.................................... 22
    There Is a Better Way to Live.. 25
    Christians Need to Be "All In" 28

Reflections on Our Identity and Purpose in Christ.........................31
    Christ Died so He Could Live through Us...........................35
    Christ Must Increase—"I" Must Decrease........................ 38
    Embrace Your Full Relationship with Christ........................41
    Christ in Us—The Hope of Glory 44
    Holiness Is What We Need..47
    Know God's Purpose for Your Life................................ 50
    Born-Again Christians Are Supernatural! 53
    Are You a Son of God?.. 56
    The Royal Priesthood Must Arise 59
    God Measures Greatness in a Different Way 62
    We Must Stop Cursing and Start Blessing......................... 65
    Will You Hear the Lord Say, "Well Done?" 68

Reflections on the Church of Jesus Christ..71

The Church of Jesus—Some Assembly Required.....................75

The Church Must Return to the Formula That Works 78

You May Need to Tear Down to Build Up 81

Where's the Love? Where's the Power?....................................83

The Problem Is We Don't Love God...86

The Church Must Be Made Salty Again 89

The Church Must Rediscover the Bible.....................................92

We Must Yoke with Christ, Not Unbelievers...........................95

Standing Shoulder to Shoulder 98

The Light Shines when the Colors Come Together 101

A Chosen Race and Holy Nation...104

We Don't Know What We're Doing 106

The Church's Guiding Hand Needs All Five Fingers.............109

We Need the Folk Who Rock the Boat....................................112

If You're Happy and You Know It, Clap Your Hands 115

*Reflections on the Great Gifts of God: Love, Hope, Grace,
Faith, and Truth*..119

God Offers Just What You Need 123

God Made and Loves Us All 126

We Need a Better Understanding of God's Love.....................129

Live in the Love of God..132

Raising the Ceiling of Our Hope 135

Where Is the Mercy of God?..137

Thank God for His Amazing Grace! 140

Forgiveness Will Free You from the Anger That's
Killing You...143

Mustard Seed Faith 146

It's Not Theology—It's Reality! 148

God's Truth Is Not Whatever Floats Your Boat......................151

They Suppress the Truth and Offer Lies.................................154

Drink from God's Fountain, Not Broken Cisterns 157

Christians Have Only One Rabbi 160

Reflections on Marriage, Family, and Community 163

Love Your Loved Ones with God's Love 167

Divorce Is a Preventable Disease 170

The Devil's Strategy: Divide and Conquer 173

Mary Had a Spiritual Mother 176

God Is Good All the Time 179

Women are the Key to the Next Great Awakening 182

God Bless America, Land That I Love 186

Let's Get Disdain out of Our Politics 189

Serve This Country Like Our Veterans Served 192

Freedom and Independence Are Not the Same 195

Reflections on Revival and the Kingdom Coming 199

The Kingdom of God Is Still Near 203

Kingdom Problems Require Kingdom Solutions 206

Take Your Position in the Kingdom of God 209

Ask What You Can Do for His Kingdom 212

It Is Time to Fan Our Own Flame 215

God Cares How Much We Care 218

God Is Willing to Heal Us 221

An Enemy Too Long Ignored 224

We Must Learn to Cast Out Demons 227

The Lord Will Shake Things Up 230

God Will Lead Us into Righteousness 233

The River of Revival Runs through Us 236

Visions of What Revival Will Bring 239

Imagine God's Kingdom in our Community 242

Heaven and Earth Come Together 245

Reflections on Intimacy with God Through the Holy Spirit 249

Christ Prayed for Intimacy with You and Me 253

God's Most Important Gift to Us Is Himself 256

Jesus Says, "Come And See." 259

I Am Glad Jesus Left 262

The Lord Will Walk with You and Talk with You.................... 265

Sanctification Is an Inside Job 268

God Sent His Spirit to Lead Us, Not Just Help Us 271

Start Unwrapping Those Unopened Gifts 274

Partner in Life with the Holy Spirit 277

Reflections on Prayer 281

Enter into the Presence of the Lord 285

The People of God Need to Encounter God 288

Go to Your Tent of Meeting... 291

"Thank You" Is More Than Good Manners 293

We Need Some Desperate People to Pray 296

We Must Learn to Pray Together.. 299

Turn On the Power of Your Prayer Faucets 302

We Need More Watchmen on the Walls................................. 305

Join Us in a Declaration for Our Land.................................... 308

Special Reflections... 311

Otherland 315

The Deacon, the Child, and the Slave.................................... 319

Walkertown.. 322

Susie and Angelique 328

Enoch 332

A Christmas Diary.. 335

The Color of Church 337

This book is dedicated to my beautiful wife, Christie.

MOON IN THE DARKNESS

My Father, please make me a moon in the darkness
reflecting the light of Your Son;
and leave me no dark side,
no half-moon or half-truth,
that hampers Your will being done.
Let my service, through Your grace,
shift the tide of men's lives
and help draw them closer to You,
where Your love and Your light
will eclipse all their fears
and transform who they are, what they do.

My Father, please make me a star in Your heavens,
just one in a host of small sons;
with Your daughters, creating a great constellation
that sings of the victory won!
Let our lights be a guide
when men sail on Your sea
in the dark,' fore the morning's red sky.
Let them find the Safe Harbor
Who is marked by the cross,
and be saved from the storm 'ere they die.

My Father, please make me a part of the Body,
a part of the Christ now on earth—
an Aaron who helps others hold up Your prayer staff,
a clown who distributes Your mirth;
a carpenter restoring homes for the poor,
a fund-raiser collecting alms;
a disciple in service to people in need
of a love that left holes in His palms.

My Father, please make me Your lover forever,
more intimate each wondrous day;
sharing the truth of Your Word and Your works,
sharing the price that Christ pays;
sharing Your love with all people around me
that they might be Your lovers, too;
sharing my Jesus, my Father, my All
in a new world where all worship You!

My Father, please make me an Adam of love
who would never partake of that tree,
and make my wife Eve, who,
not tricked by the serpent,
abides in Your garden with me;
where we tend to Your creatures
and nurture Your plants,
and give birth by becoming one flesh.
The children are Yours!
It's a marriage of three—
love of God, man and woman that mesh.

My Father, please make me a flower ... a songbird ...
a beaver ... a tiger ... a tree ...
for reflecting Your Beauty,
for singing Your praise,
for work, war, or waiting on Thee.
I give You my life,
You give my life back,
perfect freedom for those who obey.
Use me! I thirst
For the rightness, the truth
that comes when I am what You say.

My Father, please make me whatever You will,
I ask it with all of my heart!
Let me move toward the oneness
that Christ prayed we'd have
where no one can tell us apart.
Let me speak of Your wonder
to all whom You love,
of a vastness far more than I know—
power bound by no rules
But Your wisdom and grace,
our faithlessness, our only foe.

My Father, please make me a moon in the darkness!
Please make me a star in Your sky!
Please make me the salt of Your world that preserves!
Please make me a love that won't die!
Please make me Your temple!
Please make me Your priest!
Please make me a man who will pray
every night, every day, for the rest of my life,
for those who don't choose to obey.

My Father!
My Jesus!
My Spirit!
My Life!
Please make me,
please make me, I pray,
to become all the things
I can be that will please You
on this and each following day.

Amen

Doug Tweed
1994

Introduction

Both this poem and this book deserve an introduction, which in turn requires a brief snapshot of the author. In 1996, J. Ellsworth Kalas, a wonderful preacher, teacher, and author, introduced me to the concept of "soul preaching"—God's story coming through my story into your story. My prayer is that this poem and book will be "soul writing."

My sister, Janet, and I were military brats—Dad was a career marine aviator—so we moved often. But wherever we moved, we were always raised in a loving home by two wonderful parents. Mom and Dad were married sixty-two years, and at the time of this writing, Dad is ninety-four and still with us: a decorated veteran of World War II, Korea, and Vietnam. There are not many like him left.

Both of my parents were Christian, and they made sure, at least until our high school years, that my sister and I were raised in church. I responded to an altar call in my maternal grandfather's country Baptist church at the age of nine. But like so many other people who respond to an altar call, I was never discipled. By the age of seventeen, I had drifted away from any focus on faith as a guidepost for life.

I struggled for a few rebellious years in college as a "child of the sixties" before settling into pursuit of what I understood to be the American man's dream: beautiful wife and children, professional and material success, recreational sports and early retirement. My path included law school and five years as a US Marine JAG attorney before joining a prominent law firm in a small city called Kingsport, Tennessee. In a relatively short time, I achieved much of what I was pursuing.

But it didn't make me happy, and the continued failure of that dream to make me happy left me frustrated and confused.

I wrestled with alternating bouts of stress and depression, abused alcohol, and became more and more self-centered in my relationships, particularly with my family. I felt alone, misunderstood, and unloved—the classic symptoms of the deplorable condition called self-pity. And I had no answer for my problem.

Then, at the request of a close friend, I went on a Christian spiritual retreat called the Walk to Emmaus. It started Thursday, October 31, 1991, and ended Sunday, November 3, 1991. On Friday afternoon, God turned my life right side up!

During a break in the retreat, all alone in the midst of seventy men, I called out to God for help. I finally knew I couldn't help myself. The finger of God went through me, and I knew in that moment that God is exactly who He says He is. His Son Jesus did exactly what He says He did. The Bible is exactly what it says it is. God is near. God understands. God loves me, and has always loved me, with an everlasting love.

There were some shock waves when a radically changed Doug returned home to my wife, Christie, and my two daughters, Jennifer and Jessica. But it didn't take long for the healing to begin. And the healing has never stopped. As I write this, my marriage is the best it has ever been, and my daughters are two of my very best friends, with healthy, faith-filled families of their own.

On the day I returned home, I bought a study Bible, began reading, and didn't stop until I had read it cover to cover. It has become the book I just can't put down.

I also immediately engaged with the downtown Methodist church where my family had become members. Before, Christie and the girls would head to church on Sunday mornings while I headed for the golf course. But now I led the way to Sunday school and every service scheduled. Almost immediately, I found myself on the "Sunday school circuit," sharing my testimony. This was soon followed by opportunities to serve in a prototype contemporary worship service and both youth and adult mission retreats. The Emmaus community was at the same time inviting me to serve on both their fall and spring retreat teams.

After about eighteen months of this, I walked into my Methodist church lobby one day and thought to myself, *I would really like to work here.*

The thought of leaving law and going into full-time Christian ministry seemed very appealing. I could spend my days among people who loved Jesus, help lead worship and mission teams, and maybe even preach some.

I shared my thoughts with Christie, and then with my dear friend and senior law partner, the late Ed Norris. Both told me the same thing: "Doug, you can go places a minister can't go." My bubble was burst!

In prayer, the Lord revealed that I wanted to be in ministry for the wrong reasons. I was looking to live on the mountaintop (Matthew 17:4). God sends His ministers into the valley (John 20:21). I was asking God to help me live my dreams. God wanted me to live His dream.

I repented. Like Psalm 51 in the aftermath of David's repentance over his sin with Bathsheba, the poem "Moon in the Darkness" came forth. It is the only poem I have ever written, and flowed out of me so fast that 95 percent of it was written within twenty minutes. I know that although it comes through the filters of my story, it is a poem from the Lord.

As for the one hundred reflections that make up the rest of this book, well ... Six months after "Moon in the Darkness" was written, God called me into full-time ministry. Now my heart was right! In 1995, like Brer Rabbit jumping into the briar patch, I left the practice of law and entered Asbury Theological Seminary. Since then, the Lord has allowed me to pastor four congregations, including twelve years as the pastor of St. Mark House of Prayer, a primarily African-American congregation that was one of the best small churches on the planet. He has also involved Christie and me in volunteer chaplain ministry, youth and children's ministries, prison ministry, healing and deliverance ministry, and citywide prayer ministry.

In the midst of this lifestyle of ministry, God opened the door in 2006 for me to write a monthly column for the religion section of our city newspaper, the *Kingsport Times-News*. It is a responsibility I treasure, and the reflections in this book are from that treasure chest. Like "Moon in the Darkness," they come through my story and my filters, but I believe with all my heart they also come from God. I encourage you to read the Scriptures cited in each of the reflections so the Lord can speak to you not just through me, but directly through His Word.

God has given many people a piece of the puzzle, and I don't believe anyone but the Lord has the whole puzzle. We need each other. My prayer is that *Moon in the Darkness* will inspire you to fully surrender to God's unique dream for your life and provoke you to thoughtful prayer about the role you can play in seeing God's kingdom return to earth.

Reflections on Being
a Disciple of Jesus

My Father, please make me a moon in the darkness

reflecting the light of Your Son;

and leave me no dark side,

no half-moon or half-truth,

that hampers Your will being done.

Let my service, through Your grace,

shift the tide of men's lives

and help draw them closer to You,

where Your love and Your light

will eclipse all their fears

and transform who they are, what they do.

My sheep hear my voice, and I know them, and they follow me. I give them eternal life, and they will never perish, and no one will snatch them out of my hand. My Father, who has given them to me, is greater than all, and no one is able to snatch them out of the Father's hand. (John 10:27–29)

Jesus Has Many "Believers" but Few Disciples

Then Jesus told His disciples, "If anyone would come after me, let him deny himself and take up his cross and follow me. For whoever would save his life will lose it, but whoever loses his life for my sake will find it."

—Matthew 16:24–25

So therefore, any one of you who does not renounce all that he has cannot be my disciple.

—Luke 14:33

For the gate is narrow and the way is hard that leads to life, and those who find it are few.

—Matthew 7:14

As Jesus Christ prepared to ascend to heaven in the aftermath of His resurrection, He gathered His disciples to Himself and gave them these closing instructions: "Go and make disciples of all nations" (Matthew 28:19).

Peter, Andrew, James, John, Matthew, and the others understood all too well what Jesus was saying. He had called each of them as a disciple through the seemingly easy invitation, "Follow me." But following Jesus had been anything but easy.

Jesus taught truths that required them to abandon their religious traditions. Jesus insisted they lay aside their personal ambitions and live the life of a servant. Jesus performed feats of power that were not humanly possible and then asked them to do the same. Jesus had enemies who

5

became their enemies, and sometimes those enemies were family and friends.

Peter summed it up to Jesus this way: "See, we have left everything and followed you" (Mark 10:28). Now Jesus was asking Peter and his fellow disciples to go invite others to do the same.

And that is exactly what those first disciples did. It began with a core group of 120 disciples, both men and women, who devoted themselves to prayer and fellowship while eagerly awaiting the promised power of God's Holy Spirit (Acts 1:1–15). When God's Spirit was poured into them ten days later, they went out manifesting the spiritual gifts of language (tongues) and anointed preaching (Acts 2).

Three thousand people came to faith that first day, and over five thousand more came to faith a few days later in response to the spiritual gift of healing (Acts 3; 4:4). Just as Jesus commanded, the disciples were making new disciples who received the Holy Spirit and devoted themselves to learning and obeying everything Jesus had taught (Matthew 28:20; Acts 2:42–47).

If you are looking for some inspiration, read the book of Acts. It is the story of disciples of Jesus—a story of men and women who, in the face of tremendous opposition, changed the world.

Where are our world-changing and community-changing disciples for today?

Let's be honest with ourselves. The Christian churches in America are not disciple-making organizations. We invite people to "be saved" or become "church members." We may go so far as to politely ask people to "get involved." But when is the last time you heard an altar call using the Scriptures cited at the beginning of this chapter? When have you heard your pastors demand of a congregation what Jesus demands of everyone who would follow Him?

According to 2006 Barna Group research, only 15 percent of regular church attendees rank their relationship with God as the top priority in their life. Only one in six believe spiritual maturity is meant to be developed in the context of a local church or community of faith. This is not disciple making!

We have invited people to come with open hands and open hearts to receive the free gift of eternal life. But we have not told them of their

King's demand that they also come with open minds, open wills, and open daily planners.

I wonder who will be held accountable on the day of judgment for those virgins whose lamps ran out of oil, those servants who buried their talents, and those "goats" who failed to address the needs of others (Matthew 25). Is it their failure alone when we never taught them all Jesus required and never held them accountable?

Most of all, my heart aches for what is lost when we lose the "Way"— the way of a disciple who fellowships with Jesus through the Holy Spirit, learns everything He teaches, obeys His every command, and does "even greater works than these" (John 14:12).

The life of a disciple is the life of an apprentice to the Son of God: a life filled with love, truth, purpose, and power; a life that transforms you so you can bless and transform the world around you. It is the only life worth living, and it lasts forever.

Resolve to become a disciple. Link up with other disciples. And see what happens as a result!

God bless you, and God bless our community.

We Need the Full Message
of the New Life

*They arrested the apostles and put them in the public jail. But
during the night an angel of the Lord opened the doors of the jail
and brought them out. "Go, stand in the temple courts," he said,
and tell the people the full message of this new life."*

—Acts 5:18–20 NIV

Amazing! Exciting! That is always my reaction to the exploits of the church
in the book of Acts. Ordinary people do extraordinary acts of love and
power because they are filled with and led by the Holy Spirit.

Our Scripture from Acts 5 tells of a time when all the apostles were
arrested in Jerusalem. The religious and civic leaders wanted to shut them
down, but the Lord sent an angel to set them free. This angel then gave
them (and us) the Lord's command: Go! Stand! Tell!

What we are to tell is the full message, the whole word, of the "new
life." The Greek word translated here as *new life* is *zoë*—a word used in
the New Testament to describe life in Christ, the life of a person born not
just of man but of God (John 1:13).

So, what is the full message of the new life that we are supposed to tell
everyone? As I study different streams of Christian thought, I seem to find
different answers, so please let me pose this test to you.

Question: What is the full message of the new life in Christ?

(A) God is love. God loves all people and wants everyone to have
    eternal life. We are to share in this love and desire, even with
    people very different from us. Jesus is our example of a life in love,

8

but people who don't know about Jesus have also received some understanding about God. We express our love for them and all people through acts of charity and by the pursuit of social justice and peace for everyone.

(B) The Bible is God inspired and totally trustworthy. Jesus is the Son of God. His death on the cross paid the price for all sins for all people for all time. Jesus has risen from the dead and now has all authority in heaven and earth. No one comes to the Father except through Him. If we repent of our sins and receive Jesus as Lord and Savior, we will be saved by grace through faith. God will send us the Holy Spirit as a seal of salvation, and we will go to heaven rather than hell when we die.

(C) When you put your trust in Jesus as Lord and Savior and ask to receive God's Holy Spirit, the very presence and power of God comes to dwell within you. You experience Him as you worship and as you walk and talk with Him every day. Being God's son or daughter, you receive authority to bring healing to people and deliver them from demonic oppression. God can work miracles through you. God will speak personally to you with dreams, visions, and prophetic words of wisdom and knowledge as He empowers your life and leads you into all truth.

(D) Faith in God and His Son, Jesus, is a very personal matter of the heart. It is not about going to church or other religious activities. It is about a person's daily relationship with a God who always loves you, always understands you, and never leaves or betrays you—one who can help you and give you hope in times of need.

Which answer would you pick? Answer (A) seeks to capture the modern or liberal stream of Christian thought. Answer (B) seeks to summarize the conservative or evangelical stream. Answer (C) looks at the charismatic stream. Answer (D) acknowledges the many Christians who no longer participate in any church because they have been wounded or have become disenchanted.

My prayer is that you will pick none of these four and that you are holding out like me for Answer (E): "All of the above."

Answers A, B, C, and D are all absolutely verified in the Bible. They are also verified in the lives of many wonderful Christians worldwide. No one of these answers represents the full message of the new life in Christ, but when these four streams of truth are brought together into one river of life, we have a message that everyone needs to receive.

Prayerfully examine your own faith. What do you really believe and why? How do you live your faith? If any of these four *zoë* streams of new life are missing, then you are missing out. Reach out and drink the fullness of all God has for you. Then share it with everyone you meet.

God bless you, and God bless our community.

Be with Jesus, Be like Jesus, Be for Jesus

Therefore, since we have so great a cloud of witnesses surrounding us, let us also lay aside every encumbrance, and the sin which so easily entangles us, and let us run with endurance the race that is set before us, fixing our eyes on Jesus, the author and perfecter of faith.

—Hebrews 12:1–2 NASB

We live in an age of bumper stickers, flash ads, and text messaging: one-liners and catchy slogans that compensate for shortening attention spans. They are effective, much as mottos in my past like "Be prepared" (Boy Scouts) and "Semper fidelis" (US Marines). It is helpful to have a phrase that is easy to remember and yet captures the essence of what you wish to communicate.

For that reason, I propose a motto of Christian discipleship. "Be with Jesus. Be like Jesus. Be for Jesus."

To "Be with Jesus" recognizes His promise that He is with us always (Matthew 28:20). Through the Holy Spirit, Jesus abides in us (John 14:23). We can walk through life with Him just like Enoch walked (Genesis 5:22; Micah 6:8). It is the daily intimate relationship with Jesus that caused Paul to cry out with joy, "Christ lives in me!" (Galatians 2:20; Colossians 1:25–27).

To "Be like Jesus" is to recognize God's plan to restore the image of God in us that has been broken by sin. We can't change ourselves, but the Spirit of God will transform us into the likeness of Jesus one step at a time, "from glory to glory" (2 Corinthians 3:17–18). The fruits of the Spirit in

Galatians 5:22 are the character of Christ being formed in us—what David called a clean heart and a steadfast spirit (Psalm 51:10).

To "Be for Jesus" is to deny ourselves, take up our cross daily, and follow Him (Luke 9:23). It is to be sent by Jesus as Jesus was sent by the Father (John 20:21), to be His witnesses (Acts 1:8), make disciples (Matthew 28:19–20), "wash feet" as servants to all (John 13:14–15; Matthew 25:31–46), and even do what Jesus called "greater things than these"—the signs and wonders He did on earth (John 14:12). Through us, His kingdom on earth spreads like leaven in the loaf and grows from small to great (Matthew 13:31–33; Ephesians 3:20–21).

It is absolutely essential that we see how the three prongs of this Christian motto are interwoven. At the risk of offending, let me suggest that some in the mainline tradition try to be like Jesus, seeing Him as a great teacher and model for living, but struggle with the ideas of being with Him (too supernatural) or for Him (too theologically exclusive and politically incorrect). Some in the evangelical tradition are passionately for Jesus but struggle with the idea of His manifest presence with them (too charismatic) and becoming like Him (too contrary to being "sinners saved by grace"). Some in the charismatic tradition fervently seek God's presence and the gifts of His Spirit, but may neglect the fruit (being like Jesus) and His call to focus more on the needs of others than one's personal experiences (being for Jesus).

There is a lot we can teach each other, with one's strength bolstering another's weakness. The more we are with Jesus, the more like Him we become. The more like Him we become, the more effective we are in serving Him. The more effectively we serve Him, the more we find ourselves with Him. And so it goes until one day as the Lord has promised, our service will be complete because His kingdom has come on earth as it is in heaven. We will see Him as He really is because we will be just like Him, and we will be with Him forever (1 John 3:1–2)!

Break out the bumper stickers! Be with Jesus! Be like Jesus! Be for Jesus!

God bless you, and God bless our community.

Dive into The Deep End Of God

*Then he brought me back to the door of the temple, and behold,
water was issuing from below the threshold of the temple toward
the east (for the temple faced east). ... Going on eastward with a
measuring line in his hand, the man measured a thousand cubits,
and then led me through the water, and it was ankle-deep. Again
he measured a thousand, and led me through the water, and it was
knee-deep. Again he measured a thousand, and led me through
the water, and it was waist-deep. Again he measured a thousand,
and it was a river that I could not pass through, for the water had
risen. It was deep enough to swim in, a river that could not be
passed through.*

—Ezekiel 47:1, 3–5

Like most people in our region, I am thrilled about our new Kingsport
Aquatic Center. In offering yet another expression of healthy quality of life
for our region, it fits right in with Bays Mountain City Park, the Greenbelt,
Meadowview Conference Center, the Renaissance (and Senior) Center,
Funfest, Darrell's Dream Boundless Playground, and other wonderful
decisions our civic leaders have made over the years.

The new aquatic center reminds me of Dollywood's Splash Country,
where I spent two wonderful days with my grandchildren last summer. And
it inspires me to imagine an even more spectacular water park: the Living
Water Park of God, where Jesus is the lifeguard and the Holy Spirit is the
swimming instructor.

When you enter the Living Water Park, you immediately enter the
kiddie pool area. We need a kiddie pool—the place where people can first
wade into the living water and see how delightful it is. But the kiddie pool

is supposed to be only a brief visit on our way to learning how to swim. Unfortunately, our kiddie pool today is packed with Christians who have never moved beyond this first step.

Here we find those who were told to get "saved" but were never taught that the invitation is to follow Jesus, not just "believe in" Him. Here we find those who are simply told that God loves them and everyone, and to feel good about themselves.

The kiddie pool includes a splash pad where you can have high-tech praise music, stimulating videos, and dramatic short messages of encouragement wash over you while you wade.

And there are waterslides in the kiddie pool, although they do not work like you wish they would. You see, people who stay too long in the kiddie pool become disenchanted with the shallowness of this living water they were told was so wonderful. Many of them backslide right out of the kiddie pool and back onto the hot, hard concrete of the world. Some will later find their way back. Others will not.

A more recent addition to the Living Water Park is the Lazy River. The water moves here because these people have learned they can experience the presence of the Lord. However, the Lazy River is almost as shallow as the kiddie pool, because the people are not looking to swim. They just want the blessings of a pleasant experience of God, without having to engage in His kingdom purposes through personal effort or sacrifice.

Farther inside the Living Water Park, you find the lap pool. Here the water is chest deep, staying in contact with your heart, and you can finally do some swimming. There are plenty of lanes for you to choose from because there are not many people here—only that small percentage of the church who engage in the work of the kingdom. Some are "professionals" and swim many laps a day, and others swim a couple of laps a week. Regardless, we praise God for these few who do the work of many.

At the same time, we must recognize that when people stop swimming their laps in the lap pool, they stand on their own two feet. Much of the work accomplished in the church today is done in reliance on our own strength and resources rather than the power of the Holy Spirit. And most Christian lives are compartmentalized, with times of faith and ministry set apart from times of work and recreation.

Beyond the lap pool, in the very heart of the Living Water Park, you will find the deep end. Here you can't stand on your own two feet, and must rely on the water to hold you up. Here you can immerse your whole being. As you overcome your fear, you even use the high dive, soaring down even deeper and discovering there is no end to how deep you can go.

As you go deeper, you discover things you never imagined a water park could offer—coral reefs of heavenly beauty, sunken treasures of truth and wisdom, and even the ability to live under water by relying on the breath of God. This is the Way that leads to Life, but few are finding it (John 14:6; Matthew 7:14).

Our admission price to the Living Water Park has already been paid, with full access to every part of the park we choose to enter. I encourage you, even urge you, to dive into the deep end of God.

God bless you, and God bless our community.

Repentance May Be Your Missing Ingredient

Jesus came into Galilee, proclaiming the gospel of God, and saying, "The time is fulfilled, and the kingdom of God is at hand; repent and believe in the gospel."

—Mark 1:14–15

We all know what happens when you are missing a key ingredient. The food doesn't taste good. The chemical compound doesn't perform like you want. The medicine doesn't heal.

This principle of missing ingredients applies to our life of Christian faith just as much as it does our cooking and concocting. After all, our relationship with the Lord is supposed to taste good (Psalm 34:8)! God intends for us to perform incredible things through Christ (Romans 8:31; Philippians 4:13)! Jesus came to heal us all from evil's oppression (Luke 4:18–19; Acts 10:38)!

Are these things happening in your Christian life? If not, you may be missing a key ingredient. And based upon what I have learned in my personal struggles, that key ingredient may be repentance.

We should begin with a word study. There are two Hebrew words in the Old Testament and one Greek word in the New Testament that are primarily translated as *repent*.

The Hebrew word most frequently translated as *repent* is *shub*. It means "to turn." You repent by turning away from sin and turning back to God. This is a change in behavior by an act of choice.

The other Hebrew word used for *repent* is *naham*. It indicates remorse or regret—a change of heart that can motivate a change of behavior.

16

The New Testament Greek word is *metanoeo*, which means a change of mind. This can, like *naham*, refer to a feeling such as remorse, but it more often refers to a transformation in understanding: a change in how you view what is true, real, or important.

We need to remember that under the Old Testament covenant of the law, the central issue was obedient versus sinful behavior. But in the New Testament, Jesus asks us not just to turn from sinful behaviors, but to modify our understanding about who God is and what God wants. As set forth in Mark 1:14–15, Jesus connects "repent and believe."

Here is how I put all this together. My behavior is based on my choices. I make my choices on the basis of two things: what I think and how I feel. How I feel and what I think are in turn based on my view of what is true, real, and important. If I change my mind about what is true, real, and important (metanoeo), it will change the way I think and feel (naham), which will in turn change my behavior (shub).

Modern psychology calls this cognitive behavioral therapy. Changing how you think changes how you feel and behave. The Bible calls this same principle repentance.

Another way to look at it is "You will know the truth, and the truth will set you free" (John 8:32).

My most important time of repentance came when I turned back to God in 1991. God used my circumstances and His Holy Spirit to reveal to me that I could not fix my problems on my own. He then used His people and His Word to reveal that He loved me and wanted to help. I didn't repent from sin so much as I repented in my view of what was true about me and God. As a result, I chose to cry out to God, and like it says in the old hymn, "He touched me!"

Since that awesome day, I have continued to experience the blessings of repentance time and time again. Many of these occasions have simply been the experience of guilt after I said or did what I knew I shouldn't say or do. But many others have been those wonderful times when God uses His Spirit, His Word, His people, and my circumstances to further transform what I view as true, real, and important.

For example, when I first thought of leaving the practice of law for full-time ministry, God revealed how selfish my motives were. Like Peter at the transfiguration, I thought I could go live in a mountaintop experience

(Matthew 17:4). After I repented of this foolishness and realized the need to walk with God in the valleys of people's lives, I was ready for ministry.

Other God-triggered changes of mind have led me to become a man of prayer and a more appreciative, less critical husband. I am still very much a work in progress, but because I remain willing to let God "change my mind," my life and ministry continue to change for the better.

Repentance is a crucial ingredient in the ongoing recipe of my life, and I highly recommend it to you.

God bless you, and God bless our community.

We Need Both the Blood
and the Cross

*So they took Jesus, and He went out, bearing His own cross, to
the place called the place of a skull, which in Aramaic is called
Golgotha. There they crucified Him.*

—John 19:16b–18

Easter Sunday is two days away. On that morning, the anniversary of the
resurrection of Jesus Christ, our churches will experience their largest
attendance of the year. Everyone wants to participate in the resurrection.

A significantly smaller group of believers gather in advance of Easter
to focus on the ghastly and glorious event that makes resurrection possible:
the crucifixion of Jesus. It is not that the others don't remember this
sacrifice. It will be declared on Easter, as it is throughout the year: "Jesus
died for our sins!" "We are washed in the blood of the Lamb!"

But people have a hard time gathering to "celebrate" death, particularly
death on a cross. And we like to believe that because He died, we don't
have to. That's where we are wrong.

The question I pose for us this day is "Why both the blood and the
cross?" And before you dismiss that question, let me remind you that it is
the blood, and not the cross, that washes away our sins (1 John 1:7).

In the Old Testament sacrifices that foreshadowed Christ, it was the
shedding of blood and giving of life that made atonement for sin (Leviticus
17:11). Jesus is the Passover lamb for the world, the one-time sacrifice for
eternal redemption (1 Corinthians 5:7; Hebrews 9:12–15). But the Passover
lamb and the other animals sacrificed in the temple were never crucified.

Their deaths were swift and merciful. So why was the cross, rather than a swift and merciful death, required for Jesus?

All of us know crucifixion was a very painful, prolonged, and shameful mode of execution. What many may not know is that the Roman Empire did not use crucifixion for every condemned prisoner. Crucifixion was reserved for slaves, enemies of the state, rebels, and revolutionaries. In later times, they added foreigners and the vilest of criminals.

To understand why a holy and loving God chose this mode of execution for His Son, we must travel two avenues of Scripture and find where they merge.

First look at the declarations of Jesus Himself: "If anyone would come after me, let him deny himself and take up his cross and follow me" (Matthew 16:24). Our Lord explained that if we do not do this, we are not worthy of Him (Matthew 10:37). The only way to save our life is to first lose our life for His sake (Luke 9:24).

Next look at the declarations of the apostle Paul: "I have been crucified with Christ. It is no longer I who live, but Christ who lives in me" (Galatians 2:20).

Paul is describing something here that goes way beyond forgiveness of sin. Those who belong to Jesus must crucify our "old self," and the flesh with its passions and desires, so we can "put on the new self, created after the likeness of God in true righteousness and holiness." Then we can "live by the Spirit" and "walk by the Spirit" (Ephesians 4:22–24; Romans 6:6; Galatians 5:24).

Now merge these Scriptures. To follow Christ, be worthy of Christ, become like Christ, and be led by Christ's Spirit, we must go beyond forgiveness of our sins. We must bear our own cross to our own crucifixion, dying to the "I" that is self-centered, self-righteous, self-reliant, self-occupied, and self-directed. Only then is there enough room in our life for Christ to live and rule. Only then can we live out the humble, loving role of servanthood that is the calling of every disciple.

This "self" we die to is a slave to sin and Satan. It is a rebellious enemy of the kingdom. It is a foreigner to heaven and a vile criminal against God's holiness. Crucifixion is the death it deserves.

At the outset of His earthly ministry, Jesus was baptized with water for repentance (Matthew 3:13–17). He didn't need to do that for Himself. He had nothing to repent. He did it because we needed to follow Him there.

Likewise, Philippians 2 tells us how Jesus emptied and humbled Himself, taking on the form of both man and slave. His obedience took Him to death on a cross not because He needed to go there, but because we need to follow Him there.

Paul prophesied that in these last days, many of the people of Christ's church would be "lovers of self ..., having the appearance of godliness, but denying its power" (2 Timothy 3:1–5). The prophecy has come true and will remain true until we all recognize that we need both the blood and the cross.

God bless you, and God bless our community.

It Is Time to Evaluate Ourselves

*Search me, O God, and know my heart! Try me and know my
thoughts! And see if there be any grievous way in me, and lead me
in the way everlasting!*

—Psalm 139:23–24

The Christian life is not focused on self. We are to be Christ centered and
focused on the needs of others.

Occasionally, however, we must examine ourselves and evaluate how
well our lives conform to God's biblical mandates for His people. Other
organizations do these self-assessments on a regular basis as a part of good
quality management. Since our Lord is all about goodness and quality, it
behooves us to do the same.

When we conduct this self-evaluation, we should do so at every relevant
level. Since there is only one body and one bride, we are all part of one
church. How is the one church doing?

In addition, most of us are part of a local congregation—what we often
call "our church." How is your church doing?

Finally, each Christian family and individual is an important
representative of the Lord in their own right. How are you doing?

Please let me propose seven areas of assessment:

God's rule: The gospel is the good news of the kingdom of God (God's
rule) being restored to the earth by being restored to the hearts of mankind.
Jesus died for our sins as Savior, but it is only by acknowledging and
trusting Him as Lord and King that you receive His eternal life.

Is Christ the King of your heart? Do you seek His direction for your
major and daily decisions of life? Is His kingdom actively proclaimed

and honored in your church? Do you offer people "salvation" or church "membership" without requiring their submission to His Lordship?

God's love: The fundamental law of the kingdom is agape: the unconditional, sacrificial love of God. Agape is always forgiving, sometimes tough, and never-ending. It is an essential ingredient of everything God's people are to do.

Do you know God loves you? Do you experience that love often? Do you really love Him back? Do you love Him with all your heart, mind, soul, and strength? Do you love and care about everyone God loves, including those who have hurt or disappointed you? Do you love yourself?

God's truth: Truth is not whatever we choose to believe is true. Truth is reality, and truth is revealed by the God who created reality. Some truth is revealed to our human senses and science, but we often misunderstand, and other truth cannot be "seen" by us at all. So God reveals truth by His Word and through His Spirit.

Do you trust the Bible as God-breathed scriptural revelation—that is, as the written Word of God? Have you read it or do you rely on others to tell you what it says? Do you trust all of it, or just the parts that make sense to you? What about "No one comes to the Father except through Me"? What about the baptism and gifts of the Holy Spirit?

God's presence: God's people are invited into God's presence—the Holy of Holies. We live in Christ and Christ lives in us. He has promised to be with us always, and whenever we gather together in His name, He is in our midst.

Do you expect to experience God's presence when you gather for worship, or when you enter your secret place for prayer? Can you sincerely sing "He Touched Me" or even better, "He walks with me and talks with me …"?

God's purpose: God's purpose is to reconcile all things in Jesus Christ, and so we are given the Great Commission of Matthew 28:18–20 and Mark 16:15–20.

Are you a disciple or just a believer? Are you making disciples, or just believers? Are you witnessing to Jesus Christ and His kingdom in your daily life by your love, service, testimony, and demonstrations of kingdom power such as healing and deliverance?

God's divine order and strategy: God's structure for ministry in the New Testament is very different from the Old Testament, because every Christian is God's child and receives His Holy Spirit.

Are you organized as priests and laity, or as the one royal priesthood? Are you organized as ministers and laypeople, or as a family of saints all spiritually gifted and engaged in ministry? Do you honor all the equipping ministries described in Ephesians 4? Is your leadership composed of mature elders filled with and led by the Holy Spirit? Are you truly a house of prayer?

God's peace and joy: Do you have peace in your heart even in difficult circumstances? Do you have a continuing joy in your salvation that strengthens you in times of suffering and disappointment?

How are we doing? Is there room for improvement? Need for change?

God bless you, and God bless our community.

There Is a Better Way to Live

*Come to me, all you who are weary and burdened, and I will give
you rest. Take my yoke upon you and learn from me, for I am gentle
and humble in heart, and you will find rest for your souls. For my
yoke is easy and my burden is light.*

—Matthew 11:28–30 NIV

Have you even wondered why so many Christians live defeated or at least
somewhat dissatisfied lives?

From my vantage point, it appears that the biblical concept of "abundant
life" is something a high percentage of believers have read about in "the
book", but not actually experienced (John 10:10). New believers tend
to fall back into their old problems. Even long-term believers seem to
struggle with stress, frustration, depression, and family problems as much
as nonbelievers do.

In short, many Christians are not very happy, not very peaceful, not
very fulfilled, and not very hopeful that things will improve this side of
heaven. Why?

I believe a fundamental problem is our failure to get past the theology
of salvation by grace as "a free gift of God" and to understand that Jesus
calls for those He saves to take on His yoke and learn from Him.

To "take on His yoke" means we submit to Jesus as Lord. We live each
day the way He wants, not the way we think we want (John 14:6).

To learn from Jesus means we continually let Him teach us about this
new way of life so we can do a better and better job of living it. This is
how we mature to the full stature of Christ and see our lives transformed
from glory to glory (Ephesians 4:13, 2 Corinthians 3:18, Hebrews 5:11–14).

A ticket to heaven may be a free gift we receive by faith, but "rest for our souls" on earth comes through this process of submitting and learning. Being blessed for living life God's way is a principle proclaimed throughout Scripture (Exodus 33:13, Deuteronomy 5:32–33, Psalm 119, Isaiah 30:18–21, Matthew 28:18–20)

Please let me suggest a short list for living the way Jesus wants:

1. Start each day with at least one half hour of prayer. Submit your day to the Lord. Tell Him you love and trust Him. Be reminded that you are a child of your heavenly Father and a dwelling place for God's Holy Spirit. Pray for your loved ones, your community, your nation, the church, and whatever God puts on your heart.

2. Seek to remain attentive to God's presence throughout your day. Bless each place you go in the name of Jesus. Every blessing you speak pours out living water on this world. And refrain from harsh and judgmental words, because they pour out curses on people who are loved by God (James 3:2–10).

3. End each day in prayer. Review the day. Repent and be forgiven where necessary. Submit your time of sleep and dreams to Him.

4. Own a study Bible in a translation you can understand. Read it often. Read it cover to cover so you know the whole of it, not just parts.

5. Commit to living a life of love. Focus on humbly serving others, not yourself. Consistently forgive those who hurt or disappoint you, including yourself.

6. Spouses, pray together every day. Several Christian marriage ministries make reference to a 1997 Gallup poll by the National Association of Marriage Enhancement that revealed an amazing statistic: less than one percent of Christian couples who pray together daily will divorce.

7. Parents, lay hands on your children every morning and pray for blessings and protection. Spend one half hour with them every day sharing prayer and Bible stories. You will grow closer to God and each other. This is much more important than sports or academics.

8. Do not neglect gathering for corporate worship. Expect to encounter God, not just a sermon. Sing to Him from your heart.

9. Actively share your faith—what Jesus has meant in your life—with family, friends, and the struggling people God puts in your path. Invite and encourage others. There is no better gift you can give.

10. Get involved and remain involved in a ministry that trains you in Christian discipleship. Include involvement in a team ministry to others, whether it's food pantry, prison ministry, hospital visitation, intercessory prayer, or something else.

11. Have at least one or two friends in Christ who encourage you and hold you accountable.

Your first reaction to this list may be "That's too hard," or "I don't have time." But Jesus calls this yoke easy and light. It is just radically different because it is His way, not the world's way you have always known.

And as to time, don't let the Devil deceive and distract you with your busyness, TV, and the Internet. Simply reprioritize your time and energy according to what God says is important.

There is a better way to live. Let's start living it.

God bless you, and God bless our community.

Christians Need to Be "All In"

"You will seek me and find me when you seek me with all your heart."
—Jeremiah 29:13 NIV

The Super Bowl is over. Most sports fans will be turning their attention to basketball. But another "sport" will continue to share the spotlight on many TV sports channels (and even the Travel Channel). I am talking about the "sport" of poker.

The recent phenomenon of televised poker focuses on one particular card game: Texas Hold 'Em. Millions of people are watching it, playing it on the Internet, and flocking to casinos to participate in tournaments.

Why has this particular game become so popular so fast? Most of the game's rules are similar to other poker games, but one rule of betting stands out and causes all the excitement. At some point in any hand played, a player can push all of his or her chips into the pot and announce, "I'm all in."

Folks, thousands of years before Texas Hold 'Em, television, or the Internet, God spoke through His prophet Jeremiah. You have to seek the Lord with your whole heart. God's people need to be "all in."

This is the meaning of God's Great Commandment: love the Lord God with "all" your heart, "all" your soul, "all" your strength, and "all" your mind (Luke 10:27).

This is the meaning of the Matthew 13 parables about the kingdom of heaven. The men sold "all" they had to obtain the treasure and the pearl of great value.

So, is the church "all in" today? Are we wholehearted in our engagement with God and His will, or would it be more honest to say that we are, at best, halfhearted?

Think back to the 2007 Super Bowl. Imagine David Tyree making a halfhearted stab to catch that game-changing Eli Manning pass. No way that would have happened for that play or any play with the Super Bowl rings at stake. You might even say those players presented their bodies as living sacrifices for the chance to be football champions (Romans 12:1).

Yet God's people have much more at stake than football, money, or Super Bowl rings. We have a Father in heaven who wants to give us and those around us eternal treasure—a ring from His hand, His finest robe, sandals for the feet that carry the good news, and a fatted calf served at a heavenly banquet (Luke 15:22–23). Our stakes are eternal life and death. Compared with that, everything else is rubbish (Philippians 3:7–11).

Jesus told us how He felt about halfhearted Christians in His message to the lukewarm church in Laodicea (Revelation 3:14–19). He threatened to spit them out, and none of us want that. So why do we continue to struggle with being "all in"?

One problem is that we compartmentalize our lives. I have my religion, my family, my work, and my hobbies, and I try to spend some time involved with each of them. It is as if my life has many rooms, and I have my relationship with God in one of them.

To be "all in," the Lord needs to be Lord in all the rooms of my life.

A second problem is that we think "church activity" rather than "kingdom life." "All in" does not mean being at church every time the doors open. In fact, "church" in that sense can become empty religious practice or legalism.

"All in" is about love. What greater love can someone have, Jesus asked, than to sacrifice his life for a friend (John 15:19)? Jesus went "all in" for all of us on the cross. Now He calls on us to be "all in" for Him and for the world (Luke 9:23–25).

A third problem is comparison. "I may not be perfect, but I'm more faithful than he is. I pray more, give more, and sin less than she does. They need to repent!"

"All in" does not mean "more than my neighbor." Often the standard set by our neighbor is pretty low. And there is a terrible danger we face whenever we compare ourselves with others: the sin of pride. The minute I take pride in the belief that I am "all in," I lose the pot.

Instead, our standard is Jesus, who went "all in" by obediently and humbly emptying Himself to the point of death (Philippians 2:5–11). Even before He died, Jesus was "all in" as a foot-washing servant to "all" (John 13:3–17; Mark 9:35). We are called to be the same.

"All in" is not about being mistake-free—praise God—but it is about being as loving and faithful as you can be to all people all the time (Philippians 3:12–16). Each of us has to choose.

Dear friends, as best I can, I'm choosing "all in." What about you?

God bless you, and God bless our community.

Reflections on
Our Identity and
Purpose in Christ

My Father, please make me a star in Your heavens,

just one in a host of small sons;

with Your daughters, creating a great constellation

that sings of the victory won!

Let our lights be a guide

when men sail on Your sea

in the dark 'fore the morning's red sky.

Let them find the Safe Harbor

Who is marked by the cross,

and be saved from the storm 'ere they die.

And we know that for those who love God all things work together for good, for those who are called according to His purpose. For those whom He foreknew He also predestined to be conformed to the image of His Son, in order that He might be the firstborn among many brothers (and sisters). And those whom He predestined He also called, and those whom He called He also justified, and those whom He justified He also glorified. What then shall we say to these things? If God is for us, who can be against us? (Romans 8:28–31)

Christ Died so He Could Live through Us

"I have been crucified with Christ. It is no longer I who live, but Christ who lives in me."

—Galatians 2:20

Why did He do it? Why did the heavenly Father send His beautiful, immortal sinless Son to be cursed, beaten, and murdered on that cross? We know His motivation was love because God is love, but what was His purpose? What is His plan?

Some would point to John 3:16 and say God simply wanted to establish a way (Jesus is the Way) by which people could receive eternal life through faith. Those who believe will "go to heaven," and everyone else will not.

There is, of course, truth in that statement, but it is incomplete truth. John 3:16 reveals that God loves the world, not just people, and certainly not just some elect group of people. God desires all people to come into salvation (1 Timothy 2:4; 2 Peter 3:9). He intends to completely renew both heaven and earth (2 Peter 3:13; Revelation 21:1–5). His glorious purpose is to reconcile all things on heaven and earth to Himself through Jesus Christ (Colossians 1:19–20)!

How do the crucifixion and resurrection enable this glorious purpose? Well, as I heard one speaker put it to Christians recently, "We are the plan, and God has no other plan." The key is to understand where the risen Christ is living now.

Forty days after His Easter resurrection, Jesus ascended to heaven and took His place at the right hand of the Father (Mark 16:19). Although the fictional accounts of the Left Behind series suggest otherwise, the Bible says the Lord Jesus will remain there until the Father makes His enemies into a footstool for His feet (Psalm 110:1; Hebrews 10:12–14).

On the other hand, the Bible proclaims that Christ is here with us always (Matthew 28:20). This miracle of Christ in heaven and Christ at the same time with us is accomplished through the gift of the Holy Spirit—the Spirit of Christ (Romans 8:9–10). In Christians, the plan of God that has been the mystery of the ages is revealed: "Christ in you, the hope of glory" (Colossians 1:25–27). Because Christ died on the cross, you and I can now proclaim, "Christ lives in me" (Galatians 2:20)!

Jesus is the grain of wheat that fell to the ground and died so He could reproduce many grains of wheat (John 12:24). In His resurrection, He became not only the One born from the dead, but the firstborn from the dead—a beginning that is producing many born-again brothers and sisters (Colossians 1:18; Romans 8:29). Before His death, Christ walked the earth in a single body. Now Christ walks the earth in millions of bodies that are, corporately, His one Body filled with His one Spirit (1 Corinthians 12).

I repeat, the crucifixion and resurrection process is not just about people going to heaven. It is about the kingdom of God—the reestablishment of the rule of God on earth as it is in heaven (Matthew 6:10). When Christ came two thousand years ago, the kingdom of God came near because the King had come (Luke 10:9–11). Now the King is King of Kings and Lord of Lords because He lives in you and me as our King, and because He has reestablished in us an authority, a lordship, that we lost when sin came into the world (Matthew 16:19; John 20:21–23).

Adam and Eve were told to be fruitful and multiply, and to rule over the earth under God's rule (Genesis 1:28). Through sin they failed, and the kingdom of darkness entered the earth. But by His crucifixion and resurrection, Christ has disarmed and condemned the forces of darkness (John 16:11; Colossians 2:15). Through Jesus, the rule of God has been planted anew in the earth, and Christ, the grain of wheat, is being fruitful. He multiplies every time another person becomes a born-again Christian (John 3:3).

God's glorious purpose of reconciliation through Christ—the restored kingdom on earth—is now the purpose of all who have Christ in them (2 Corinthians 5:18–21). As we begin living the truth that the risen King is within us, the kingdom of God will spread over all the earth (Matthew

13:31–33; 28:18–20). There will be no end to the increase of His rule and peace (Isaiah 9:7).

On Easter mornings when we gather to worship, many of us sing the great hymn "He Lives." Embrace the truth of what you sing. "He lives within my heart." "He walks with me and talks with me." "Jesus Christ the King!"

Then let's take Easter and all it means into the world around us. We have prayed the Lord's Prayer countless times—"Your kingdom come." United under His Lordship and empowered by His Spirit, let's go out and make it happen.

God bless you, and God bless our community.

Christ Must Increase—"I" Must Decrease

"He must increase, but I must decrease. He who comes from above is above all."

—John 3:30–31a

He was, for his time, Billy Graham, Tiger Woods, and Bruce Springsteen all rolled into one. Two thousand years ago, John the Baptist was "the man." His altar calls had national impact! All the people of Jerusalem and Judea went to him to confess their sins and be baptized (Mark 1:5).

John the Baptist was the first prophet the Jewish people had seen in four hundred years. The anointed power of his preaching was unsurpassed. To a people who remembered the greatness of Abraham, Moses, David, and Elijah, Jesus declared none was greater than John the Baptist (Matthew 11:11). Heady praise indeed!

Yet this greatest of prophets, while still young and at the height of his fame, looked at the rising ministry of Jesus Christ and said, "He must increase—I must decrease." Wow!

"Christ must increase—I must decrease." It is profound truth, and we must examine it in three ways.

First, we must understand that John the Baptist knew his purpose. He was a voice crying in the wilderness, preparing the way for the Lord (John 1:23; Isaiah 40:3–5). He came to get people ready to receive Jesus, and when Jesus showed up, he directed their attention to Him, not himself (John 1:29–37).

In the Old Testament, priests and prophets acted as intermediaries between the people and God. But John the Baptist prepared the way and then got out of the way so people could have their own intimate relationship with Christ the King.

John's measure of success was not about gaining a following or building a personal kingdom. It was about having people more connected to Jesus and less dependent on him. The church today could use more of that attitude. Fellow pastors and preachers, Christ must increase and we must decrease.

Second, we need a deeper understanding of how the transition from John the Baptist to Jesus represents the transition from the old covenant of law to the new covenant of the Spirit (2 Corinthians 3:6).

John himself pointed out the difference: "I baptized you with water; but He will baptize you with the Holy Spirit" (Mark 1:8). In saying this, he was not pointing to the cross. He was pointing beyond the cross to the outpouring of God's Spirit at Pentecost.

Remember—John's baptism was for repentance, but his preaching went well beyond repentance. He declared that the kingdom of God was at hand, just like Jesus, and he declared that Jesus was the Christ, the Lamb of God who takes away the sins of the world (Matthew 3:2; John 1:29). People accepted Jesus as Savior on the basis of this message, but John's water baptism was not all they needed (Acts 19:1–7; 8:5–17). They needed to be baptized (the word means "immersed") in the Holy Spirit, and so do we.

Many churches today do not talk about or pursue the baptism of the Holy Spirit. They repent of their sins. They believe that when Jesus died on the cross, He paid the price for their sins so they can go to heaven. But that is not all Jesus came to do. I say to these good people, Christ must increase! Receive the baptism of the Holy Spirit that Jesus instructs you to receive (Acts 1:4–8). Then and only then will you have the power to live a truly godly life.

Third, we must recognize how trapped we all are in that big word *I*.

In these challenging times, the prevailing mantra of modern America remains, "What's in it for me?" And many people apply that same attitude toward their faith. "Do I like the worship? The preaching? The attire? If I give this, what will I get in return?"

Jesus said we must lose our life to find it (Matthew 16:25). Paul said, "It is no longer I who live, but Christ lives in me" (Galatians 2:20). In short, "I" must decrease by setting aside self-centeredness and personal agendas so Christ can increase in my life. We are called as a lifestyle to follow and serve Him, not just believe in Him. In doing so, we find our true identity and purpose along with the abundance of life Jesus came to give us (John 10:10).

In my prayer time, I have heard God saying to His people, "Stop being selfish!" Until Christ increases in our lives, He will not increase in our nation. And without an increase in Christ, no stimulus package will be sufficient to save America.

Christ must increase in you and me. "I" must decrease for that to happen. Oh Lord, help us make it so!

God bless you, and God bless our community.

Embrace Your Full
Relationship with Christ

For God knew his people in advance, and He chose them to become like his Son, so that His Son would be the firstborn, with many brothers and sisters.

—Romans 8:29 NLT

Relationships are the heartbeat of life. From the moment of birth, we are moved and shaped by our relationships.

It starts with parents (or surrogate parents), siblings, extended family, and peers. As we grow older, the network of relationships expands to include marriage, children, and work.

Much of our identity is wrapped up in these relationships: I'm this person's wife, or that person's son, or his friend, or work for her. All along the way, we can generally measure the quality of our life by the quality of these relationships.

For a Christian, there is no relationship more important than your relationship with Christ. Jesus insisted that our relationship with Him have first priority (Luke 14:26). But for most of us, that doesn't happen. We simply do not give Him the time, attention, and affection He deserves. Why not?

I believe much of our problem comes from our failure to embrace all the relationships we are invited to have with Jesus.

Many simply define themselves as believers. They have embraced the biblical promise that if you believe in your heart and confess with your mouth, you are saved (Romans 10:8–11). That is their only goal, and so their faith is religion far more than relationship. They have not yet learned that we must both believe and love (1 John 3:23–24; Luke 10:25–28). We must be doers of the Word, not just hearers (James 1:22–25).

Many others have moved beyond "believer" to the role of servant. Jesus modeled and taught the importance of being a servant (John 13:3–17). As King, He is worthy of our service. Frankly, some service seems only fair in light of all Christ has done for us, so we engage in various forms of church work—choir, usher, Sunday school teacher, trustee, mission team—and expect that others should do the same.

The problem here is that we are called to follow, not just serve (John 12:26). We are called to be a disciple, a relationship that embraces a life of following and learning with the goal of becoming just like our Teacher (Luke 6:40). Even several hours of service every week will not meet the expectation of Christ, which is that you deny yourself, forsake all you have, take up your cross daily, and follow Him (Luke 9:23, 14:27, 33).

For those who have embraced the identity of disciple, another wonderful identity is offered. What Jesus said to those first disciples, He will say to you: "I no longer call you servants ... Instead, I have called you friends" (John 15:15).

Note: this isn't about Jesus being your friend, as the popular hymn celebrates. This is about you being His friend, just as Abraham and Moses were called friends of God (Isaiah 41:8; Exodus 33:11). A servant simply does what he or she is told, but a friend of Jesus has learned what Jesus and His Father are working toward: the salvation of mankind and redemption of Creation. A friend joyfully joins in that work not because they have to but because they want to. They share the vision. They are friends of the King.

Last but not least, Christians are invited to live in their identity as brothers and sisters of Jesus (Romans 8:29, as set forth above). When we are born again, we become children of God (John 1:12–13, 3:3). We share the same Father with Jesus, who is the firstborn and our eldest brother. As Jesus is King, so we are royal sons and daughters in the kingdom (1 Peter 2:9).

The caution here is that we not remain infant siblings of Jesus requiring the King's constant care with bottles of milk and diaper changes (1 Corinthians 3:1; Hebrews 5:11–14). We are called to grow up to the maturity of the full stature of our eldest brother so we can do our part in the work of the kingdom that is our joint inheritance (Romans 8:16–17; Hebrews

6:1–3; Ephesians 4:11–16). He is Lord of Lords, and we become His lords, with authority and power in the Holy Spirit to speak and act in His name (John 14:12–14).

When I first married my wife, Christie, she was my lover, mate, and friend. She then became my co-parent. But now she is my wife, lover, mate, co-parent, best friend, and sister in Christ! Our marriage is the best it has ever been.

Likewise, we need to embrace all our relationships with Jesus Christ: believer, servant, disciple, friend, and Spirit-filled brother or sister of the King. In the multifaceted richness of that relationship, there is no limit to how good life can be.

God bless you, and God bless our community.

Christ in Us—The Hope of Glory

I became a minister according to the stewardship from God that
was given to me for you, to make the word of God fully known, the
mystery hidden for ages and generations but now revealed to His
saints. To them God chose to make known how great among the
Gentiles are the riches of the glory of this mystery, which is Christ
in you, the hope of glory.

—Colossians 1:25–27

Colossians 1:25–27 has to be one of the most challenging and exciting passages in the Bible.

First, this passage is exciting because the answer to an ages-old divine mystery was being revealed by God to His people. Paul's readers appreciated the significance of this Greek term, *mysterion*, because the Greco-Roman culture in which they lived was saturated with mystery cults. Those cults always keep their secret "truths" and rituals to their own inner circle, but now everyone who put their faith in Jesus was receiving the correct answer to the real mystery from the one true God.

Second, this passage is exciting because the word of God being made fully known here answers an extraordinarily important mystery. What is the hope of glory?

The Greek word *elpis* can be translated as *hope*: our expectation for a good thing to happen, or as "basis of hope": the reason we can expect that good thing to happen.

The Greek word *doxa* can be translated as *glory* or *divine, majestic radiance*. The word points toward the manifest presence of the Lord and the atmosphere of His kingdom.

The tendency of the institutional church is, particularly in the Western world, to focus on the individual and, thereby, see "the hope of glory" as our personal tickets to heaven and everlasting happiness. However, the gospel that Jesus preached was the good news of the kingdom of God returning to earth as it is in heaven (Matthew 4:23, 6:10, 24:14). I am convinced "the hope of glory" in our passage refers to nothing less than the time described by Moses, Solomon, and Habakkuk when "all the earth shall be filled with the glory of the Lord" (Numbers 14:21; Psalm 72:19; Habakkuk 2:14).

This leads to the third reason our passage is exciting, and the reason it is also incredibly challenging. We are told the basis for this hope: why we can expect a time when all the earth will be filled with God's glory. The basis for our hope, according to the Lord, is "Christ in you" and Christ in me—Christ in us!

It is absolutely crucial for us to understand what Paul says, and doesn't say, in this revelation. The hope of glory is not just "Christ" or "Christ Jesus." It is Christ *in us*!

It is also crucial to understand this word *Christ*, because unfortunately, there are many Christians who think this is simply the last name of Jesus. In fact, it is not His name at all. Instead, *Christ* is His divinely assigned purpose. And I propose here that *Christ* has become the assigned purpose of His disciples as well.

Christ is the Greek translation of the Hebrew word *Messiah*, which means, "the Anointed One." The Hebrew people understood the anointing of someone with oil to signify that that person had been approved, appointed, and empowered to do a special task for the Lord. They also understood from the prophets that God would one day anoint someone with His Holy Spirit—the Messiah approved, appointed, and empowered to save God's people and be their everlasting King (Daniel 9:25–26; Isaiah 9:6–7, 11, 61:1–9).

Scripture and history are clear that Jesus is that Messiah—the Christ (Luke 4:16–21; Mark 14:61–62). He died for the sins of mankind, rose from the dead, and sits as King at the right hand of the Father with all authority in heaven and earth.

But that is not the end of the story. Scripture says Jesus will remain at His Father's right hand until His enemies are made a footstool at His feet (Hebrews 10:12–13). And there has been another anointing!

First John 2:20 and 2 Corinthians 1:21 tell us as disciples of Jesus that we have been anointed by the Lord with the same Holy Spirit who anointed Jesus, which means we have been approved, appointed, and empowered like Jesus for a special task. This is why Jesus says, "As the Father sent me, I send you" (John 20:21). "I give you the keys of the Kingdom" (Matthew 16:19). "You will do the works I do, and greater works" (John 14:12). This is why Paul says the ministry of reconciling the world to Jesus has now been given to us (2 Corinthians 5:18–19).

This is also why we are called the body of Christ. We are not the body of Jesus, in which Jesus sits by the Father and will one day return to the earth. We are the body of the Messiah, the Anointed One, with Jesus now as the head of the body. As we "grow up in every way into Him" who is the head by maturing in our faith, love, unity, and trusting obedience, we will together attain the full stature of Christ, and the Holy Spirit will be able to complete His mission on earth just like Jesus completed His (Ephesians 4:1–16; John 16:8–11, 19:30).

The Greek word *pleroma* can be translated as *fullness* or *completion*. As radical as it may sound, Ephesians 1:23 could be best translated as *His body, the completion of Him who completes everything in every way.*

The hope of glory for the earth rests in the reality that Christians have become a part of Christ. It is time to fully embrace our identity and mission.

God bless you, and God bless our community.

Holiness Is What We Need

As obedient children, do not be conformed to the passions of your former ignorance, but as He who called you is holy, you also be holy in all your conduct, since it is written, "You shall be holy, for I am holy."

—1 Peter 1:14–16

You are a ... holy nation, a people for His own possession, that you may proclaim the excellencies of Him who called you out of darkness into His marvelous light.

—1 Peter 2:9

Many of you may be familiar with the praise song "Holiness," by Micah Stampley. The key lyric is "Holiness is what I long for; holiness is what I need." And I say, "Amen."

In preparation for seven days of worship, prayer, and fasting this week, I have diligently studied the scriptural meaning of the word *holy*—a word used in the Bible even more than the word *love*. These studies have convinced me that holiness is the key missing ingredient in the church today.

The Old Testament Hebrew word for *holy* is *qadash*. The New Testament Greek word for *holy* is *hagios*. Both words have the same core meaning: to be separated from, set apart, or consecrated.

The word *holy* appears for the first time in Genesis 2:3, when God blesses the seventh day and makes it holy. God separated the Sabbath from the week so His people would be separated from work and focus only on rest and on Him.

The Lord then proceeds to separate not just a day but a people. Speaking from the top of Mount Sinai to a Hebrew people just freed from bondage

47

in Egypt, God pronounces, "You shall be for me a kingdom of priests and a holy nation" (Exodus 19:6). The Lord set the Hebrew people apart from the rest of the world to be His people and His priests ministering in the world. This foreshadows our calling as the church.

God proceeded to train His Hebrew people in the concept of being set apart through the designation of holy items for worship, holy diet, and other rules of "clean" and "unclean." Then He explained to them why they were being set apart and what it really meant to be holy. "I am the Lord your God. Consecrate yourselves therefore and be holy for I am holy" (Leviticus 11:44–45).

For an object to be holy, it was set apart from mundane and profane use, dedicated solely to the purposes of the Lord. For a people to be separated to the Lord requires the same thing and more. As persons (God is Person), they also had to become like Him. What separates God from the world is not just that He is Creator. God is also separated in that this broken world is full of evil and God is good—perfectly good. God calls His people to the goodness that is the essence of His glory (Exodus 33:18–19).

Conclusion: the true meaning of *holy* is to be separated from the world and its evil, and to be joined together with God and His goodness.

Are Christians—the people of God under the new covenant, called to holiness—to be separated from the world and joined to God? Absolutely! Our Scriptures from 1 Peter totally embrace the language of Leviticus 11. And Peter is not just speaking of the "holiness" that comes from being forgiven of our sins. He writes to people who are already Christians and directs them to be holy in all their conduct—holy in everything we do.

The difference between the Hebrew and Christian calls to holiness lies in our awareness that the heart of God's goodness is selfless agape love. And we now have the power to walk in this holy separation and holy agape goodness because we have new birth in Jesus and the baptism of the Holy Spirit.

Once we understand this meaning for the word *holy*, all of the other Scriptures for holy living fit right in. We are to be separated from the things of the flesh and walk according to the Spirit (Romans 8, Galatians 5). We are cautioned against loving the world and the things of this world even when those things are not sin (1 John 2). Why? Because the cares and pleasures of the world choke what the Lord has planted in us, and keep our fruit from becoming mature (Luke 8:14).

Friends, how much God I get depends on how much room I make for Him in my life. Jesus says we are in this world but not of this world (John 17:15–16). If we will embrace that truth and devote ourselves to God and His goodness like the Acts 2 church, we will begin to live in the love, joy, and power they experienced.

God bless you, and God bless our community.

Know God's Purpose for Your Life

Commit your work to the Lord, and your plans will be established. The Lord has made everything for its purpose.
—Proverbs 16:3–4

"For I know the plans I have for you," declares the Lord, "plans to prosper you and not to harm you, plans to give you hope and a future."
—Jeremiah 29:11–13 NIV

And we know that for those who love God all things work together for good, for those who are called according to His purpose.
—Romans 8:28

In a few days, I will be sixty-two years old and qualify for early Social Security benefits. My wife, Christie, is, dare I say it, only nine months behind me.

Most people our age are retired, semiretired, or planning for retirement in the near future. But the only thing Christie and I are planning is a new kingdom of God adventure, opening a Friends of the King ministry site at 112 Shelby Street, Kingsport, where we will offer prayer, healing, teaching, and mediation ministries. The Tweeds are excited!

Why is retirement so appealing to some, yet so unappealing to others? I believe for many, the answer is simply this: You retire from a job. You don't retire from your purpose.

It took me a long time—forty-three years—to find my purpose. I will spend the rest of my time on earth gratefully and passionately living out that purpose. And a part of my purpose is helping others find the purpose the Lord has for them.

To each person out there who has not yet found their divine purpose, I offer encouragement and the following clues.

First, it is never too late and never too early. Samuel and David both started as children, and Moses didn't begin until he was eighty.

Second, God will not waste your past as He leads you into your future. Joseph learned a great deal from slavery and imprisonment. Mary Magdalene's incomparable love for Jesus burst forth from a life of prostitution and demon-possession. My experiences as a child of the sixties, a marine officer, and a trial lawyer have each become part of how the Lord works through me.

Third, your foundational purpose has nothing to do with "doing." You were designed, first and foremost, to experience God's indescribable love and to love Him back with all your heart, mind, soul, and strength. This intimate love relationship is intended to be now, constant and eternal. The Holy Spirit and your spirit become one and cry out together, "Abba! Father!" (Romans 8:15, 1 Corinthians 6:17). You are in Christ and Christ is in you (Galatians 2:20, Ephesians 2:4–10)!

Dear friends, when you live in the intimate awareness of God's love, it becomes second nature to both humbly love yourself and love others. The greatest shortcoming of the church has been the failure to show believers how to truly become lovers of God.

Fourth, as explained in 1 Corinthians 12 and Ephesians 4, all disciples of Jesus Christ are ministers with callings and spiritual gifts. We are all Christ's witnesses, all members of the royal priesthood, all citizens of the kingdom, and all members of the King's assembly (*ecclesia*, the Greek word we translate as *church*).

In other words, we all have both an important purpose in the body of Christ and an important kingdom purpose in the world. Pew sitting is not an option. Failure to share your faith is not an option. And although some may be teachers, others healers or pastors, others prophets, and others helpers or administrators, we are all called to pray. Make prayer your priority, both to be with your loving Father and to petition your powerful Lord, so we can at long last deserve to be called "a house of prayer" (Isaiah 56:7).

Finally, read Ephesians 3:8–21 so you will remember your purpose is not ministry for God. It is God's ministry in and through you, and it unfolds as a supernatural by-product of that foundational love relationship between you, your heavenly Father, your Savior King, and the Holy Spirit.

It unfolds into your marriage. It unfolds into parenthood and caring for your parents. It unfolds in the workplace, school systems, branches of government, cultural centers, and wherever else the Spirit of God leads you.

God's purpose for us is life together in the kingdom of God: "righteousness, peace and joy in the Holy Spirit," Sunday through Saturday, now and forever (Romans 14:17). This is the "life abundant" Jesus was talking about (John 10:10). This is heaven expressing itself on earth. And there is no limit to what the Lord can do through the people who embrace it.

So know God's purpose for your life, and live it!

God bless you, and God bless our community.

Born-Again Christians
Are Supernatural!

*Jesus answered him, "Truly, truly, I say to you, unless one is born
again he cannot see the kingdom of God."*

—John 3:3

The prevailing fascination of this decade is the supernatural person.

Look at our top box office movies, which are so often a cultural
barometer. The latest rage is the return of the superhero: *The Avengers,
Thor, Captain America, Green Lantern, Iron Man* (*1* and *2*), *The Dark
Knight Rises, The Amazing Spider-Man,* and more.

Before that was the teenage romanticizing of vampires and
werewolves—the Twilight series. Before that were the X-Men, with their
mutant powers. And blended in amidst them all were the eight Harry Potter
movies, in which both magic and a good heart are needed to overcome evil.

Turn on the Saturday morning cartoons and see more of the same. Our
fascination begins at an early age and extends to computer games and other
media entertainment as well. Why?

I believe we long as a culture for supernatural abilities because we have
at long last recognized that our natural human strength and understanding
are insufficient to meet the challenges of life. The problems are simply too
many and too great. Evil is too prevalent and too strong.

This recognition is a valid insight. Unfortunately, it is one thing to see
the need for supernatural abilities and quite another thing to obtain them.
Even as we flock to these movies and identify with these characters, we
know they are make-believe. We are not going to get Thor's hammer or

Harry Potter's wand. We are not going to be bitten by a radioactive spider or good-looking vampire. So where can we look?

The answer is found in the only reliable "Book of the Supernatural" there is: the Bible. But before we turn there, we need a definition for the word *supernatural*, since that word does not actually appear in Scripture. The Google dictionary offers, "attributed to some force beyond scientific understanding or the laws of nature." Merriam-Webster Online adds, "of or relating to an order of existence beyond the visible observable universe."

Based upon these definitions, is God supernatural? Absolutely! What about His power? Certainly! What about His Holy Spirit? No doubt!

What about Jesus, the only begotten Son of God, born of a virgin, who died for the sins of mankind and was resurrected to become King of Kings with all authority in heaven and earth? What about the works of Jesus as He walked the earth—miraculous healings and deliverances, raising the dead, walking on water, and calming storms? What about His kingdom, which is in the world but not of this world (Luke 17:21; John 18:36)?

All of the above is clearly and wonderfully supernatural, which leaves one very important question for every Christian reading this column. What about you?

The tragic truth is that although all Christians believe in a supernatural God, the vast majority have never considered themselves to be supernatural in any way. But that is not what the Bible tells us!

Those of us who believe in and receive Jesus become children of God, no longer born just of man, but of God (John 1:12–13). We receive the Holy Spirit, who becomes one with our human spirit, so that we are truly born of the Spirit—"born again" (Acts 2:38; 1 Corinthians 6:17; John 3:3–8).

Does this make us supernatural? We are now partakers of God's divine nature, no longer of the world (2 Peter 1:4; John 17:16). According to 1 John 3:6, God's seed abides in us (think DNA). We are siblings of Jesus (Romans 8:29). Christ lives in us (Colossians 1:27). All of that is incredibly supernatural!

What about supernatural abilities? Scripture says God can do abundantly more than we can ask or imagine, through His power at work within us (Ephesians 3:20). Jesus said we are to do the supernatural works He did, and even greater works, and that He stands ready to do anything we ask in His name (John 14:12–14). The Holy Spirit gives us gifts of healings and miracles, and the power to receive prophetic knowledge and wisdom directly from God (1 Corinthians 12).

People in New Testament times used these supernatural abilities just like their Lord did. And, praise God, there are some people who still use them today—just far too few.

The worldwide community of born-again Christians represents the kingdom of God on earth (Revelation 1:6). The kingdom of God is about supernatural power, not just words (1 Corinthians 4:20). But as indicated at John 3:3, we will not see the power of the kingdom until we know we are "born again" and fully accept what that really means.

My friends, it is time for Clark Kent to enter the phone booth.

God bless you, and God bless our community.

Are You a Son of God?

For the creation waits with eager longing for the revealing of the sons of God."

—Romans 8:19

Two of the most misunderstood Greek words in the New Testament are *huios*, which our English Bibles translate as *son*, and *huiothesia*, which we translate as *adoption*.

The proper understanding of *huios* is not simply *male child*. It is a child who has matured in his father's opinion to the point that he can be identified publicly as his heir and begin to be entrusted with his inheritance.

Huiothesia is the public declaration by the father that his matured child is now officially his heir, and that he will begin to entrust him with inheritance.

The most important example of huios is Jesus, the only begotten Son of God (Mark 1:1; John 3:16). The most important example of huiothesia is Jesus' baptism, where the Father publicly declared Jesus His beloved huios (Matthew 3:16–17). At that time, Jesus received from His Father the anointing of the Holy Spirit, who would empower His ministry on earth as the Christ (the Anointed One).

The next most important examples of huios are supposed to be you and me. We become God's child (Greek word *teknon*) when we embrace Jesus by faith as our Savior and King (John 1:12–13). But we are not supposed to remain infants (Greek word *nepios*) in Christ (1 Corinthians 3:1). It is our Father's predetermined plan for us to mature and become sons of God who are entrusted with divine inheritance on this earth like Jesus was (Romans 8:14–29).

These are the Christians who walk as Jesus walked, do the works He did, and embrace His purpose to reconcile all things to God (1 John 2:3–6; John 14:12; 2 Corinthians 5:17–21). Creation is eagerly waiting for them to show up so this broken world can be set free.

Are you maturing as a child of God? Are you developing the faith and character God can trust with kingdom inheritance? Are you a son of God?

I have room here to list only a few of the characteristics of a son of God. Join me in prayerful self-examination. How many of these are developing in your life?

Sons of God are male or female. It is a matter of your heart, not your gender (Genesis 1:26–28; Galatians 3:25–29; Acts 2:17–18).

Sons of God know themselves to be new creations, born of God and no longer just of man—in this world but no longer of this world.

Sons of God trust God, Jesus Christ, and the Bible completely.

Sons of God know God's love, and love God deeply in return. They are reverent, intimate worshippers.

Sons of God hunger for God's revealed presence. They watch constantly for God's activity around them.

Sons of God know God's love for others and, through the Holy Spirit, have agape love for everyone God loves.

Sons of God are devoted disciples of Jesus Christ. They want to follow Him everywhere He leads them and learn everything He has to teach them. They aspire to be just like Him.

Sons of God are led by the Spirit of Christ. They have eagerly received the baptism of the Holy Spirit, including the spiritual gifts the Lord has for them.

Sons of God are friends of Jesus who understand and share His vision.

Sons of God live humble lives as servants and living sacrifices, laying down their personal agendas daily to embrace God's agenda. They never seek glory for themselves, only for their Lord.

Sons of God seek the kingdom of God and His righteousness for themselves and the world around them. They do not focus on treasures of earth.

Sons of God are peacemakers who help others find healing and wholeness. They embrace their purpose as the royal priesthood, ambassadors for Christ, salt and light.

Sons of God are knitted properly together in the body of Christ and accountable to each other. They are not lone rangers.

Sons of God pray all the time, both for intimacy with God and to intercede for others.

Sons of God earnestly and prayerfully study Scripture. They never stop learning truth.

Sons of God are resolved to shed every encumbrance and sin, as the Lord reveals them, so they can be sanctified completely in spirit, soul, and body.

Sons of God love good. They hate evil and stand against it.

Sons of God know their authority under the Lord's authority. They use the keys of the kingdom.

Sons of God live in the peace and joy of their salvation.

Jesus once said, "Many are called but few are chosen" (Matthew 22:14). You and I have been called to be sons of God. Will we be chosen? Do we want to be chosen?

All creation awaits our answer.

God bless you, and God bless our community.

The Royal Priesthood Must Arise

Come and, like living stones, be yourselves built into a spiritual house, for a holy, dedicated, consecrated priesthood, to offer up those spiritual sacrifices that are acceptable and pleasing to God through Jesus Christ. . . . You are a chosen race, a royal priesthood, a dedicated nation, God's own purchased, special people, that you may set forth the wonderful deeds and display the virtues and perfections of Him who called you out of darkness into His marvelous light.

—1 Peter 2:4–5, 9 AB

Four weeks ago, I wrote about the sons and daughters of God. This week, I write about the royal priesthood. Then I wrote about identity. Today I write about purpose.

The roles of priest and priestess were a part of human culture long before the birth of Christianity. Archeologists have uncovered evidence of priesthoods in Mesopotamia existing before 3,000 BC. These priests, male and female, did what priests have always done: mediate the relationship between mankind and their god or gods.

Yet, even though priests have been a part of virtually every people group throughout history, only in the Bible do we see the possibility of a people group where all are priests. The first example occurs when Moses takes the Hebrew people out of Egyptian bondage to Mount Sinai. God makes an incredible offer to the Hebrews, inviting them to become His "kingdom of priests," "holy nation," and "treasured possession" (Exodus 19:5–6).

The second example, set forth in 1 Peter 2, is the very similar invitation made by the Lord to you and me.

The track record for the Hebrews as a kingdom of priests was spotty at best. Instead of being a godly influence on the world around them, they were too often influenced by the world, even being seduced away to idols both man-made and demonic. By the time of Jesus, they were back in bondage, this time to Rome.

But keep in mind they were operating at a distinct disadvantage. They had the law, but not the truth and grace that would come with Jesus (John 1:17). And although the Holy Spirit rested on some of their judges, prophets, and kings, the Holy Spirit did not dwell within them. It is for this reason that Jesus said the greatest of the Old Testament would be exceeded by the least of those in His kingdom (Luke 7:28).

So what is the track record for the church as a dedicated royal priesthood? We have more people professing Christianity than ever before: about two billion people in a world population of seven billion, with one quarter billion (250,000,000) of those in the United States. Yet how many of these people are functioning as the royal priesthood? How many are actually showing forth powerful deeds and displaying the godly virtues of our Lord?

The answer, my friends, is "Not many!" If we had one quarter billion people functioning as the Lord's priesthood in America today, our nation would look extraordinarily different. But according to 2011 Barna Group research, we can't even get half of our professing Christians to a worship service in any given week. And our national statistics for Bible literacy and daily prayer are worse than that.

Peter's portrait of a priesthood people is perfectly consistent with Paul's portrait of a body of Christ where everyone is spiritually gifted and knitted together in ministry (1 Corinthians 12; Ephesians 4). Since Jesus is both King and High Priest and we are His siblings, this priesthood is royal—we have authority (Hebrews 5:5–10; Romans 8:29; Matthew 16:18–19). Add the amazing fact that Christ dwells within each of us, and there is really no limit to what we can accomplish (Colossians 1:27; Ephesians 3:20–21; John 14:12–14).

So isn't it time to get rid of selfish, lazy, ill-informed Christianity and start holding each other accountable to our divinely appointed purpose? Isn't it time to dismantle the traditions that create a few overworked "clergy," a few more "volunteers," and a crowd of pew-sitters? Isn't it time for the royal priesthood of Jesus Christ to arise?

Old Testament priests were anointed with oil. This royal priesthood is anointed with Holy Spirit and power. We learn and teach God's Word. We function as a team where everyone's contribution is important. Our daily service is a living sacrifice pleasing to the Lord.

We enthrone the Lord in our praise. Our love and faithfulness witness to the lost. Our prayers move mountains, heal the sick, and protect our schools and neighborhoods from evil. Our prophetic words of wisdom provide sound solutions to all kinds of problems.

Arise, royal priesthood. Just as the Old Testament priesthood carried the ark of the covenant, we carry the Lord's presence with us wherever we go. Darkness is covering the earth. Our time is now.

God bless you, and God bless our community.

God Measures Greatness
in a Different Way

Great is the Lord and most worthy of praise; His greatness no one can fathom.

—Psalm 145:3 NIV

God is great! And because we Christians are His sons and daughters, made in His image and called to be godly, I have no problem saying Christians should also be great.

We are to be the light of the world (Matthew 5:14–16). We are to love like God loves (Matthew 5:48). We are to be transformed into the Lord's likeness with ever-increasing glory (2 Corinthians 3:18). We are to do greater works than the miracles Christ did (John 14:12).

In other words, Christians are called to be great. The Marine Corps challenges recruits to "be all you can be." God challenges us to be all we can be through Him (Ephesians 3:16–21).

Unfortunately, there are several obstacles in our path to greatness. The church struggles with complacency, divisiveness, unbelief, and worldly distractions. We also suffer from a lack of knowledge, which gets us off course and leads to destruction (Hosea 4:6).

By lack of knowledge, I mean we substitute a worldly viewpoint for biblical truth. In the pursuit of greatness, we fail to understand how God measures greatness and, instead, apply the world's measure. So we get off course.

How does the modern world measure greatness? We all know the answers: money, popularity, skill, and power.

Donald Trump is a TV star because he is the symbol of "rich." Oprah is so popular, her opinions change public opinion. Tiger Woods may be the most recognized person on earth because of his extraordinary golf skills. (I love golf, but it is just hitting a little white ball into a hole.)

Finally, although we are all captivated by the intense interplay of personalities in our presidential election process, we should not lose sight of the fact that, at its root, this is a battle for power. Much of the intensity of our candidates comes from their ambitious desire for the most powerful political position in the world. That is where they hope to find greatness.

How does the church measure greatness? Do we not look to the megachurches with their high-tech programs and high-profile pastors—people such as T. D. Jakes, Rick Warren, and even Jeremiah Wright? Do we not look to media popularity—James Dobson, Joyce Meyer, Max Lucado, Frederick Price, and so many others? For more charismatic Christians, do we not look to signs and wonders, such as the ministry of Benny Hinn, and bold prophetic ministries such as that of Chuck Pierce?

Please understand. It is not my purpose to address whether these particular Christian leaders are really great. All I am trying to challenge is how we measure that greatness. My concern is that, far too often, we measure by the world's measure. How popular are they? How skilled are they at keeping us engaged and excited? How much national power do they wield? How much supernatural power? For those who preach prosperity, how prosperous is the preacher?

Even on a local level, are we not tempted to measure greatness by attendance, facilities, budget size, and skilled preachers, choirs, or worship teams?

God has given us His measure for greatness. He takes the world's message and flips it right side up. The measure of greatness in the kingdom of God is humble, selfless, sacrificial service to God and others.

Matthew 18:1–4 says those who humble themselves like little children are greatest in the kingdom. Philippians 2:1–8 expands on this theme, encouraging us to the same attitude as Jesus, who humbly "emptied Himself" and became bond servant to the world.

Jesus washed feet, and so must we. "The greatest among you will be your servant" (Matthew 23:8–12). "Whoever wants to be first must be last of all and servant to all" (Mark 9:35). We must deny ourselves (I repeat, deny ourselves!) and take up our cross daily and follow Him (Luke 9:23).

Few things excite me as much as the spiritual awakening we see bubbling up in the church today. Intimacy with God! Power to heal and deliver! Power of prayer to change lives and nations!

Few things concern me more than the need for this awakening to be led by men and women who are humble, selfless servants.

Do people who seek treasures on earth for themselves fit this description (Luke 12:33–34; Matthew 6:19–20)? What about those who seek recognition or those who seek power over others? Or those who seek to always please and never offend their audience?

To the church and its leaders, I say, "Dare to be great!" Dare to be humble and selfless. Dare to become a sacrificial servant to everyone loved by God. Dare in your love to speak unpopular truth. Dare to be like Jesus.

God bless you, and God bless our community.

We Must Stop Cursing
and Start Blessing

From the same mouth come both blessing and cursing. My brethren, these things ought not to be this way. Does a fountain send out from the same opening both fresh and bitter water?
—James 3:10–11 NASB

A few weeks ago, Christie and I attended an excellent conference in our area hosted by Shekinah Church. The featured speaker was John Kilpatrick, former pastor of the church in Pensacola, Florida, where the Brownsville Revival broke forth in 1995.

The Brownsville Revival was, like all major revivals, both powerful and controversial. It lasted more than five years and drew millions of people, including thousands of pastors, from around the world. I was very grateful for the opportunity to hear from the pastor who led a church through such an incredible experience.

Brother Kilpatrick had many good things to share, but what really grabbed me was his teaching on blessings and curses. I purchased his CD sermon series on the subject and let those launch me into personal Bible study. My conclusion: we have as Christians grossly underestimated the power of our words to bless and curse the people, places, and circumstances around us.

Remember the old childhood saying "Sticks and stones may break my bones, but words will never hurt me"? Most of us have learned by now how untrue that saying is. Harsh and critical words hurt the heart, destroy self-image, alienate, and isolate. *Verbal abuse* has become part of our modern psychological terminology for good reason.

Likewise, we all appreciate the positive effect of a kind and encouraging word. Mother Teresa, an expert on kindness, put it this way: "Kind words can be short and easy to speak, but their echoes are truly endless."

At this level of emotional and psychological effect, we Christians understand our responsibility to control our tongues. We may not be very faithful at it, but we understand. It is a part of our call to love and goodness.

What we have not understood sufficiently is the spiritual power unleashed by our words, for good or for evil. Our words can bless or our words can curse—a heavy responsibility and a tremendous opportunity.

As so often in this column, I can hit only the highlights.

The word *bless* in the biblical languages meant to invoke by your words the power for someone to prosper or succeed in an endeavor. The word *curse* meant to invoke by your words an opposite result: failure, misery, or destruction.

No one blesses more than God, starting with Adam and Eve (Genesis 1:28). But people are called to bless as well, and that does not just mean praying for God to bless someone.

Melchizedek blessed Abraham and God (Genesis 14:19). Fathers like Isaac and Jacob blessed their children (Genesis 27:27–29, 49:28). And they did so by faith, which means they expected the blessings to work (Hebrews 11:20–21)!

Moses, David, and Solomon all blessed the people (Deuteronomy 33; 2 Samuel 6:18; 1 Kings 8:55–66). And the people blessed Solomon.

Our greatest model, Jesus, blessed the children (Mark 10:16). His last act before ascending to heaven was to bless His disciples (Luke 24:51). And He called on us to bless even our enemies—to bless and not curse (Luke 6:27–28).

Do our words have power? God spoke creation into existence, and we are made in His image. Jesus said the words He spoke "are spirit and life" (John 6:63). Then He reminded us that what comes out of our mouths will also bring forth good or evil (Luke 6:45).

For me, the most persuasive Scriptures on the matter of blessings relate to the purpose of God's priests. In the Old Testament, the Lord declared the priests were chosen by Him to serve Him and "to bless in His name" (Deuteronomy 10:8, 21:5; Numbers 6:22–27).

Now, as Christians, we live in the New Testament. Who are the priests? We are! We are the royal priesthood, the priests of the kingdom of God on earth (1 Peter 2:9; Revelation 1:6). A crucial part of our priestly role must be to speak blessings into this world in the name of our Lord Jesus.

Start speaking blessings on your spouse, your children, your home, your job and workplace, your pastor and congregation, your problems. And see what happens.

Stop speaking harsh, negative, and judgmental words toward your children, spouse, job, and so on, and toward your nation's leaders. They are curses. They are sin, and they bring about evil.

Where you remember you have spoken words in the past that curse, choose to repent, recant, and revoke. Then replace them with words of blessing.

God's power is within us. Our words can change the spiritual atmosphere around us. Let's become people who bless.

God bless you, and God bless our community.

Will You Hear the Lord
Say, "Well Done?"

His master said to him, "Well done, good and faithful servant. You have been faithful over a little; I will set you over much. Enter into the joy of your master."

—Matthew 25:21

Almost all of us know the story, but have we really heard what Jesus is saying when He tells it?

A master leaves on a journey, entrusting each of his three servants with talents while he is away. Upon his return, the master finds that two of the servants have used the talents given them to produce more. But one servant has failed to invest his talent, instead burying it.

The two faithful servants are commended and rewarded, entering the joy of their master. The unfaithful servant is rebuked and cast into the outer darkness (Matthew 25:30).

This is one of four stories in a row Jesus tells His disciples when they ask what will happen at the end of the age (Matthew 25). Scripture is clear that we will all appear before the Lord Jesus for an accounting of our life and what we have done with it (2 Corinthians 5:10; Revelation 22:12). Each of these four stories in Matthew depicts such an accounting, and they do not suggest a "free ride" for everyone who has been to church, been baptized, or responded to an altar call.

What do you believe your Master Jesus would say to you if you were to appear before Him today? Would you get a "well done"? Have you been "good and faithful," or do you have buried talents?

This is a challenging question most Christians (and preachers) in the American church avoid asking. Part of the problem, I think, is that in the church's effort to emphasize salvation by grace, we have left people with the impression that works are not important to God. This isn't true. Although works cannot save us, we are also not saved by grace unless that grace is received through faith (Ephesians 2:8–9). And faith without works is dead and useless (James 2:14–20).

Otherwise put, if you are not demonstrating love and service to God, don't be too sure you have a sincere and saving faith in your heart (Galatians 5:6; 1 Timothy 1:5).

Another misunderstanding occurs when people are led to believe that eternal life is simply the same ticket to the same heavenly reward for everyone who is saved. Jesus advises us that some will be great and some will be least in the kingdom of heaven (Matthew 5:19). He urges all of us to store up treasures in heaven, not treasures on earth (Matthew 6:19–21). But too many Christians still focus their time and energy (and even their theology) on the earthly riches we are told not to pursue (1 Timothy 6:6–11). Their choices will have eternal consequences.

Please understand. I am not suggesting our faithful service will make God love us more. He already loves each of us perfectly and unconditionally.

I am also not suggesting we serve God simply so we can receive rewards in return. The church already has too much "what's in it for me" as it is.

What I am saying is this: God has already given us His Son, forgiveness of sin, a reconciled relationship, the gift of His Holy Spirit, and eternal life. He is asking us, out of love, trust, and gratitude, to give Him back a life of faithful service for our remaining few years on this earth. Doesn't He deserve that from us? Isn't He worthy?

We all have spiritual "talents" and godly missions on this earth (1 Corinthians 12; Ephesians 2:10). Most of these missions are outside the church walls: the home, workplace, community, and for some, the ends of the earth (Acts 1:8). All of these missions work together to bring others into the kingdom of God, and to bring the kingdom on earth as it is in heaven.

It is no wonder the Master feels outrage when a servant buries the talent(s) he or she has been given. Only He can picture how much could be accomplished for the kingdom if everyone did their part. We must start holding each other accountable. We must begin stirring one another up to love and good works (Hebrews 10:24–27).

I've had some tremendous things said to me over the years. My wife, Christie, said, "I do." My daughters have said, "I love you, Dad." My parents have said, "We're proud of you, son." And above all, my Father and Lord have said, "I love you, Doug. You are forgiven and restored. Welcome home."

Looking forward, I cannot think of anything I want said to me more than "Well done, good and faithful servant" when I stand before Jesus. How about you?

God bless you, and God bless our community.

Reflections on the
Church of Jesus Christ

My Father, please make me a part of the Body,

a part of the Christ now on Earth—

an Aaron who helps others hold up Your prayer staff,

a clown who distributes Your mirth;

a carpenter restoring homes for the poor,

a fund-raiser collecting alms;

a disciple in service to people in need

of a love that left holes in His palms.

"He said to them, "But who do you say that I am?" Simon Peter replied, "You are the Christ, the Son of the living God." And Jesus answered him, "Blessed are you, Simon Bar-Jonah! For flesh and blood has not revealed this to you, but my Father who is in heaven. And I tell you, you are Peter, and on this rock I will build my church, and the gates of hell shall not prevail against it. I will give you the keys of the kingdom of heaven, and whatever you bind on earth shall be bound in heaven, and whatever you loose on earth shall be loosed in heaven." (Matthew 16:15–19)

The Church of Jesus—Some Assembly Required

Jesus said to them, "But who do you say that I am?" Simon Peter replied, "You are the Christ, the Son of the living God." And Jesus answered him, "Blessed are you, Simon Bar-Jonah! For flesh and blood has not revealed this to you, but my Father who is in heaven. And I tell you, you are Peter, and on this rock I will build my church, and the gates of hell shall not prevail against it. I will give you the keys of the kingdom of heaven, and whatever you bind on earth shall be bound in heaven, and whatever you loose on earth shall be loosed in heaven."

—Matthew 16:15–19

Identity crisis is defined in the Free Dictionary by Farlex (Online) as follows: "Distress and disorientation (especially in adolescence) resulting from conflicting pressures and uncertainty about one's self and one's role in society."

In other words, you cannot function effectively unless you know who you are.

It is crucial for every disciple to understand his or her true identity in Christ. I addressed that identity crisis in other reflections.

It is equally crucial that we address the identity crisis of the church. Until we know who the church truly is, we will never function effectively in our purpose. We have been in a disoriented adolescence far too long.

In our Matthew 16 passage, Jesus tells us several things about the church. The church is His. There is only one. He builds her. His identity is her foundation. Responsibility and authority for the kingdom of heaven on earth are delegated to her. The powers of darkness cannot defeat her. And her name, which is at the core of her identity, is the Greek word *ekklesia*.

First, the church belongs to Jesus and no one else. He is the head, and we are the body, which means we are all diversely gifted members of the team He owns and coaches. This team is not for sale or trade to any political regime or religious hierarchy. And He doesn't want any benchwarmers.

Second, Jesus has only one church. Local churches are to exist in every community, but they must operate in teamwork as the one church. Jesus is not a bigamist. He has only one bride.

I am as grateful as anyone for leaders like Martin Luther, John Calvin, and John Wesley. But there is no Gospel of Luther, Calvin, or Wesley. Christ has not been divided, and for too long we have been ignoring His command of loving unity (1 Corinthians 1:11–13; Ephesians 4:1–6; John 17:21–23).

Third, Jesus builds His church. Unless the Lord builds it, we build in vain (Psalm 127:1).

The Lord doesn't build by catering to our corporate strategies, short attention span, and musical preferences. He builds by baptizing people in the Holy Spirit and teaching them to live in total obedience to Him (Matthew 28:19–20; Acts 1:4–5). When the church lived in reverence to Christ and the empowering presence of the Holy Spirit, the church thrived (Acts 9:31).

The building foundation is Jesus' identity as the only begotten Son of God, the Christ who is the Savior of the world. Those who do not believe these truths about Jesus are simply not part of His church. They are not standing on the only foundation He builds on.

Fourth, the church has been given the keys of the kingdom: responsibility, authority, and the ability to bring about the purposes of King Jesus on earth.

This is not theology. It's reality! We are supposed to be winning ground for righteousness, not losing it.

These principles of identity and purpose all tie together when we understand the name Jesus gives to His church—the Greek word *ekklesia*, which means "assembly."

The Old Testament often speaks of leaders such as Moses, Joshua, David, Solomon, Ezra, and Nehemiah who would assemble God's people so they could hear from the Lord or celebrate His goodness to them. Jesus carries that concept into His new covenant when He speaks of His assembly.

But Jesus also embraced a more specific meaning for assembly when He used the name ekklesia.

Each city in the Roman Empire had an ekklesia of the Roman citizens living there. They would assemble to hear the will of Caesar (their king). It was then their collective responsibility and authority to communicate and enforce Caesar's will in that city.

Likewise, when the New Testament speaks of local churches, they are never denominations or competing congregations. They are simply the ekklesia of that city—citizens of God's kingdom who assemble to discern and bring about His purposes in the community where they live.

Kingsport, like every other community, needs a network where all our churches can belong, connect, and assemble. When we begin operating as the ekklesia of Kingsport, we will begin walking in our identity and fulfilling our purpose.

God bless you, and God bless our community.

The Church Must Return to the Formula That Works

Peter said to them, "Repent, and let each of you be baptized in the name of Jesus Christ for the forgiveness of your sins; and you shall receive the gift of the Holy Spirit ..." So then, those who had received his word were baptized; and there were added that day about three thousand souls. And they were continually devoting themselves to the apostles' teaching and to fellowship, to the breaking of bread and to prayer. And everyone kept feeling a sense of awe; and many wonders and signs were taking place through the apostles. And all those who had believed were together, and had all things in common. ... And day by day continuing with one mind in the temple, and breaking bread from house to house, they were taking their meals together with gladness and sincerity of heart, praising God, and having favor with all the people. And the Lord was adding to their number day by day those who were being saved.

—Acts 2:38, 41–44, 46–47

Acts 2 describes the explosive birth and early development of the church built by Jesus Christ (Matthew 16:15–19; Psalm 127:1). Contained within this birthday story is the formula the baby church used to grow healthy and strong. It is a formula the church must return to if we are to fulfill our purpose on this earth.

Ingredient number one in this formula is repentance. The Greek and Hebrew words for *repentance* mean "change of mind" and "change of direction." True faith includes a change of mind about how we view our relationship with God and a change of direction in how we live our lives. No change indicates no real faith (Matthew 7:17; James 2:14–18).

Ingredient number two is baptism into the name of Jesus Christ. The sacrament is not what saves us, but baptism expresses our entry into a new covenant relationship with God where we are trusting God's Son as our Savior and Lord (Acts 2:36). It also expresses our new birth as a new creation and child of God. We should feel new and act new because we are new. The old is supposed to pass away (2 Corinthians 5:17).

Ingredient number three is the forgiveness of our sins, which removes the barrier sin has been to our intimate relationship with God. Our glorious reconnection with God then takes place through ingredient number four, receiving the gift of Holy Spirit—the Spirit of Life (Romans 8:2)!

This is the most important ingredient of all, emphasized in Peter's birthday speech at the beginning, in the middle and at the end (Acts 2:17, 33, 38). Without Holy Spirit, the other ingredients have minimal effectiveness, and some will not work at all. That is why Jesus told us not to leave home without it (Acts 1:4, 8)!

The final four ingredients of our formula come with an instruction on dosage. The early Church "continually devoted themselves" to these four ingredients because the Lord and His kingdom were their first priority every day. As we all know, if you don't take your meals and medicine as prescribed, they will not provide the health and energy you desire.

Ingredient number five is the apostolic teachings, which means nothing more or less than what Jesus commanded before He ascended to the Father: "… teaching them to obey all that I have commanded you" (Matthew 28:20). The key words here are *all* and *obey.*

Ingredient number six is fellowship, first and foremost, with the heavenly Father and His Son Jesus Christ (1 John 1:3–4). The early church knew the intimate presence of God. They then made that loving fellowship complete by including each other in it. You cannot say you love God if you don't love each other (1 John 4:20).

"The breaking of bread" is ingredient number seven. Some propose that this refers to Holy Communion, but even though I cherish the remembrance and power of that sacrament, it is more likely that this "breaking of bread" combines two other traditions: the cherished Hebrew family meal, where the bread was always broken rather than carved, and the bread of the presence that was in the Holy Place of the tabernacle (Exodus 25:30). The early church gathered together in their homes daily as the family of faith. They knew as they broke bread together that Jesus, the Bread of Life, was present with them (John 6:48–51; Luke 24:30–31).

Our final ingredient, number eight, is prayer, both for intimacy with God and intercession in the world. The early church was the household of unceasing prayer we are supposed to be (Matthew 21:13; 1 Thessalonians 5:17).

And what were the results of this formula? There was a deep daily reverence for the Lord. Wondrous miracles occurred all the time. Their trust in God and love for each other motivated them to share so that no one remained in need. They were people of joy, integrity, and humility who had the admiration of the lost around them, attracting more and more people into the kingdom every day.

In other words, the early church was exactly what the world needs today. And today's church can be the ones, in far greater numbers, who meet those world needs if we return to their Acts 2 formula for life.

God bless you, and God bless our community.

You May Need to Tear Down to Build Up

See, today I appoint you over nations and kingdoms to uproot and tear down, to destroy and overthrow, to build and to plant.
—Jeremiah 1:10

On my first day of US Marine Corps basic officer training, they led us to the exercise field and ordered us to do all the pull-ups, sit-ups, and push-ups we could do. I was coming out of a college life where I had played basketball four to five times a week. I did pretty well. Second day, same order: I didn't do so well. Third day, same order: I could barely do one pull-up. Welcome to the Corps' building plan: tear you down so they can build you up better. It was painful but effective. Within a few weeks, I was in the best shape I will ever know.

Years later, we moved to Kingsport to begin civilian law practice, purchasing a modest home on a beautiful "country road" four-acre lot just ten minutes from my office. After a few more years, we were making enough money for a bigger house. In all our looking, we could find no location better than where we lived. The problem was that the design of our existing house would not allow us to simply add on and have the home we wanted. Substantial portions of our existing house had to be torn down to accommodate the "bigger and better" house design. It was very costly but, again, effective. By the grace of God, we still live at that beautiful location in a home that blesses our needs.

Ecclesiastes 3:3 reminds us there is "a time to tear down and a time to build." It is a lesson we apply in sports or business when we see that our past practices are no longer adequate to meet the new challenges of competition or marketplace. We are willing to learn. We are even willing to unlearn so we can learn more and better.

But when it comes to our faith—what we have been taught about God, the church, and the world—our attitude toward change is, to put it mildly, much less receptive. Tell me something new that fits comfortably with what I already believe, and I praise the Lord for my additional understanding. But try to teach me something that doesn't fit, that requires me to abandon something I have already chosen to believe to accept something new, well, that is simply too painful and too costly, no matter how persuasive the "new" truth is.

Jesus addressed this problem in the parables of the old wineskin and old cloth patch (Mark 2:21–22). Many devout Jews were unable to accept a Messiah who didn't behave like they had been taught, and so they missed the time of the Lord's visit (Luke 19:44). Their temple was destroyed, and the church was built.

Earlier in Jeremiah's time, God warned His people that they were living independent of Him and in pursuit of idols (Jeremiah 2:11–13). God allowed Jerusalem and that temple to be torn down, promising that He would build it back better in the new covenant we know to be Jesus (Jeremiah 31:31–34).

Does the church today pursue idols, treasures of earth rather than treasures of heaven? Do we act independently by, for example, leaning on our own understanding, with "liberals" trusting intellect over Scripture and "conservatives" insisting Scripture be read in conformity with man-drafted doctrines rather than the power of the Holy Spirit?

God is the builder of our lives and of His church (Hebrews 3:4, 11:10). Only what is built on the foundation of Jesus Christ will stand (Matthew 16:18). Who He is, what He has done, and what He has said create the cornerstone that positions everything true (Ephesians 2:20). I urge us all to stay willing to unlearn (tear down) anything that does not conform to this divine building plan. As we relearn, the Lord will build us "bigger and better" and bless all peoples through us (Genesis 12:3; John 14:12).

God bless you, and God bless our community.

Where's the Love?
Where's the Power?

For this reason I bow my knees before the Father, from whom every family in heaven and on earth is named, that according to the riches of His glory He may grant you to be strengthened with power through His Spirit in your inner being, so that Christ may dwell in your hearts through faith—that you, being rooted and grounded in love, may have strength to comprehend with all the saints what is the breadth and length and height and depth, and to know the love of Christ that surpasses knowledge, that you may be filled with all the fullness of God. Now to Him who is able to do far more abundantly than all that we ask or think, according to the power at work within us, to Him be glory in the church and in Christ Jesus throughout all generations, forever and ever. Amen.

—Ephesians 3:14–21

Wendy's Old Fashioned Hamburgers had a truly memorable television commercial twenty-five years ago in which a little old lady would stare down the servers at various hamburger joints and growl, "Where's the beef?"

The message was clear. As quality management guru Stephen Covey once said, "The main thing is to keep the main thing the main thing." The main thing in a hamburger is the beef. So where is it?

Now imagine a little old angel arriving at your church one Sunday morning on a quality control assignment from the head of your church, Jesus Christ. She quickly (and supernaturally) examines your times of worship, your fellowship with one another, and last but not least, your hearts. Then she growls, "Where's the love? Where's the power?"

The church is called to express the gospel brought by Jesus: the good news of the kingdom of God returning to earth (Matthew 4:23, 24:14). The fundamental principle of life in the kingdom is love of God and love of others (Matthew 22:36–40). The fundamental manifestation of the kingdom is power of good over evil (Luke 11:20, 1 John 3:8). That is why Paul's great prayer in Ephesians 3 focuses so much on love and power.

In other words, love and power are the "main things" about the kingdom of God we are to express on earth as His church. Where are they?

As for power, I have written before about our scriptural mandate to provide ministries of divine healing and deliverance from demonic oppression (Mark 16:17–20; John 14:12). Even if your doctrines reject that biblical reality for some reason, you should still be able to recognize the powerlessness of a Christian community with a high divorce rate and countless individuals, young and old, struggling with anxiety, depression, loneliness, poverty, pornography, adultery, promiscuity, and substance addiction. "God gave us a spirit not of fear but of power and love and self-control" (2 Timothy 1:7).

As for love, Jesus said the world would know we are His disciples by how we love one another (John 13:35). Yet how many congregations demonstrate that loving fellowship? In our larger congregations, people don't even know most of the other people in "their church." There is a lot of "duck in" and "duck out." And in smaller congregations, where the call to be one loving family might be easier to accomplish, we too often have cliques and factions instead (1 Corinthians 1:10–13).

Finally, and most important, how many professing Christians really love God and love Jesus from the depths of their heart? The Lord's Great Commandment is that we love God with all our heart, mind, soul, and strength (Mark 12:30). But everywhere I go, what I hear people say is simply, "I believe in God." "I believe in Jesus." It is much harder to find those who earnestly proclaim, "I love Jesus!" "I love my heavenly Father!"

Anyone who thinks our Lord doesn't do quality control inspections of His church needs to read Revelation 2 and 3. Let's not wait to be "spit out" or "blotted out." Instead let's honestly examine ourselves, and if God's awesome love and power are not present and growing in our hearts and ministries like they were in the Acts 2 church, let's change our ways.

Get rid of "religion." Don't be satisfied with intellectual, unemotional assent to the faith. Don't be satisfied with goals that are based on your own power and resources.

Begin to live out the fulfillment of Paul's prayer that by the incredible gift of His Holy Spirit, you will experience both the wonder of God's love for you and the awesome availability of His power within you. Become the "more than conqueror" you have read about, and then help others do the same (Romans 8:37).

Be filled with all the fullness of God, and see what happens!

God bless you, and God bless our community.

The Problem Is We Don't Love God

Love the Lord your God with all your heart and with all your soul and with all your strength.

—Deuteronomy 6:5

I bought a new carpet steam cleaner recently. We have big dogs that bring the outside inside, and our old carpet cleaner had worn out.

Some assembly was required, but it was just putting one top part onto one bottom part. I did it quickly, put hot water and detergent in the appropriate compartment, and began cleaning. Since it was a new machine highly rated by *Consumer Reports*, I was looking forward to a like-new carpet.

After several minutes of work, I was very disappointed. The carpet wasn't getting clean. I touched where I had been cleaning. It was dry. Somehow no steam or detergent was getting to the carpet, so I was giving maximum effort with minimal results.

Inspection revealed I had committed a basic assembly error, almost as bad as failing to plug the machine in or turn it on. When the problem was fixed, the carpet got even cleaner than I had hoped.

My carpet cleaner experience illustrates a significant problem we are experiencing in the church.

Our churches are, at least in some ways, giving maximum effort. We spend lots of time and money scheduling services and developing programs. But frankly, we see minimal results. The culture is not becoming more Christian. Many of our congregations will lead no one to Christ. Depression, stress, divorce, and addiction are epidemic within our own families. Why?

I believe our problem is basic. Most of us don't really love God. We believe in Him. We're grateful for the ticket to heaven. And we know He loves us. But we don't love Him back—the most basic thing He asks us to do. Loving others is wonderful, but it is not a substitute for loving God.

We call it the Great Commandment. Love God with all you are. Jesus said that if we get this one right, and love our neighbor, then everything else falls into place (Matthew 22:37–41).

Note: Jesus also said that if we love Him, we will obey Him, but if we don't love Him, we won't obey Him (John 14:15.23–24).

To understand this, just remember the difference between a job you love and a job you don't love. When you have a job you don't love, it is hard to get up in the morning. You do what is required to get your paycheck, but your heart isn't in it. You give yourself some slack when you can get away with it. If it gets too tough, you quit.

But when you have a job you love, it is not really a "job" at all. It is a joy.

The Old Testament provides another great example. Have you noticed the Great Commandment is not one of the Ten Commandments?

When the Hebrews received God's Ten Commandments, they barely knew Him. They had lived hundreds of years in a culture of pagan gods and were not ready to grasp the idea of a divine love relationship. So God offered them a "paycheck" relationship. Do what I tell you and I will bless and protect you.

The Hebrews got by in this relationship, despite a lot of complaining, until they were about to cross into the Promised Land. Then, when it looked too tough to go on, they quit.

Forty years later, the Hebrews returned to the Jordan River, but those who quit had died. This new generation had spent their entire lives in the wilderness experiencing the loving provision of God. Their clothes and sandals never wore out. Their enemies never defeated them.

These Hebrews were ready for a greater commandment, and Moses gave it. Love God with all you are (Deuteronomy 6:5). And then see what He does for you and through you.

They crossed the river, took Jericho, and divided the land God had promised. Faith in God plugged them in. Love for God turned them on.

Take some time to ask yourself, *Do I really love God? Do I treat Him like others I have loved deeply? Do I long to be with Him and draw closer to Him? Do I want to know more about Him? Do I willingly give up other things for Him? Does making Him happy make me happy?*

If you have not loved God like He deserves, ask Him to help. He is the source of love. No one has earned our love more. And when you get to know Him, no one is more lovable.

What does God want? He wants a church that truly loves Him. That church will be assembled correctly, "turned on," and change the world.

God bless you, and God bless our community.

The Church Must Be
Made Salty Again

*"You are the salt of the earth. But if the salt loses its saltiness,
how can it be made salty again? It is no longer good for anything,
except to be thrown out and trampled by men"*
—Matthew 5:13 NIV

Salt is almost a bad word in today's USA. Medical science tells us some salt is necessary for life, but our nation's excessive salt intake has led to serious warnings.

Salt causes high blood pressure, which leads to strokes and heart attacks. Salt can cause excessive fluid retention and even promote weight gain. As fast-food restaurants and snack vendors know, the taste for salt is addictive. We end up eating far more French fries, chips, popcorn, and so on than we should. Then the salt makes us thirsty for sugary drinks such as soda and beer, which do further damage.

We are directed to low-sodium and salt-free diets, even salt substitutes, to avoid this potentially hazardous condiment. In short, the less salt you have, the better off you are.

In the days of Jesus, however, the word *salt* had only good connotations. Salt kept you alive. Salt flavored your food. Salt was necessary to preserve meats and other foods so they wouldn't spoil. Salt was such a universal necessity that it could be used as currency to buy things or pay wages.

When Jesus told God's people they were "the salt of the earth," He was saying that we are essential to the well-being of the earth. We have purposes that go all the way back to creation.

For five days, God created things and called them "good," but on the sixth day when God created us in His image, He called it "very good" (Genesis 1:31). We provide the flavor of creation: the family relationships of a Father and His children.

God also assigned us the task of preservation—family growth and, under God's authority, stewardship and dominion over all the earth (Genesis 1:26–28). These two purposes of relationship and stewardship—flavor and preservation—go hand in hand.

The problem, as we all know, is our failure to fulfill our purposes. Sin broke our relationship with God and each other, which in turn destroyed our ability to be effective stewards. The salt lost its saltiness, and the world has been a mess ever since.

To know how to become salty again, it helps to understand how salt loses saltiness. Salt is sodium chloride, a chemical compound we obtain in crystal form from the earth (rock salt) or the sea. Unlike chewing gum or stale bread, a salt crystal does not simply lose its flavor. Instead, salt loses its saltiness when salt crystals become mixed with nonsalt crystals like sand. Who would want to try separating nonsalt from salt crystal by crystal? No one, so you just throw it away.

When mankind loses saltiness, how does God avoid throwing us away? The first steps in this plan of salvation were God's. He sent Jesus to pay the price for all sin, and He sends His Holy Spirit to all who receive Jesus as Savior and Lord.

But the next step in regaining saltiness is ours. I encourage you to carefully read Luke 14:25–35 and Mark 9:38–50. In Luke, Jesus describes how our love of possessions and other worldly relationships can become "nonsalt" that distracts us from discipleship and destroys our saltiness. In Mark, Jesus teaches how a spirit of "them versus us" among God's people can do the same damage.

The Father prunes us (John 15:1–2). The Son of God can be "like a refiner's fire or a launderer's soap" in our lives (Malachi 3:2–3). But what God does in His initiative is not intended to excuse us from our own initiative. As the salt of the earth, we are called to purify ourselves just as Jesus is pure (1 John 3:1–3). We are called to examine our lives and cut out anything that interferes with our relationship with God or our stewardship in His name.

We Christians in modern America are, as a whole, much too self-seeking. We spend far more "church money" on ourselves than we do on the poor. We seek music we like and preaching that makes us feel better about where we are. We ask, "What can God do for me?" rather than, "What can God do through me?"

How many of us take the time each week to share love and the gospel with the lost? How many spend more time with God than they spend with TV, computers, and other distractions?

The church (every Christian!) must reclaim our divinely assigned purpose. We must purify our structures, routines, and priorities to meet that purpose. Creation is waiting in eager expectation for the salt to regain its saltiness so the world can be liberated from decay (Romans 8:19–20).

God bless you, and God bless our community.

The Church Must
Rediscover the Bible

*Go, inquire of the Lord for me, and for the people, and for all
Judah, concerning the words of this book that has been found. For
great is the wrath of the Lord that is kindled against us, because
our fathers have not obeyed the words of this book, to do according
to all that is written concerning us.*

—2 Kings 22:13

... Speaking the truth in love ...

—Ephesians 4:15

Josiah was a good boy who became a good king. His story, told in 2
Kings 22–23, is the story of revival that came to God's people when they
rediscovered God's book and reformed their ways to fit His blueprint.

Josiah was twenty-two years old when the "Book of the Law" (probably
the Pentateuch, the first five books of our Bible) was found somewhere in
the temple. We do not know how long it had been buried or laid aside, but
it had clearly been long enough for the people to forget what it actually
said. For many years they had practiced their faith according to doctrines
taught by men, without recourse to Scripture, and many of those practices
would have been developed during the fifty-five-year reign of Josiah's
wicked grandfather Manasseh.

Now a fresh reading of Scripture revealed to Josiah how many of their
existing practices were contrary to God's will, and Josiah took immediate
steps to correct that. He discontinued practices that Scripture prohibited,

including demonic idol worship, and reinstituted practices that Scripture described, including the celebration of Passover.

The Scripture Josiah honored would, in turn, honor him. The Bible says Josiah turned to the Lord "with all his heart, might and soul," and that there was no other king like him, before or after (2 Kings 23:25). High praise indeed for one whose ancestor was King David.

Friends, I am deeply convicted of our need today to learn from King Josiah. Virtually every "wing" of today's church in America has abandoned Scripture in some significant way. These failures to follow God's blueprint have both crippled and divided us.

Several mainline denominations have lost the belief that all Scripture is the divinely inspired Word of God. As a result, there are behaviors such as the practice of homosexuality that they call God's creative will even though Scripture calls it sin. And they say Jesus is simply one way, not the Way, to eternal life. As in the days before Josiah, Scripture has been laid aside.

Other Christian institutions hold fast to the God-breathed nature of Scripture but declare traditions of man, such as papal decrees, to be of equal authority. As a result, people are asked to call a man their spiritual father when the Bible says only God in heaven is our spiritual father (Matthew 23:9). They declare Mary to have been sinless like Jesus and pray to her, even though Scripture says only God is sinless (Mark 10:18; Romans 3:23). They maintain a system of God, priests, and the people when Scripture reveals the Old Testament system abolished in the new covenant of Christ, in which all Christians are the royal priesthood (1 Peter 2:9; Ephesians 4).

These traditions are contrary to Scripture, not in addition to them. Scripture has been displaced and misplaced.

Finally, although no one has more vigorously defended the Bible than the evangelical wing of the church, many of these defenders of Scripture have abandoned Scripture as well. They have effectively "torn out" the hundreds of biblical passages that speak of our need to be baptized, gifted, empowered, and led by the Holy Spirit.

This doctrine of "cessationism" argues that because the frequency of reported healings, miracles, and other spiritual gifts declined a few hundred years after the birth of the church, those types of Spirit-empowered practices are no longer intended by God to be part of His church. There is no, I repeat, no scriptural support for this conclusion.

There is no "post-Spirit" or "post-Power" dispensation of God! The declining frequency of healings, miracles, and other gifts was the result of man's increasing unbelief, not God's eternal will, and we have the same problem today. Remember what our Lord said about the "power from on high" being sent to us: don't leave home without it (Acts 1:4–8)!

Friends, I love the church and the many Christians who have, as members of these denominations and traditions, lived out their lives in loving service to others. Nevertheless, love includes speaking the truth in love.

We must rediscover the Bible as our blueprint, stop doing what Scripture prohibits, and start doing everything Scripture directs us to do. Stop living Sinatra's "I did it my way" and do it God's way—the way of His Spirit and His truth!

Then revival will come.

God bless you, and God bless our community.

We Must Yoke with Christ,
Not Unbelievers

Do not be unequally yoked with unbelievers. For what partnership has righteousness with lawlessness? Or what fellowship has light with darkness? "... Therefore go out from their midst, and be separate from them," says the Lord, "and touch no unclean thing; then I will welcome you, and I will be a father to you, and you shall be sons and daughters to me," says the Lord Almighty.

—2 Corinthians 6:14, 17–18

My last three columns have focused on our need as Christian disciples to seek righteousness and spiritual maturity, becoming sons and daughters of God so we can function effectively as the Lord's royal priesthood in a world that desperately needs Him.

I recently encountered a Scripture passage that brings home how important this is. At Romans 2:23–24, the apostle Paul speaks to fellow Jews who were part of the church but still proud of their status as God's old-covenant people: "You who boast in the law dishonor God by breaking the law, for, as it is written, 'The name of God is blasphemed among the Gentiles because of you.'"

Paul was reminding these Jews that they had been called to be a holy nation and kingdom of priests so God could demonstrate His righteousness and power to the Gentile world through them (Exodus 19:5–6). However, the failure of the Jews to obey the law of which they boasted—their failure to "walk the talk"—had produced an opposite result. Instead of being respected and feared among unbelievers, the name of Jehovah God was treated with disdain.

Now apply this principle to two periods of church history. In the earliest years, the church in Jerusalem was a community of devoted disciples. Their lifestyle was reverent worship, prayer, learning and obeying the teachings of Jesus, loving fellowship, generosity, and a faith that produced awesome demonstrations of God's power. They had "favor with all the people" and day by day, the lost came into the kingdom (Acts 2:42–47).

Compare that with America today. Is the name of the Lord respected and feared, or blasphemed?

Folks, the names Jesus and God are spoken millions of times per day in America, but most often as a curse or epithet. The sexual and marital morality taught in Scripture is seen as a prudish restriction of personal freedom. Belief in supernatural events such as prophecy, healing, deliverance, and miracles is viewed as ignorant superstition. People fear being unfriended on Facebook more than they fear God.

What happened? The church has failed to "walk the talk." Why? In large part because we have been "yoked to the wrong folk"!

Scripture gives Christians two instructions about the yoke. First and foremost, be yoked to Christ. Be in submission to His authority and teachings, and in union with His powerful presence within you (Matthew 11:29–30). Second, as set forth in 2 Corinthians 6, do not be yoked with unbelievers.

This warning is not about marriage, as many have treated it. Paul tells believers married to nonbelievers to stay married (1 Corinthians 7:12–17). But he tells Christians yoked to unbelievers to separate from them so they can draw close to their heavenly Father and become sons and daughters of God. Only Christians who are rightly fitted together will grow to full spiritual maturity (Ephesians 4:11–16).

Tragically, the church has a long history of becoming unequally yoked. In the second century, many Christian "theologians" began to yoke biblical revelation to Greek philosophy. In the third century, the institutional church became yoked to the politics and greed of the Roman Empire. Those patterns of yoking Christians to man's intellectual limitations and desire for personal power and wealth have continued in various forms ever since.

As a result, we have religious practices rather than divine intimacy, church division rather than loving fellowship, little faith rather than great faith, and powerless lives that resemble the unbelievers around us more than they resemble Jesus.

Remember—the yoke in this context concerns a strong bond and alignment of shared purpose, not just friendship or family. Such unbelief is a problem whether it is in whole or part.

So ask the Lord if you are unequally yoked. Are you yoked to a denomination that has abandoned biblical standards for sexuality and marriage? Are you yoked to a congregation that enables pew sitting instead of the biblical mandate of witness and sacrificial service? Are you yoked to those who have rejected Christ's command that His disciples be baptized in the Holy Spirit so they can receive His presence, power, gifts, and holy character?

There are only two yokes we should wear. One is the yoke of Christ. The other is a yoke shared with others yoked to Christ: people who embrace the authority of Scripture, the leadership of Holy Spirit, and the call to re–present Jesus in the world.

Then our light will shine!

God bless you, and God bless our community.

Standing Shoulder to Shoulder

"Then will I purify the lips of the peoples, that all of them may call on the name of the Lord and serve Him shoulder to shoulder."
—Zephaniah 3:9 NIV

The people of God have an ungodly tendency to be divisive. This may be rooted in the first brotherhood when a jealous Cain killed Abel (Genesis 4:1–16).

We see the enmity in Abraham's lineage between Isaac and Ishmael, Jacob and Esau, Joseph and his jealous brothers. Moving forward to the time of the kingdom of Israel, we have Saul versus David. Then David deals with rebellion by his son, Absalom. And upon the death of David's son, Solomon, the one kingdom divides into two kingdoms: Israel and Judah. Eventually both are destroyed. As Jesus would later instruct, "A house divided against itself falls" (Luke 11:17).

In the midst of this Old Testament divisiveness, the prophet Zephaniah foresees a time when God's wrath will be expressed against the sins of the world and His disobedient people. God will gather a people humble toward Him and each other. They will be cleansed of their sin and be one people serving one Lord "shoulder to shoulder."

Zephaniah was foreseeing the church. In her infancy, we seemed to meet this "shoulder to shoulder" standard (Acts 2). Unfortunately, the New Testament people of God soon proved to have the same divisive tendencies as their predecessors. Paul cries out, "My brothers, some from Chloe's household have informed me that there are quarrels among you. What I mean is this: One of you says, 'I follow Paul'; another, 'I follow Apollos'; another, 'I follow Cephas'; still another, 'I follow Christ.' Is Christ divided?" (1 Corinthians 1:11–13 NIV).

Despite the many theological and political conflicts that followed, there was no formal division in the church for a thousand years. Then church authorities in Rome and Constantinople split into what we call the Roman Catholic Church and the Eastern (or Greek) Orthodox Church. About five hundred years later, resistance to "reformation" led to the Protestant Church. Church splits have continued to abound since that time. Today there are thousands of denominations and "nondenominations."

We don't work together often, and frequently compete. We hardly ever pray together. "Shoulder to shoulder" is not how the non-Christian world sees us or how we see each other, because it is not what we do.

How do we become one body working together (Ephesians 4:1–16)? How do we answer Jesus' prayer that we be one so the world will finally know God sent Jesus and God loves them (John 17:20–23)? Zephaniah 3 indicates that God's gathered people will possess these traits:

1. Obedience (verses 9, 12): They will understand unity is a command, not an option. If we are truly standing shoulder to shoulder with our Lord and cornerstone, Jesus, we will stand shoulder to shoulder with each other (Ephesians 2:19–22).

2. Transparency (verse 3): They will be honest, "real," and vulnerable with each other (1 Corinthians 12:24–26). Deceit is a weapon of the enemy.

3. Humility (verse 11–12): We are called to serve the Lord, each other, and the world, not focus on "me" and "mine" (Mark 9:35). Pride and selfishness are character traits of the enemy.

4. Accountability (verses 9, 13): They will be made righteous by the blood of Jesus (Isaiah 6:5–7). They will humbly and lovingly help each other stay that way (Proverbs 12:1). Lawlessness is the banner of the enemy.

5. Mercy (verses 9, 11): We must forgive one another to receive our Father's forgiveness (Matthew 5:7, 6:14–15). We must love each other in the same way Jesus loves us (John 13:34). Accusation is another weapon of the enemy.

6. Agreed Purpose (verse 9): Teamwork evolves from a common purpose, a common Lord, even a common enemy. We have all of those. We are not called to compete for members and build our own

"house" (Haggai 1). We are called to further the prayer that His kingdom will come and His will be done on earth as it is in heaven.

A divisive church will continue to fall short, but when we stand shoulder to shoulder, the Lord will be with us and turn back our enemy so completely, we will never again fear harm (verse 15; Matthew 16:18).

And please hear this! The most exciting promise of all is how the Lord will respond to those who stand shoulder to shoulder: "He will take great delight in you, He will quiet you with his love, He will rejoice over you with singing" (verse 17).

I yearn to be part of a church where God rejoices over us with singing! Let's become congregations who network together and stand shoulder to shoulder for the King in our Kingsport community. Let God rejoice over us!

God bless you, and God bless our community.

The Light Shines when the Colors Come Together

And He opened his mouth and taught them, saying: ... "You are the light of the world."

—Matthew 5:2, 14)

Again Jesus spoke to them, saying, "I am the light of the world."
—John 8:12a

So, which way is it? Is Jesus the light of the world, or are we the light of the world?

Obviously the Lord said both, and He took the time to explain what He means. While Jesus was in the world, He was the light of the world (John 9:5). After He ascended to the Father, His light remained on earth within those who follow Him: His disciples, the family of faith He calls His church (John 8:12b).

Imagine with me what the light of Jesus looks like. In one way it is about truth—revelation and transparency. The darkness recedes and the blind see!

In another way, it is about brilliance and radiance—the majestic glory of the King of Glory. Breathtaking!

Now ponder with me how as the church and as individual Christians, we have made this incredible light within us appear so dim to the world around us. Darkness is everywhere. The blind are everywhere. And the name of Jesus Christ is probably used in profanity more often than it is used in reverent worship. Heart wrenching!

I researched how God forms visible light. In simple terms, it is a spectrum of colors—various wavelengths of light—brought together. There are six basic colors: red, orange, yellow, green, blue, and violet. We see them divided in a rainbow or through a prism. But usually we see them together as bright white, far more radiant than they could ever be apart.

I then reflected on the spectrum of a Christlike life. With the help of a book by Richard Foster called *Streams of Living Water*, I envisioned six "colors" of Christian focus.

For red, think of the evangelical tradition with its emphasis on the Word and the blood of Jesus. If we don't believe the whole Bible is divinely inspired, we are left to figure out who God is and what He wants based on our own puny understanding. If we don't embrace the truth of how the cross provided salvation by grace through faith, we are left with the need to save ourselves. The world needs red.

For orange, think of the charismatic tradition and the fire of the Holy Spirit. I write often about the Spirit-filled, Spirit-led life. That is how Christ walked the earth. When Jesus assigned us to be His witnesses, He warned us not to leave our room until we were empowered with His Holy Spirit (Luke 24:48–49). The world needs orange.

For yellow, think of the holiness tradition and the pure gold of a pure heart. We are called to be a holy people (1 Peter 1:14–16). The pure in heart see God (Matthew 5:8). This is a life of agape—selfless and unconditional love. If we don't get love right, we don't get anything right (1 Corinthians 13). The world needs yellow.

For green, our "change the environment" color, think of the social justice tradition—a lifestyle of compassion for the poor and marginalized. Those who think Jesus was interested only in getting people to heaven need to reread Matthew 25:31–46: "What you do for the least of these, you do for me." God's prophet declared God's expectation: "Do justice, love mercy and walk humbly with your God" (Micah 6:8). The world needs green.

For blue, the color of the heavens above us, think of the contemplative tradition: the life of prayer. Prayer is many things, but at its root, prayer is simply being with God and staying lovingly attentive to the One who is always lovingly attentive to you. Prayer holds everything else together. The world needs lots of blue.

Finally, for violet, the spectral version of purple, think of the sacramental tradition and how the royal mysteries of God are expressed in baptism and Holy Communion. If we listen hard enough during the baptism of a true convert, we can hear our eternal Father declaring, "This is my beloved, in whom I am well pleased." If we look deep enough, we can see the hand of the King of Kings serving us the broken bread and the cup. The world needs violet.

Dear friends, what would happen if as congregations and individuals, we stopped limiting ourselves to a couple of colors and brought all these "colors" of the Christlike life into our lives? We would finally shine brightly—the light of the world! Everyone and everything around us would be touched by the glory of God.

In the beginning, the Lord said, "Let there be light!" Let's be light!

God bless you, and God bless our community.

A Chosen Race and Holy Nation

You are a chosen race, a royal priesthood, a holy nation, a people for God's own possession, that you may proclaim the excellencies of Him who has called you out of darkness into His marvelous light; for you once were not a people, but now you are the people of God.

—1 Peter 2:9–10 NASB

The community of Christian faith we call the church has many names in Scripture: the body of Christ (1 Corinthians 12:27), the Bride of Christ (Revelation 19:7–9), the fellowship (1 John 1:3–7), the assembly (*ekklesia*, Matthew 16:18, which we translate as *church*). One of my favorite descriptions is found at 1 Peter 2:9–10 cited above.

The phrase *royal priesthood* points to our purpose, addressing issues of ministry and authority. But the other phrases—*chosen race, holy nation,* and *people of God ... for God's own possession*—all point to our collective identity. Throughout human history, men and women have grouped themselves in a collective identity based on family, tribe, nation, ethnic heritage, or language and culture. Through Christ, God has established a new people group—His people set apart for His purposes.

Different English translations of the Bible may translate Peter's Greek words for people groups (*genos, ethnos,* and *laos*) in somewhat different ways. The key is to recognize that Peter has basically used all of the Greek "people group" words available to him. In essence, God is saying that it doesn't matter how you previously identified yourself ethnically, culturally, or politically. Now, as a Christian, you identify yourself first and foremost with all other Christians.

And Paul, who loved his Hebrew heritage, added that we are to consider all other forms of identity rubbish compared with being in Christ (Philippians 3:8; Galatians 3:28).

These are challenging words for us. If we're honest, we admit it is easier to be united in our American patriotism than to come together across denominational lines in the name of Jesus. But are we not more connected to another Christian, regardless of nationality, than to a nonbelieving next-door neighbor?

Perhaps the most visible expression of our identity problem is how we are with rare exception still white churches, black churches, Hispanic churches, and Asian churches. Employment and educational barriers of race have been diminished by law, but in our churches, segregation is alive and well.

Again, I ask, who is my brother and sister? The one who is my color, or the one with whom I share Jesus (Mark 3:31–35)?

I am not proposing here the elimination of national loyalty or the immediate abolishment of denominations. And I am not suggesting we mandate "church busing" to desegregate existing congregations. But I am suggesting we need to begin living out the priority of our collective identity in Christ in ways that will show the rest of the world we are truly "one" people (John 17:20–23).

When we come together for the glory of God, we openly challenge the conflicts of racism, politics, and socioeconomics, manifesting the reconciliation that can come only through Jesus Christ (2 Corinthians 5:16–21; Ephesians 2:13–22)! If we don't do it, no one will.

God bless you, and God bless our community.

We Don't Know What We're Doing

When they came to the place called the Skull, there they crucified him, along with the criminals—one on his right, the other on his left. Jesus said, "Father, forgive them, for they do not know what they are doing."

—Luke 23:33–34

I was asked during Easter week to participate in a service remembering "the seven words" Jesus spoke from the cross. The first word from—Luke 23:34—was my assignment.

This Scripture was one I have preached on many times. There are profound truths in the passage about both the necessity and power of forgiveness. But this year what I heard in my heart was "Father, forgive us, for we don't know what we're doing." "Father, forgive your people, the church, for we don't know what we're doing."

The Hebrew people became God's people by entering a covenant we now call the "old covenant" or "Old Testament." As the people gathered at the foot of Mount Sinai, God descended on the mountain in fire and smoke, and spoke the Ten Commandments (Exodus 19; Hebrews 12:18–21). The people agreed to be God's people, but declared in their fear that they did not want God to speak directly to them anymore. They asked Moses to be their go-between (Exodus 20:18–19, 24:3).

God had, of course, anticipated their response. And so was born the tabernacle system in the wilderness that would later become the temple system in Jerusalem. The tribe of Moses, the Levites, became the caretakers of the tabernacle/temple, and the family of Moses, through his brother Aaron, became the priests who would "go between" the people and God.

These priests were given access to places in the tabernacle where the people could not go. They performed rituals and other functions the people were not permitted to perform. They were given special garments—robes and vestments—that would distinguish them from the people.

Almost 1,500 years later, Jesus showed up with a new covenant and a new system. When Jesus died on the cross for our sins, the veil in the temple was torn down, signifying that all God's people would now have direct personal access to God's presence (Matthew 27:50–51; Hebrews 9, 10:19–22).

This new covenant created not only a new access to God but a new priesthood and a new temple. No longer would priests "go between" God and His people, because all of God's people were now a royal priesthood (1 Peter 2:9). And no longer would a building be the structure where God would dwell, because now His house would be built of living stones— again, all God's people (1 Peter 2:9).

The inauguration of this new covenant system was Pentecost when reminiscent of that earlier time at Mount Sinai, God once again descended in fire and power (Acts 2; Hebrews 12:22–29). This time God's people joyfully received God's Holy Spirit within them. They were all assigned ministries and spiritual gifts (1 Corinthians 12:4–7). Some were to be given ministries that equip others for ministry, but all would grow together in intimacy with God and maturity of faith (Ephesians 4:4–13).

So what happened? Why, instead of a unified people filled with God's Spirit and power, does so much of the church today look like the old-covenant system?

Instead of one people of God, we talk again about the priests and the people, or alternatively, the "laity" and "clergy." Instead of being the church, we go to church: in templelike buildings with pews for the people and special areas up front for the priests/clergy. These priests/clergy are the "ministers" and perform duties and sacraments the people can't do. They often wear special robes and vestments the people can't wear. What happened?

One thing that happened is that about three hundred years after Pentecost, the Roman emperor Constantine gave his official approval to the Christian faith. With his worldly approval came his worldly influence and affluence. Christians had met in homes and common public areas, but now ornate church buildings were built. Official priests were appointed to oversee these facilities and the services conducted in them. These priests were provided special robes to distinguish them and special places in the building to perform. All of a sudden, much of what was intended by the new covenant reverted to the old covenant.

Some 1,700 years later, the church is in many important ways still more influenced by Emperor Constantine than we are by King Jesus. We preach new-covenant theology, but it is caged in old-covenant institutional structures that encourage hierarchy rather than brotherhood, religion rather than divine relationship, and performance rather than power. If we want abiding revival, this must change.

Father, forgive us. We don't know what we are doing. Lord, tear down the veil again.

God bless you, and God bless our community.

The Church's Guiding Hand
Needs All Five Fingers

And he gave the apostles, the prophets, the evangelists, the pastors and teachers, to equip the saints for the work of ministry, for building up the body of Christ, until we all attain to the unity of the faith and of the knowledge of the Son of God, to mature manhood, to the measure of the stature of the fullness of Christ.

—Ephesians 4:11–13

The human hand is amazing. With the nineteen joints of its five fingers and palm, we can touch, feel, hold, grasp, caress, manipulate, and gesture. Our hands allow us to sign our names, paint pictures, play musical instruments, wield chain saws, and type newspaper columns.

Too often, we take the hand for granted. But then we meet someone whose hand has been crippled by the loss of one or more fingers, and we begin to appreciate how much each of those fingers, from thumb to pinky, means to us.

The Lord gave His church five fingers as well. They are the five equipping ministries described in Ephesians 4—apostles, prophets, evangelists, pastors, and teachers. Their purpose is to empower their fellow Christians for ministry in the world.

The promises of Ephesians 4 are staggering. If the whole body of Christ is united by these equipping joints, with each member doing their part, then we will be built up in love and attain "the stature of the fullness of Christ" (Ephesians 4:13–16).

I read these promises and say, "Wow!" Then I reflect on why we have, after almost two thousand years, so utterly failed to grasp what those promises offer.

We are missing fingers, church! In fact, most congregations are trying to function with just one finger: the "head pastor," who is expected to preach, teach, nurture, administrate, and do it all. But one pastor can't. The Lord didn't design the body that way. And because we are operating by human design rather than the Lord's, research studies reported by the New York Times in 2010 reveal a third of our pastors feel burned out within their first five years of ministry. Seventy percent do not have any close friends, and 75 percent report severe stress.

As for the members of our congregations, only a minority are engaged in any ministry, and those who are focus primarily on keeping their own church doors open. The vast majority of Christians are, in a nutshell, ill equipped for the ministry God has for them.

We cannot fully address the functions of the five equipping ministries in this column, but here are some "springboard" thoughts.

First, we need preachers and evangelists. They proclaim with exhortation the gospel of Jesus Christ, the Holy Spirit, and the kingdom of God (Acts 2:14–41). Even after we receive Jesus, we need that exhortation. It recharges our batteries.

But we have to recognize that exhortation is not discipleship. We must be taught to obey everything Jesus commanded (Matthew 28:20). And we need to acknowledge that the best pastors are usually not great preachers, and vice versa.

Second, our teachers (preachers, pastors, or others) need to be freed to teach the whole counsel of God (Acts 20:27).

As it stands, the teaching most Christians receive is limited to the doctrines prescribed by their denomination or tradition. But there is no gospel of Luther, Calvin, Wesley, or Smyth. Although we can be instructed by the teachers of yesterday, we cannot let them edit what we read in the Word or insist on an interpretation that may be contrary to what the Spirit and Word speak into our heart. Jesus said we have only one teacher (Matthew 23:8–10). These winds of doctrine are what have too often divided us.

Third, we must recognize that prophecy is vitally important for the church being built by Jesus Christ (Matthew 16:18; Acts 2:17–18). God doesn't just want us to read His Word. He wants us to hear His voice.

Prophecy encourages, comforts, and builds up the church (1 Corinthians 14). It can direct people to their calling and gifting (1 Timothy 1:18, 4:14). Let us test prophecy but not despise it like we have (1 Thessalonians 5:20–21).

Fourth, our pastors need to understand how, in addition to their love of God and people, they can be equipped with divine gifts of wisdom and healing (1 Corinthians 12:8–9). Guidance and healing are part of what shepherds do.

Finally, we must shed our institutional hierarchies and reestablish the biblical model of apostolic leadership. *Apostle* means "one sent out." The Lord sends out apostolic servants just like He was sent out by the Father (John 20:21). The true ones will always look like Jesus—humble yet courageous, and sacrificially selfless (Matthew 20:25–28).

Some are sent to penetrate new territory, such as Paul, Barnabas, William Carey, and Hudson Taylor (Acts 13:1–3, 14:14). Some are called upon to confront error and redirect the church, such as Paul, John, Martin Luther, and John Wesley. Others, such as James, influence and connect congregations in a region or city (Galatians 1:19). Like a thumb enhances the other fingers, apostolic servants magnify the productivity of the other equipping ministries.

In these days of increasing darkness, the guiding hand of the church must use all five fingers. Only then will we be equipped for the ministry this world so desperately needs.

God bless you, and God bless our community.

We Need the Folk Who Rock the Boat

"And blessed is the one who is not offended by me."
—Matthew 11:6

As part of our thirty-fourth wedding anniversary celebration, Christie and I went this week to see *Pirates of the Caribbean 3: At World's End.* Despite the intriguing subtitle, we were not expecting to receive any spiritual insight from this lighthearted adventure comedy. But God continues to work in mysterious ways.

There is a scene in the movie when our heroes on their ship, the *Black Pearl*, are sailing on a sea in the Land of the Dead. They desperately want to return to the Land of the Living, but do not know how to get there. Then Captain Jack Sparrow gets an idea.

He begins running back and forth from one side of the boat to the other. At first the others think he is crazy. Then they realize that he is trying to rock the boat, and that his plan is to rock the boat so violently, it will capsize and turn upside down. Then they realize that upside down on the sea in the Land of the Dead may be right side up on the sea in the Land of the Living. (This is Disney fantasy, after all.)

So they all decide to join him, running back and forth like crazy until the boat is rocked and turns upside down. Praise the Lord: what they had thought was upside down does turn out to be right side up. They are no longer stuck in that dead zone. They are alive again!

After hearing this modern parable, some of you could write the rest of this column. We know what it is like to live for a season in a spiritual dead zone. We want to feel spiritually alive and vibrant, experiencing the righteousness, peace, joy, and presence of the Lord that is promised in Scripture (Romans 14:17). We are not content with where we are. But we seem stuck.

What really adds to the challenge is the fact that we are not stuck alone. A significant part of our personal spiritual life is interwoven into the life of our local church. This is as it should be. We are part of a "body," not lone rangers (1 Corinthians 12:12–13). Our greatest expectation of reaching Christian maturity comes as we serve in the unity of the faith (Ephesians 4:11–13). But what do we do when our church family is stuck?

We all know churches can struggle with lifelessness. There are many ways to measure that: few or no conversions to faith, shrinking membership, poor giving, dull or routine worship. Count the smiles. Feel the energy and sense of expectation in your gatherings. Are people growing in their knowledge of the Word and the power of their prayer life? Are they moving from being pew sitters to being active members in ministry?

Another measure might be the evidence seen outside the church. Are the families of the church healthy in their home life? Is the community you serve improving or deteriorating? The church is, after all, the light and salt of the world (Matthew 5:13–16). If we are doing our job, things get better, not worse.

I point this out because as you know, there are always people in the church who are in dead zones but don't acknowledge it.

This brings us back to Captain Jack Sparrow. He sees that the boat needed rocking, but unless the others join him in his efforts, the boat is never going to budge. We know a boat rocker can never "get 'er done" on his or her own, even if he is the pastor.

On the other hand, nothing happens if Jack doesn't try to rock the boat. They would all still be in that dead zone. We need our boat rockers. They are a gift from God.

Moses was a boat rocker. So were Elijah, John the Baptist, and Paul. Jesus was the biggest boat rocker of all, and He didn't stop when He ascended to heaven. Read what our King had to say to the Asian churches in Revelation 2–3. "You've lost your first love!" "You are lukewarm when I want you to be on fire!" "Let Me back into My church!"

Let's stop attacking those pastors and visionary laypeople who are trying to rock the boat. Better yet, let's resolve to protect them from the attacks made by others—the ones who would rather stay in a dead zone than change. God is planning to turn the world upside down (Hebrew 12:25–29; Haggai 2:6–9). If we listen to some of our boat rockers, we may be able to get ourselves and some others right side up before that great and terrible day (Malachi 4:5).

God bless you, and God bless our community.

If You're Happy and You Know It, Clap Your Hands

How lovely are Thy dwelling places, O Lord of hosts! My soul longed and even yearned for the courts of the Lord; My heart and my flesh sing for joy to the living God.

—Psalm 84:1–2 NASB

My wife, Christie, is a gifted preschool and children's Sunday school teacher. She enjoys sharing her work with me, so I know a lot of children's songs, including this favorite:

"If you're happy and you know it, clap your hands!" (Clap twice.) "If you're happy and you know it, clap your hands!" (Clap twice.) "If you're happy and you know it, then your face will surely show it! If you're happy and you know it, clap your hands!" (Clap twice.)

The subsequent verses provide additional ways to show your happiness. "Stomp your feet!" "Shout 'Amen'!" The concluding verse brings all three activities together in one resounding expression of joy. And the whole time "your face will surely show it."

So, church, let's all stand right now and sing together: "If you're happy and you know it ..." Whoa! Stop! We have a problem, church. Your faces are not showing you're happy. And many of you are refusing to sing, clap, or shout "Amen!"

Church, where is your happiness? Christians are called *blessed*, a word that means "happy" or better yet, "happy all over." Happy all over are those who trust in the Lord (Psalm 84:12)! Happy all over are those whose strength is in God (Psalm 84:5)! Happy all over are those whom God welcomes into His presence in praise, thanksgiving, prayer, and mission (Psalm 84:4; Psalm 100; Hebrews 10:19–25)!

Church, where is your joy? Psalm 84:2 declares we should be singing for joy with our hearts ("inside") and our flesh ("outside"). As citizens of the kingdom of God, we are invited to live in joy by the presence and power of the Holy Spirit (Romans 14:17). The joy of the Lord is our strength (Nehemiah 8:10)!

No joy, no strength. Nothing weakens our witness to nonbelievers more than our apparent lack of joy and happiness—both in church services and throughout the week. Too often we have turned the water of His Word into whine—expressing worry about our personal futures, the nation's future, and the world's future even more than those who don't know the victory of the cross and resurrection. Like David, we need to have the joy of our salvation restored (Psalm 51:12). How do we do that?

First, we must not allow our day-to-day circumstances to dictate how we view life. I don't like high gas prices or inflation. And there are problems much worse than the economy: godlike judges who seek to change the natural fabric of marriage and family with the stroke of a pen; abortion; an intolerant oil-financed religion of Islam that breeds terrorism while its so-called moderate leaders refuse to speak out; cancer, AIDS, Alzheimer's, and the other illnesses we are still struggling to cure.

Jesus warned that in this world, we will have trouble, but He told us to take heart. He has overcome the world (John 16:33)! Even in hard times, we are urged to rejoice in the Lord and our salvation (Habakkuk 3:17–18; Philippians 4:4). We can do this for two reasons.

First, we know our destiny. Our salvation is sealed by God's Spirit and secure in His faithfulness. Death has no sting for us or our loved ones who know Jesus. Life is eternal, and it will be in a new heaven and earth without pain or darkness. This earthly life is a blip on the screen for Christians. We are going to live with our heavenly Father and our glorious King forever! Can't we be happy about that now?

Second, while we walk this broken earth, we do not walk alone. God is with us. Nothing can separate us from His love. We belong to a family of millions of His children. If God is for us, no one can ultimately prevail against us, because we can do all things through Christ. Even when we are persecuted, we are blessed by the accumulation of treasures in heaven. Can't we have joy in that?

This is not a column about worship styles. But please understand that this joy issue is both "inside" (heart) and "outside" (body and voice), because what the world around us sees is what they "get."

Do we have happiness and joy in our hearts? Does it show on our faces? Is it reflected by our behaviors in our congregational gatherings and the daily gatherings of life?

Church, if we are happy and we know it, then for God's sake, let our faces show it. The world desperately needs to know where happiness is found.

God bless you, and God bless our community.

Reflections on the Great Gifts of God: Love, Hope, Grace, Faith, and Truth

My Father, please make me Your lover forever,

more intimate each wondrous day;

sharing the truth of Your Word and Your works,

sharing the price that Christ pays;

sharing Your love with all people around me

that they might be Your lovers, too;

sharing my Jesus, my Father, my All

In a new world where all worship You!

May grace and peace be multiplied to you in the knowledge of God and of Jesus our Lord. His divine power has granted to us all things that pertain to life and godliness, through the knowledge of Him who called us to His own glory and excellence, by which He has granted to us His precious and very great promises, so that through them you may become partakers of the divine nature, having escaped from the corruption that is in the world because of sinful desire. For this very reason, make every effort to supplement your faith with virtue, and virtue with knowledge, and knowledge with self-control, and self-control with steadfastness, and steadfastness with godliness, and godliness with brotherly affection, and brotherly affection with love. For if these qualities are yours and are increasing, they keep you from being ineffective or unfruitful in the knowledge of our Lord Jesus Christ. (1 Peter 2:2–8)

God Offers Just What You Need

And my God shall supply all your needs according to His riches
in glory in Christ Jesus.

—Philippians 4:19 NASB

What a wonderful promise! God will address *all* our needs, using what is infinitely superior to the cast-off goods we often donate to the needy. God provides the best God has through the greatest gift of all.

So what's the holdup? God's Word is trustworthy, so why aren't our daily Christian lives filled with the blessings of this divine bounty?

First, some of us don't recognize that we are needy. Jesus preached good news to "the poor" (Luke 4:18), declaring that the kingdom of heaven is for them (Matthew 5:3). They know they have needs only God can meet, and accept their dependence (Romans 9:16). They ask and receive (Matthew 7:7), whereas those who don't ask don't receive (James 4:2). Those who embrace independence may think they "don't need a thing," but the Lord calls them "wretched, pitiful, poor, blind and naked," and warns they are at risk of being spit out of His mouth (Revelation 3:14–22).

This warning points to our second problem. Many of us don't identify what our needs are and what it really takes to satisfy them.

Most experts agree that mankind has three basic needs: (1) the need to belong, (2) the need for safety, and (3) the need for significance. As for meeting each of these needs, the world and God offer very different answers.

To meet our need to belong, the world offers popularity, the admiration of others, and stardom. Such answers are self-centered and ultimately isolate people. The world also offers special groups—everything from country clubs and sororities to gang membership. But everything that makes you special makes those outside the group "not special." The "them and us" mentality is as much about not belonging as it is about belonging.

God, on the other hand, offers in Jesus to make you His child (John 1:12). Through the Holy Spirit, the Father and the Son will intimately abide with you in this life (John 14:23) and extend that intimate, loving relationship into eternity (John 14:1–3; Revelation 21:1–7). As if that wasn't enough, God also offers loving fellowship with all other people who share Jesus with you (1 John 1:3–4; Acts 2:42–47).

To meet our need for safety, the world offers money and material possessions. With enough wealth, you won't fear for your next meal. You can even live in a gated community. The world also offers power. Be in charge, whether in business or politics, and you gain control. But neither wealth nor power will protect you from cancer and car wrecks. They won't prevent death or affect what happens after you die.

God offers to be your fortress and shield (Psalm 144:2). He delivers you from death and the fear of death (Hebrews 2:15; Psalm 23:4). If God is for us, who can be against us (Romans 8:31)? Nothing can ever separate us from the love of God in Christ Jesus (Romans 8:38–39)! His perfect love casts out all fear (1 John 4:18).

To meet our need for significance, the world offers … absolutely nothing. You see, what the world would propose as purpose is really just what the world already offered to meet our needs for safety and belonging. Pursue money, power, popularity, stardom, and exclusive groups. To what end? Have you ever wondered why the people we admire and reward the most are people who play games (sports) and pretend (actors and media personalities)? It is because our culture has lost its sense of purpose. We admire those who are best at things that have no purpose beyond entertainment—things that keep us from being bored with an aimless life.

From the beginning, God offered mankind a wonderful purpose: be fruitful and multiply, creating family and society, and take stewardship of the earth (Genesis 1:28–31). In short, do things that improve society and bless the lives of others, and use your creativity to build positively within God's creation. This purpose can be pursued in countless ways, not just in so-called church ministries.

Further, and in light of the fall of man through sin (Genesis 3), we are called as Christians to participate in the plan of redemption. We are witnesses to Jesus (Acts 1:8), a royal priesthood (1 Peter 2:9) sent out by Jesus in the power of His Spirit (John 20:21–22) to do "greater things than these" (John 14:12) so that His kingdom will spread throughout the earth (Matthew 13:31–32). What greater purpose in life could a person have!?

Dear friends—God has just what we need. So let's go get it! The only thing holding up the reality of Philippians 4:19 is our reluctance to truly trust and obey.

God bless you, and God bless our community.

God Made and Loves Us All

For you formed my inward parts; you knitted me together in my mother's womb. I praise you, for I am fearfully and wonderfully made. Wonderful are your works; my soul knows it very well.

—Psalm 139:13–14

Beloved, let us love one another, for love is from God, and whoever loves has been born of God and knows God. Anyone who does not love does not know God, because God is love.

—1 John 4:7–8

Maya Angelou passed away on May 28, 2014. She was a remarkable woman who, for eighty-six years, lived a remarkable life—particularly when you consider the incredible obstacles a black woman had to overcome in twentieth-century America.

Dr. Angelou was a dancer, actress, singer, poet, author, teacher/professor, and film director. Among her many honors were a Pulitzer Prize nomination, the Presidential Medal of Freedom, and three Grammys. Most of all, she was an inspirational model and mentor for the multiple generations of black women, and other people disadvantaged by prejudice and poverty, who have followed her.

This is a Christian book. Although Dr. Angelou's deep and sincere faith in God was readily apparent in her life and works, I suspect she and I would differ on several theological issues, just as we would disagree on some political and social issues. But as I listened to the eulogies being given at her memorial service, with my heart tenderized by the twelve years Christie and I spent with some remarkable black women at St. Mark House of Prayer, all I could think of is how well Maya Angelou demonstrated and proclaimed these divine truths.

She was loved by God. I am loved by God. You are loved by God (1 John 4:7–8; Matthew 5:43–48).

She was fearfully and wonderfully made. I am fearfully and wonderfully made. You are fearfully and wonderfully made (Psalm 139:14–16).

She was a person of great value and purpose. I am a person of great value and purpose. You are a person of great value and purpose (Genesis 1:26–31; Ephesians 2:10; Jeremiah 29:11).

Ever since sin entered the world, the human instinct has been to divide along the lines of "them" and "us": man lording it over woman (Genesis 3:16); Cain killing Abel (Genesis 4:1–8); this tribe or nation coveting or fearing what that tribe or nation has, and willing to kill as a result. Wars and rumors of war are the norm of human history, not the exception.

The institutional church has, in her history, been vulnerable to this instinct. We were participating in "holy wars" and cries of "infidel" long before the modern radical Muslims, and killed millions of Muslims, Jews, and other Christians as a result.

In short, the Bible reveals that God made, loves, and values all of us, and that He wants us to love and value each other. But our sinful pattern is to limit who we love and value to our "tribes," the people we feel connected with, and at most, people we don't feel threatened by. This pattern is rampant in our nation and world today, and expressing itself with increasing intensity through political, socioeconomic, ethnic, and religious conflict. Tragically many Christians are in it "up to their eyeballs"—part of the problem rather than part of the solution.

I believe in truth, in standing for the truth, and that Jesus is the truth. But the truth must be spoken in love, and love must be expressed both in word and deed (Ephesians 4:15; 1 John 3:18).

These biblical truths apply to everyone on this planet. We are all created by God in His image and likeness. We are all His offspring (Acts 17:28–29). We are all eternally loved by God even though we are all sinners who fall short of His glory (Romans 3:23). We are all people whose sins have been paid for by the blood and death of Jesus Christ (1 John 2:2). We are all people God wants to see come to repentance and everlasting life (1 Timothy 2:3–4; 2 Peter 3:9).

When I understand these things I have in common with all other human beings, it is easier for me to love and value them despite our differences. And more assistance for the right attitude comes when I recognize another biblical truth.

If you are already a disciple of Jesus Christ, you are my fellow laborer in the field of kingdom harvest. If you are not a disciple yet, you are part of the harvest into which I have been sent (John 4:34–38). I will never be part of the sowing or reaping if I do not love you (1 Corinthians 13:1–3).

I praise God for Maya Angelou today, and for how the Lord inspired us through her.

God bless you, and God bless our community.

We Need a Better Understanding
of God's Love

"You shall love the Lord your God with all your heart and with all your soul and with all your strength and with all your mind, and your neighbor as yourself."

—Luke 10:27

Beloved, let us love one another, for love is from God, and whoever loves has been born of God and knows God. Anyone who does not love does not know God, because God is love.

—1 John 4:7–8

God's love is the fundamental principle of life in the kingdom: knowing God's love for us, loving God back with all we are and all we have, and loving everyone God loves. If we don't get love right, we are nothing, have nothing, and gain nothing (1 Corinthians 13:1–3). It is critical that we have a biblical understanding of what "God's love" means.

Let's start by recognizing that *love* is the most overused word in our culture today. We love our boyfriend or girlfriend. We love our dog, our football team, our new phone, and chocolate cake. Love in this sense relates to whoever and whatever makes us feel the way we want to feel.

As for loving people, the 1960s brought us Burt Bacharach's "What the World Needs Now Is Love," followed by John Lennon's "All You Need Is Love." Soon everyone was singing along, regardless of what they believed about the reality of God. Love in this sense led to moral relativism and religious pluralism: celebrating everyone's right to be whoever they want to be, believe whatever they want to believe, and do whatever they want to do.

Add these two cultural concepts of love together, and you get "Love is god," not "God is love." What a horrible deception from the father of lies (John 8:44)!

Scripture teaches that God is love, but this does not mean *God* and *love* are interchangeable. God is love and much more. He is holy, sovereign, faithful, righteous, just, all wise, and all powerful. All these attributes of God, including His love, exist in perfect harmony (Exodus 34:6–7; Colossians 3:14).

Simply put, God's love honors His sovereignty, faithfulness, and righteousness. The most compelling illustration of this is the cross. Although God's love is everlasting and unconditional, it cannot condone sin, because sin is unrighteousness. Sin distrusts God's faithfulness and rebels against His sovereignty. Therefore, unable to ignore sin, God's love sent His Son to pay the price for it (John 3:16).

The New Testament was written in Greek, the dominant world language of that era. The two most frequently used Greek words for *love* were *eros* (romantic love) and *philia* (love of friend or brother). But God chose a much less common word, *agape*, to represent His love so we would understand that God's love is not like human love.

Agape is revealed perfectly in Jesus and described well in the Scriptures of 1 John, 1 Corinthians 13, and the story of the good Samaritan (Luke 10:25–37). Agape is selfless, serving, and sacrificial; kind and patient, but unrelenting; forgiving of wrongdoing, but never celebrating evil or sin; inviting and encouraging, but when necessary, the tough love of discipline (Hebrews 12:5–11). Agape is for friend and foe (Matthew 5:43–48). Agape never dishonors God's truth or God's rule. Agape never gives up.

These incredible qualities of agape make perfect sense when we take the time to consider how a holy God loves us. They stagger the imagination when we are confronted with God's command that we agape Him back and that we agape each other. Our human love is not enough for God.

Jesus showed His agape of the Father by trusting the Father and obeying His commandments (John 14:31; Philippians 2:1–11). We live out our agape for God in the same way—by trusting our faithful Lord Jesus and obeying His sovereign commands (John 14:15, 21, 23; 1 John 5:3). If we don't seek to trust and obey God and His Word, we don't love Him (John 14:24)!

As for agape of neighbor, we must love each other in the same way Jesus loves us (John 15:12). Jesus gave His life for us, so we are to be servants and give our lives as living sacrifices for others, all the while giving God the glory (1 John 3:16–18; Romans 12:1; John 13:3–17; Matthew 5:16 and 16:24–27). Again God says that if we don't agape the people He loves, we don't love Him (1 John 4:20–21; Matthew 25:31–46).

Agape is radical love. Agape is the narrow gate and hard way that few have found (Matthew 7:13–14). But agape is available for all who sincerely want it. God will pour His agape into you as a fruit of His Holy Spirit if you open your heart, ask Him, and then seek to live that agape out (Romans 5:5; Galatians 5:22; 1 John 3:18–22). When more of us do that, we will find the real "life abundant," and the world will truly see Christ in His Church (John 10:10; Colossians 1:27).

God bless you, and God bless our community.

Live in the Love of God

As the Father has loved me, so have I loved you. Abide in my love.
—John 15:9

As disciples of Jesus, Christians should experience a good life. I say this for two reasons.

First, the Lord has a hope and a future for all of us—plans for wholeness, not evil (Jeremiah 29:11). Jesus came that we might have life abundant (John 10:10). He is the Shepherd who leads us to green pastures and still waters while restoring our souls (Psalm 23).

Second, we must experience goodness of life if we are to be effective witnesses for Christ in this world. We are God's people, chosen to show forth the excellencies of the One who brought us out of darkness into His marvelous Light (1 Peter 2:9). The evangelistic success of the early church came not just from Spirit-empowered miracles and preaching, but from the favorable response of the lost to glad and generous hearts in the Christian community (Acts 2:42–47).

Are we living this good life Scripture describes? Are nonbelievers attracted to what they see in our lives, wanting what we have? Or do they instead see the same negatives among us that they and their friends are experiencing?

There are some studies suggesting Christians are more healthy and happy than atheists, and other studies proposing this relates to various types of spirituality, not just faith in Jesus. My assessment is that there is a difference between the lives of Christians and non-Christians in the world today, but it is, with some wonderful exceptions, not a great difference. There are far too many struggles among Christians with stress, anxiety, depression, frustration, divorce, addiction, loneliness, and escapism for us to say we are living the good life God intends for us. And this lack in our lives is reflected in our poor track record with evangelism.

Why does the problem exist? There are several factors, I am sure, but the most important one is this: we have not learned how to live in the love of God.

John is our preeminent apostolic teacher on God's love. It starts with his gospel revelation, "For God so loved the world ..." and culminates in his epistle revelation, "God is love" (John 3:16; 1 John 4:8). These Scriptures help us know that God loves us.

But when John 15:9 records Jesus' command that we should "abide" or live in His love, we are not simply being asked to know that God loves us. We are being invited to know God's love—to experience this divine love in the same way we "know" our spouse or know the hugs and kisses of our mom and dad. It is a matter of heart knowing, not just head knowledge. It is what Paul prayed we would experience: "That you, being rooted and grounded in love, may have strength to comprehend with all the saints what is the breadth and length and height and depth, and to know the love of Christ that surpasses knowledge, that you may be filled with all the fullness of God" (Ephesians 3:17–19).

Why is it so important that we know and live in the love of God?

First, we can love God only because He first loved us (1 John 4:19). The Great Commandment is to love God with all our heart, mind, soul, and strength, but you cannot simply love on command. When we experience God's love, it becomes natural to respond by loving Him back. David worshipped and served the Lord with abandon because he deeply knew God's love for him (Psalm 52:8).

Second, knowing God's love creates the right foundation for our faith. The immensity and complexity of creation make it easy to comprehend God as all powerful, all knowing, and all wise (Romans 1:20). When we know how completely He loves us, we can absolutely trust His good intentions for us, and since God is incapable of failing or making a mistake, we can absolutely trust that He will accomplish all He intends to do (Isaiah 46:8–11; Psalm 25:10).

A life of joyful obedience flows naturally from a heart that absolutely trusts and loves God. As Jesus said, "If you love me, you *will* keep my Word" (John 14:23, *emphasis is mine*).

Third, knowing the perfect love of God will cast out your fear, anxiety, and stress (1 John 4:18). We have challenges in this life, but if you know God's love, you know God is for you (John 16:33). If God is for you, what can stand against you (Romans 8:31)?

In short, the love of God that surpasses knowledge brings the peace that surpasses understanding (Philippians 4:7).

Finally, when I know God's love for me, I can better understand how much He loves you—because He loves you as much as He loves me. This is the revelation that enables us to truly love our neighbor and our enemy (Matthew 5:43–48).

Dear friends, learn to live in the love of God. Through prayer and worship, let the Holy Spirit reveal in your heart the incredible love God has for you (Romans 5:5, 8:35–39). Through His Word, remember all that the Lord has lovingly done and promised to do for you.

Every day, identify yourself like John as "the disciple Jesus loves" (John 19:26, 20:2, 21:7, 20). Then you will know a good life, and the lost will want what you have.

God bless you, and God bless our community.

Raising the Ceiling of Our Hope

*May the God of hope fill you with all joy and peace in believing,
so that by the power of the Holy Spirit you may abound in hope.*
—Romans 15:13

In 1 Corinthians 13, Paul describes the three greatest spiritual gifts: faith, hope, and love. Christians talk often of love and faith. God is love. The Great Commandment is love of God, neighbor, and self. We are saved by grace through faith, and should walk by faith rather than sight. But where does hope fit in?

We don't often teach on hope. Maybe we think all Christians are "hope-full" by definition. After all, we look forward to eternal life. We believe our God is all loving and all powerful. But for much of the church in America, the symptoms I see reflect not hopefulness but a deep need for more hope. Meeting this need is crucial, because the ceiling of our hope defines the ceiling of our effort. We will not reach (or pray) beyond what we have at least some hope for.

Even more important, Hebrews 11:1 tells us that faith is the "substance of things hoped for." The ceiling of our hope defines the ceiling for our faith. Let me explain.

Hope comes from putting together two ingredients: expectation (what we think can happen) and desire (what we want to happen). If either ingredient is absent, there is no hope. When we "expect the worst," it is not hope, because we don't desire the "worst." It is pessimism. And when we have desires but lose all expectation that we can obtain them, we have hopelessness—shattered dreams.

Faith develops when our expectation of receiving what we desire increases. We move from wishful thinking toward a level of assurance and, ultimately, God's goal of "faith without doubt" (Matthew 21:21). But this movement from hope to faith, while increasing our expectation, is still limited to the desires we were hoping for in the first place. Our faith does not reach higher than the hope from which it springs.

Proverbs 13:12 tells us, "Hope deferred makes the heart sick." All people experience this at one time or another. We wanted to be a sports star, wealthy, happily married with children, and so on, but something else happened. If that something else was okay, some of us can redirect our hope. When everything goes wrong, some of us despair and give up our dreams altogether. The majority of us, however, experience a heartsickness more subtle and difficult to diagnose: "half hope," the condition where we hope for far less than God wants to provide.

To understand half hope, ask yourself these questions. Do you hope to experience God's presence each day in prayer or worship? Do you hope for a marriage that grows closer to God and in which you grow closer to each other every day? Do you persist with optimism in daily prayers of salvation and healing for lost and hurting loved ones? Do you minister in our community as the royal priesthood of believers (1 Peter 2:9) with a hope that things will significantly change, despite all adversity, for the better? For too many Christians, the answer to some or all of these questions is "Not really," despite the fact that God's Word has promised all of those things to His people.

Let's raise the ceiling of our hope. Pray to the God of hope that by His Spirit, you will overflow with hope (Romans 15:13). Let the Bible help you desire the right things—His plan for your life rather than worldly plans (Jeremiah 29:11), treasures of heaven rather than treasures of earth (Matthew 6:20). Most of all, embrace the "hope of glory" that is already yours as a child of God—"Christ in me" (Colossians 1:27).

Jesus said we would do "greater works than these" (John 14:12) because we can do all things through Him (Philippians 4:13)—more than we can ask or imagine (Ephesians 3:20)! As the ceiling of our hope rises, so will our faith and our prayers and God's answers to them.

God bless you, and God bless our community.

Where Is the Mercy of God?

But the Lord said to Moses and Aaron, "Because you did not trust in me enough to honor me as holy in the sight of the Israelites, you will not bring this community into the land I give them."

—Numbers 20:12 NIV

Fourteen years ago I was in transition from the life of a lawyer to the life of Christian ministry. Feeling like a minister but still thinking like a trial lawyer, I encountered Numbers 20:1–13, the story of Moses and the Hebrew people at Kadesh.

Moses had led the people a long time. It wasn't his fault the people rebelled at the Jordan River, refusing to cross into the Promised Land. But when God banished the people to forty years in the wilderness, Moses went with them. Now their sentence was almost over. A new generation of the people was returning to the Promised Land—a second chance for Moses.

Then at Kadesh the people ran out of water. This generation dealt with the problem just like their parents, quarreling with Moses and bemoaning they had ever left Egypt.

Moses went before the Lord, who told him to take his staff, gather the people, and speak to the rock, which would provide water. Moses took his staff and gathered the people. But he was angry. Calling the people rebels, Moses struck the rock twice with the staff.

Water came forth for the people—good news—but the Lord's rebuke came forth for Moses—bad news. God declared that Moses had distrusted and dishonored God. His punishment was that he would not lead the people into the Promised Land.

As a trial lawyer, I was concerned about the harshness of this divine judgment. The more I investigated the situation, the more troubled I became. Where was the mercy?

From the time Moses obeyed God and left his home in Midian to return to Egypt, his faithfulness to God and the Hebrew people had been remarkable. He faced down Pharaoh with God's power. He tirelessly led thousands of people across deserts. On not one but two occasions he fasted forty days and nights on Mount Sinai while receiving the law.

Most to the point, Moses had interceded on at least five occasions between an ungrateful, rebellious people and the wrath of God (Exodus 32:31–32; Numbers 11:1–2, 14:10–19, 16:20–22, 45–46). Each time, the actions of the people angered God, but He responded to Moses' pleas for mercy.

Then, after forty years of faithful service, Moses slipped up. One time he let his personal frustration with the people show, and failed to fully follow the Lord's directions. But did anyone intercede for Moses like he had so many times for the Hebrew people? No! Did God exhibit any leniency despite the fact that the people triggered the problem (Psalm 106:32–33)? No!

Moses was given the heaviest punishment you can imagine: denied the right to place his feet on the Promised Land after forty years of walking on those feet to get there. Where was the mercy?

Back on Mount Sinai, the Lord had passed before Moses, declaring Himself merciful and gracious (Exodus 34:6). Now for Moses, it was two strikes on the rock and you're out?! I ask again, ladies and gentlemen of the jury, where was the mercy?

Well, for a long time I had the question but not the answer. Then God showed me Numbers 12:3 (NIV), which says, "Now Moses was a very humble man, more humble than anyone else on the face of the earth." And I finally understood.

God treasured Moses' humility. Humility is not timidity or weakness. It is simply the opposite of "self-centered." Moses focused his life on God and others rather than on himself. This is why he was so effective in mediating between a holy God and an unholy people. This is why God loved Moses so much that He met with him face-to-face as friends (Exodus 33:11).

Moses lost his humility at Kadesh. He became self-centered—focused on his prideful frustration with the people rather than their need and God's desire to meet their need. And God loved Moses too much to let this loss of humility continue.

To God, character and relationship are much more important than achievement. God disciplined Moses to restore his humility, and it worked. God did this out of mercy and love, not retribution. God just had a higher goal than my lawyer mind could see.

And in good time, Moses still set foot on the Promised Land (Matthew 17:3). With Jesus!

Where is the mercy of God? Mercy is, along with love and goodness, simply who God is and in everything God does: every blessing and every judgment on every person, church, or nation. Sometimes we just can't see far enough to understand.

God bless you, and God bless our community.

Thank God for His Amazing Grace!

But God, being rich in mercy, because of the great love with which He loved us, even when we were dead in our trespasses, made us alive together with Christ—by grace you have been saved—and raised us up with Him and seated us with Him in the heavenly places in Christ Jesus, so that in the coming ages He might show the immeasurable riches of His grace in kindness toward us in Christ Jesus. For by grace you have been saved through faith. And this is not your own doing; it is the gift of God, not a result of works, so that no one may boast. For we are His workmanship, created in Christ Jesus for good works, which God prepared beforehand, that we should walk in them.

—Ephesians 2:4–10

Thanksgiving has for several years been my favorite holiday. Despite recent efforts of some stores to start Black Friday on Thursday, Thanksgiving has generally avoided the materialism and pagan fables that invade Christmas and Easter. Family and gratitude to God have remained our focus, and I can think of nothing my family is more thankful for than God's amazing grace.

With the exception of *love*, *grace* is the word most often used to express the heartbeat of Christianity. "Amazing Grace" is far and away the best-known Christian hymn. Yet I suspect that hardly any of us appreciate just how amazing grace is.

The Greek word for grace, *charis*, is best defined as "benevolence or favor from one person to another that is unearned and undeserved." "God's unmerited favor" is therefore a very workable definition for God's grace to us.

140

Many understand this unmerited favor as simply an expression of God's unconditional love: a merciful God choosing to forgive our sins so we can qualify for a ticket to heaven. But grace is much more than that.

First, the grace that brought us forgiveness is an expression of both God's love and God's holiness. The gift is offered free to us, but it wasn't free to Him. This gift came with the biggest price tag ever—God's beloved Son tortured and murdered on a cross—because the holiness of God and heaven could never ignore or bypass the serious wrongness of our sins.

Those who would live in eternity with God must not simply be pardoned. They must be "justified," because the justice of a righteous God must be served (Romans 3:19–26). Our sins had to be paid for, washed away in the precious blood of Jesus.

God created Passover so the Hebrew people would remember how He brought them out of Egypt into the Promised Land, and from Passover the Lord created the Lord's Supper so we could remember the cost of the grace by which we are saved. But time and time again the Hebrew people forgot all God had done for them, taking their "chosen" status for granted and expecting God's provision and protection to continue despite their failure to love, honor, and obey Him. Far too many professing Christians follow the same pattern.

Second, the grace of God that brings us forgiveness from sin also brings us the power to stop sinning and start serving the Lord (Romans 6:1–14). We are not saved by good works, but we are certainly saved so we can begin doing them (Titus 2:11–14; James 2:14–26).

Trusting and serving the Lord is what Jesus had in mind when He told us to seek first the kingdom of God and His righteousness (Matthew 6:25–33). To empower that step, God gave us yet another grace gift—His Holy Spirit (Acts 1:8). It is only when we receive the Spirit and take this step of obedient service that we begin to fully experience the immeasurable riches of God's grace.

Ultimately, the unmerited grace gift of God to us is more than forgiveness and more than the power to live righteously. The unmerited grace gift of God to us is Himself.

God gives us Jesus as Savior, the Lamb of God who takes away our sins (John 1:29).

God gives us Jesus as Lord, the King of Kings who has all authority in heaven and earth, including authority over the evil that seeks to destroy us (Matthew 28:18–20).

God gives us the Holy Spirit, the indwelling presence of God that empowers our service and transforms our character (Galatians 5:16–25; 2 Corinthians 3:17–18). He who is in us is greater than he who is in the world (1 John 4:4).

Finally, God gives us a heavenly Father. We are born again, born of Him! And our Father is watching and waiting for us to come to our senses, stop running our own lives, and return home (John 1:12–13, 3:3–8; Luke 15:11–24). By grace, we are His family and the expression of His kingdom on earth (1 Peter 2:4–16; Revelation 1:5–6).

Amazing grace, how sweet the sound. … I could never do anything to deserve what God has given me, but I can respond, and I can do more than just be thankful. As God gave me Himself, so I can give God myself.

God bless you, and God bless our community.

Forgiveness Will Free You from the Anger That's Killing You

> *In your anger do not sin: Do not let the sun go down while you are still angry, and do not give the devil a foothold ... And do not grieve the Holy Spirit of God, with whom you were sealed for the day of redemption. Get rid of all bitterness, rage and anger, brawling and slander, along with every form of malice. Be kind and compassionate to one another, forgiving each other, just as in Christ God forgave you.*
> —Ephesians 4:26–27, 30–32 NIV

I do "prayer and counsel" ministry with individuals. I also mediate conflicts between parties, and more than 80 percent of those mediations involve families. In both situations, the most destructive single force I have encountered in people's lives is unresolved anger.

Anger is a God-given emotion with a godly but limited purpose. When we experience injustice or see evil victimizing others, a righteous anger can rise up in us to motivate action. We are created in God's image, and such emotion imitates God's wrath against evil (Psalm 7:11). Jesus cleared the temple in righteous anger (John 2:13–17).

However, what happens far too often is that we sin in our anger. We respond to evil with evil. One killing leads to another in Palestine and Iraq, and one cruel word leads to another in our living room spat. We forget that the Lord tells us to be kind to our enemy and overcome evil with good (Romans 12:18–21).

Just as destructive, we "go to bed" still angry, in violation of Ephesians 4:26. And for most of us, this unresolved anger is not a one-night stand. We hold on to that anger for years. It is killing us.

Anger comes in varied forms: rage, obsessive thoughts of revenge, bitterness, and cynicism, which is simply looking at the world through anger-colored glasses. These angers come from hurts in varied degrees of severity: injustices both real and perceived to our person, our pride, or someone we love.

Some angers are recent. Many go way back—childhood hurts from abuse or rejection. You can be angry with your parents, others, yourself, or even God.

When sincere apologies are offered, or justice is served through restitution or punishment, we can usually release our anger. But when those things don't occur, the anger remains. It will not—I repeat—it will not go away on its own. While it remains, it cripples our ability to love or receive love. It gnaws away at our whole person, resulting in physical problems such as sleeplessness, digestive troubles, headaches, or worse. As we come more and more to conclude that "things will never be made right," it even becomes the root of chronic depression.

The God of love has the answer to this bondage. The Prince of Peace is that answer. The Lord will, if we ask, remove that anger and heal those hurts. But He will not do so until we obey His command. We must choose to forgive.

Forgiveness is, to say the least, a "big deal" to our Lord. It is the only lesson Jesus reemphasizes in the prayer we refer to as the Lord's Prayer (Matthew 6:14–15). It is the first action Jesus took from the cross: "Father, forgive them ..." (Luke 23:24).

There were no apologies or restitutions taking place when Jesus forgave those who hurt Him. Their hearts were still filled with hate and evil. He forgave to keep anger and hate out of His own heart. We must do likewise.

Reconciliation and restored relationships are God's ultimate goal (2 Corinthians 5:18–19). Reconciliation, however, is mutual. It requires both parties, and in many situations, the one who hurt you will not or cannot apologize. You cannot control those circumstances or their choices. All you can do is your part (Romans 12:18). You must forgive anyway for your own health and your own relationship with God.

God wants you delivered and healed. Ask Him to reveal to you where your unresolved angers are rooted. Seek His strength and encouragement. You may benefit from the help of a mature Christian you trust. If so, seek that as well. But don't let the grass grow under your feet. The Devil has had his foothold long enough.

And when forgiving feels like it is too unfair and too hard to do, remember this: In the most important way, justice has already been served. When Jesus paid the price for your sins and the world's sins against God, He also paid the price for the sins of others against you. Any remaining issues of justice to be addressed can be entrusted to the One who will judge everyone (Acts 10:42; Romans 12:19). You must let that burden go. Then you will be free.

God bless you, and God bless our community.

Mustard Seed Faith

[This was my first piece for the newspaper.]

"For truly, I say to you, if you have faith like a grain of mustard seed, you will say to this mountain, 'Move from here to there,' and it will move, and nothing will be impossible for you."
—Matthew 17:20b

Praise God for the wonderful privilege of sharing with *Kingsport Times-News* readers some insights of Christian faith that have transformed my life. I pray, as I begin this monthly column, that God will bless you as He continues to bless me.

From 1999 to the end of 2005, I served the Lord at Mustard Seed Ministries of Kingsport—a ministry that continues under the faithful hand of my friend and former partner, Stan Leonard. In appreciation for those six years, I would like to share in my first column a thought about "mustard seed" faith.

What is "mustard seed" faith? We are told that if we have "faith like a grain of mustard seed," we can move mountains (Matthew 17:20; see also Luke 17:6). We all have mountains we would like moved in our own lives and the lives of those we love. Are those mountains being moved, or do you find yourself yearning to discover this "mustard seed" faith that will finally begin to see them moved?

The first thing we must do is shed the lie that says we need only a little faith. Although a few otherwise excellent biblical translations, such as the New International Version and New Living Translation, can mislead us by referring to faith "as small as a mustard seed" or "the size of a mustard seed," the Greek manuscripts from which we develop our English translations never mention the words *small* or *size*. The Greek preposition used means "as," "like," or "in the nature of" a mustard seed.

To understand the nature of the mustard seed, remember the other mustard seed parable told by Jesus, where he described the kingdom of God on earth (Matthew 13:31–32). The kingdom starts very small like the mustard seed, one of the smallest of seeds, but grows to be like the mustard plant, the biggest plant in the garden.

The same analogy applies to mustard seed faith. It is not small faith. It is faith that starts small but grows big.

This understanding is verified by the story that immediately precedes our parable (Matthew 17:14–20). The disciples failed to cast out a demon from a boy. When they ask Jesus why they failed, he points to their *oligopistos*—the Greek word for "little faith." And then He gives them hope through the mustard seed analogy. This time they failed, but if they will grow their faith, they will be able to move mountains!

Don't be satisfied with or resigned to whatever size faith you presently have. Instead, cooperate with the Lord as He grows your faith. Then your prayers and other acts of service for the kingdom will accomplish God-sized results.

Small steps of faith verify God's faithfulness and lead to bigger steps. Hunger for His Word, and study with a teachable spirit, will teach us more about the God we trust and the promises of God we can believe. This grows faith as well, because all of the promises of God are "yes" in Jesus Christ (2 Corinthians 1:20).

Above all, strive to love others every day, because failure to love is the most fundamental obstruction to growing faith (1 Corinthians 13:2).

As we do these things, God will grant us an ever-increasing understanding of the truth "I can do all things through Christ, who strengthens me" (Philippians 4:13 NKJ).

God bless you, and God bless our community.

It's Not Theology—It's Reality!

At that time Jesus declared, "I thank you, Father, Lord of heaven and earth, that you have hidden these things from the wise and understanding and revealed them to little children; yes, Father, for such was your gracious will. All things have been handed over to me by my Father, and no one knows the Son except the Father, and no one knows the Father except the Son and anyone to whom the Son chooses to reveal him."

—Matthew 11:25–30

"You will know the truth, and the truth will set you free."

—John 8:32

Soon after my return to the Lord in 1991, I heard a very helpful phrase: *It's not about religion—it's about relationship!*

I don't remember who first said that to me, but I heard it more than once, and I am grateful. As a warning, it saved me from falling into several "religious" traps. As a focus, it directed me into my own experience of what the apostle John joyfully declares: "Our fellowship is with the Father and with His Son Jesus Christ" (1 John 1:3).

Now there is another phrase flowing through my spirit: *It's not theology—it's reality!* I believe this phrase also carries some useful warnings and focus to help us grow as citizens of God's kingdom.

The word *theology* comes from the ancient Greek word *theologia*, which brings together the word for God (*theos*) and the word for reasoned discourse or analysis (*logos*). A good traditional definition for *theology* would be the reasoned analysis of who God is and how God relates to humanity and creation.

This obviously sounds like a worthy enterprise, but be aware of the trap. As should be expected from the culture of Plato and Aristotle, theology's emphasis is on human intellect and observation. Man figures out who God is. It can easily lead to creating God in the image we want Him to be (Exodus 20:3; 2 Timothy 4:3).

In modern times, the problem gets even worse. The traditional concept of theology has been dramatically affected by three factors: (1) the pride of scientific thought; (2) a political sensitivity to the world's diversity of religions; and (3) the confusion of competing theological doctrines within every religion, including Christianity.

A good modern definition for *theology* would be the rational study of different religious belief systems and practices. In other words, man is no longer trying to figure out who God really is. We are just studying what different groups of "man" choose to believe about God. And thus a second trap is sprung: pluralism. You figure out what you want to believe about God, and I'll figure out who God is for me. Our beliefs have equal merit.

Now compare these two definitions of theology to the definition of *reality*: the state of things as they actually exist.

What is the reality of God? Is God just whoever different groups believe Him to be? Is God whoever my intellect and experience determine He must be? Or is there a God who actually and "really" is—an "I am" (Exodus 3:14)?

Folks, Jesus Christ was not sent by His Father to start a religion. He was sent to reveal reality—truth about God that only Jesus, as the Son of God, could know (Matthew 11:27). Jesus revealed this reality during His earthly ministry, and continues to reveal reality through the Holy Spirit, who inspired all Scripture and leads us into all truth (John 16:13–15).

And Jesus didn't come to appeal to our intellect. The truths Jesus reveals are far beyond what earth-bound man could ever intellectualize. Creation speaks to God's power and majesty (Psalm 19). The law given to Moses set forth basics of right behavior that were already suggested, at least in part, by the natural conscience built into mankind (Romans 2:1–23). But only Jesus could reveal the reality of a heavenly Father's unconditional love and grace (John 1:1–18). Only Jesus could show us what being created in the image and likeness of God really means.

149

Every morning we wake up as a Christian, the greatest reality in our life should be the reality of God. More real than my house is the fact that I live in Christ and Christ lives in me. More real than my shortcomings is God's unconditional love for me every moment of every day.

More real than TV's bad news is God's good news: Jesus has paid the price for all sin of all people for all time. More real than political strife is the fact that Jesus has all authority in heaven and on earth. More real than evil is the ability of good to defeat evil—because God is for us and with us.

It's not theology. It's reality! Praise the Lord!

God bless you, and God bless our community.

God's Truth Is Not Whatever Floats Your Boat

You turn things upside down, as if the potter were thought to be like the clay! Shall what is formed say to him who formed it, "He did not make me"? Can the pot say of the potter, "He knows nothing"?
—Isaiah 29:16 NIV

Properly applied, I love the modern slang phrase *Whatever floats your boat.*

Some people like their steak rare, some like it medium, and some like it country fried. *Whatever floats your boat.*

Some people like golf. Others like computer games, and others prefer shopping. *Whatever floats your boat.*

Whatever floats your boat is a fun phrase. It recognizes that people have different tastes and preferences. *Vive la différence!* Isn't it marvelous that God has created people who are so unique and diverse?

This concept of "whatever floats your boat" can, however, be seriously misapplied. Some things are not a matter of taste or preference. They simply are what they are. This particularly applies to God and to truth.

I hope many of you were able to read the recent newspaper article about a national survey on religious faith. [For the full survey, go to religions.pewforum.org.] Some of the news was encouraging: 92 percent of Americans still believe in God, and 76 percent profess Christianity.

However, many of the survey's other indicators were troubling. Most disturbing for me: more than 70 percent of Christians believe many religions lead to eternal life; 68 percent believe there is more than one true way to accurately interpret the teachings of their own faith.

Now, for some, these statistics may seem to be a comforting sign of increased religious tolerance and humility. But it is not! It is a sign that more than two-thirds of professing Christians in our nation believe faith is a matter of taste or preference, not a matter of truth. You embrace your belief of who God is and I'll embrace mine. *Whatever floats your boat.* You have your version of what is true, or right and wrong, and I'll have mine. *Whatever floats your boat.*

Relativism is the philosophical position that there is no absolute truth—that truth for any given individual or group is relative to their point of view. Relativism applied to the issue of God is religious pluralism: your beliefs can be true for you and mine can be true for me even if our beliefs are opposite.

This may sound good at first, but when you look beneath the surface, what you see are people deciding who God is. The clay shapes the potter rather than the other way around. *Whatever floats your boat.*

God anticipated this sin in His original rules—the first and second commandments (Exodus 20:1–4). Ever since we ate of the forbidden Tree of Knowledge of Good and Evil, we have sought to "be like God" rather than just be made in His likeness (Genesis 3:5, 1:26–27). We want to keep ourselves in control so we can determine what we can do and cannot do. If we can't be our own god, we will try to make God into the image we want.

Everyone, Christian or non-Christian, should be able to understand that if there is a Creator God, He is who He is, not who we say He is. He made us, not the other way around.

Likewise, if there is a God, everyone should be able to see that religion is not just a matter of taste or preference. It is not just a matter, like language or social custom, of how you are raised. It is a matter of discovering truth—who God really is—as God reveals Himself to us.

Finally, unless God is a hypocrite and a liar, or what we call in today's politics a "flip-flopper," we can be confident that God is not going to reveal Himself one way for this person and another opposing way for that person. Hinduism believes in reincarnation and many gods. Christianity, Judaism, and Islam believe in one God and one life on earth. Both sides can't be true. Christianity believes Jesus is God's Son and our Savior. Judaism and Islam deny that. Both sides can't be true.

For those who agonize over who gets into heaven, remember, Jesus paid the price for all sin for all people for all time (Romans 5:12–19). Several Scriptures suggest God's concept of eternal accountability is beyond our "cut-and-dried" doctrines (Genesis 33:19; Romans 2:11–16; Matthew 25:31–46; 1 Timothy 2:4; 2 Timothy 2:11–13). God can be trusted far more than we can to do what is truly right and fair.

I beseech all of us: Believe there is absolute truth about God, what He is like, and what He wants from us. Then pursue it! The truth will do more than "float your boat." The truth will set you free (John 8:32, 14:6)!

God bless you, and God bless our community.

They Suppress the Truth
and Offer Lies

For the wrath of God is revealed from heaven against all ungodliness and unrighteousness of men, who by their unrighteousness suppress the truth ... Although they knew God, they did not honor him as God or give thanks to him, but they became futile in their thinking, and their foolish hearts were darkened ... Claiming to be wise, they became fools ... Therefore God gave them up in the lusts of their hearts to impurity, to the dishonoring of their bodies among themselves, because they exchanged the truth about God for a lie and worshiped and served the creature rather than the Creator, who is blessed forever! Amen.

— Romans 1:18, 22, 24–25

Truth is vitally important! Satan is the deceiver of the world (Revelation 12:9). Jesus Christ is the truth who sets us free (John 8:32, 14:6). The Holy Spirit is the spirit of truth who leads us into all truth (John 15:26, 16:13).

Because truth is so important, I am very concerned about our nation's politics. Both parties are more focused on half-truths and fear-inducing manipulation than they are on straightforward explanations of their position on the issues.

This political truth problem is, however, secondary to the foundational truth problem in our nation, which relates to God. Tragically, it is a truth problem found within the church.

In Romans 1, Paul explains how evil finds its way into our hearts and culture. Although we know God, we suppress the truth about God and exchange it for a lie.

154

This is what happened in the beginning to Adam and Eve, who exchanged what God told them for what Satan told them.

Always, this sin of suppressing the truth about God is a sin of people who know God. The lost cannot help but act lost. We, the church, are called to be the salt that preserves and the light that leads the lost to understanding (Matthew 5:13–16).

In what way is today's church suppressing the truth about God and exchanging it for a lie? For me, at least two truths cannot be compromised: (1) the truth of who Jesus is and what He did, and (2) the truth of the Holy Spirit and what He does. God has revealed in Scripture both of these truths.

Jesus is the Son of God, born of a virgin, given by His Father to be Savior of the world. As the Lamb of God, He died for our sins. As the resurrected King of Kings, He has all authority in heaven and earth. No one comes to the Father except through Him.

The Holy Spirit is the gift we can receive after we receive Jesus. The Holy Spirit is God's presence within us—the power we need to follow Jesus and witness to His gospel—a power that transforms our character, fills us with love, and destroys the works of the enemy through gifts that include prophecy, healings, miracles, and spiritual language (tongues). Together we are to be one body filled with one Spirit.

Yet many people claiming to be Christians have renounced these truths!

Many, including the leadership of several "mainline" denominations, teach that Jesus was simply an exceptionally good man who taught about love. The resurrection is symbolic, and Jesus is just one of several paths to heaven.

This suppression of the truth about Jesus offers in exchange the lie of religious humanism that worships man and his intellect (the creature) more than our Creator.

It is time to recognize that these people cannot be part of the church Jesus is building, because Jesus is building His church on the foundational truth of who God says He is (Matthew 16:15–19)!

Many other people claiming to be the church, and often claiming fervent belief in the Bible, reject God's truth about the Holy Spirit. They deny, in particular, the present reality of healing and other gifts of the Spirit, even declaring in their publications that speaking in tongues is a work of the Devil.

A similar accusation was made against Jesus when religious leaders declared His deliverance ministry a work of the Devil. Jesus' response included these strong words: "Whoever blasphemes against the Holy Spirit never has forgiveness" (Mark 3:22–30).

Read Romans 1. The evil described there is an apt description of the evil that besets our nation today. This evil succeeds because the father of lies has penetrated the church through people who do not worship and serve God "in spirit and truth" (John 4:23–24). If we do not all embrace Jesus as "the truth" and the power of baptism with the Holy Spirit as the promise of the Father to us, our light is dimmed and our salt is diluted (John 14:6; Acts 1:4-5, 8). We have lost much of our access to the divine power and authority God intended us to have.

And until we begin standing up for the truth about Jesus and the Holy Spirit in the church, we can expect this evil to increase.

God bless you, and God bless our community.

Drink from God's Fountain, Not Broken Cisterns

"But my people have changed their glory for that which does not profit. Be appalled, O heavens, at this; be shocked, be utterly desolate, declares the Lord, for my people have committed two evils: they have forsaken me, the fountain of living waters, and hewed out cisterns for themselves, broken cisterns that can hold no water."

—Jeremiah 2:11b–13

I ask with a sense of urgency what may be the most important question for the church in our day: Do you trust in God and His Word or in man and his words?

We have all been invited to drink, wash, and even swim in the living waters of our loving, Holy God (Ezekiel 47). Those "living waters" are (1) His Word—God's truth, wisdom, and grace revealed to us in Scripture and most completely, Jesus Christ; and (2) His Holy Spirit—God's presence and power manifest among us today.

Through these living waters of Word and Spirit, we receive everything we need to grow in Christ and live transformed lives (2 Peter 1:3–8; Ephesians 1:3–23). We have the liberating truth about who God is, who we are, and how He wants us to live. We have His presence so we can live in intimate, loving relationship with Him and others. We have His power within us so we can overcome even the worst the enemy throws at us.

The Lord has invited. But tragically, what the Lord has experienced both in Jeremiah's time and today is that although you can lead a horse to water, you can't make him drink.

The people of Judah chose to reject God's fountain and drink from their own "broken cisterns": to trust in the understanding and strength of man rather than the Lord (Jeremiah 17:5). As a result, they lost both God's blessings and God's protection. Their temple was torn down so the Lord could rebuild (Jeremiah 1:10, 31:28–34).

In our nation today, a great many of us are repeating Judah's mistake.

Just imagine what Luther, Calvin, Cramer, Wesley, Knox, and others of that great cloud of witnesses think when they look down on the leadership of the mainline denominations they helped to birth. Rejecting the biblical declaration of homosexual activity as sin is just the latest in a long pattern of substituting man's word for God's Word. Miracles have become metaphors. The Bible has become a religious book to be intellectually critiqued and Jesus just another way, along with Gandhi, Buddha, Mohammed, and others, to learn about a God who fits whatever our modern worldview says God should be.

Folks, this is man making up his own image of God rather than trusting God's revelation of Himself (Acts 17:29–31). This is eating anew from the Tree of Knowledge of Good and Evil, deciding for ourselves what is right and wrong (Genesis 3). Continued acts of charity and mercy, although good, do not replace the living waters of truth, holiness, and power lost in these broken cisterns.

Even within segments of the Bible-believing church, there are broken cisterns, including a word of men called the doctrine of cessationism, which asserts that the miraculous gifts of the Holy Spirit ceased after the Bible was completed.

The roots of cessationism are found in Thomas Aquinas, a thirteenth-century theologian who blended Scripture with the rationalist philosophies of Aristotle. His writings influenced John Calvin as Calvin drafted his sixteenth-century reformed theology for those leaving Roman Catholicism.

In a nutshell, neither Aquinas nor Calvin had witnessed miraculous spiritual gifts, despite being the Christian leaders of their time, and so they concluded that God didn't see a need for them anymore.

For those who have been taught cessationism, I urge you to read your Bible anew, particularly the Gospel of John and the book of Acts. Cessationism is in direct contradiction to what the New Testament says about the authority of the kingdom of God on earth and the power of the

Holy Spirit over evil. It is a doctrine of unbelief, not faith. Word without Spirit is not God's Word.

People become fully convinced that God loves them and has chosen them when they experience the gospel of God's kingdom coming in power and the Holy Spirit (1 Thessalonians 1:4–5). Because so many have drunk and invited our children to drink from broken cisterns rather than from the living fountain, we have a generation of young adults in America today where, according to 2013 Barna Group research, 60 percent will walk away from their faith or the institutional church in the first decade of their adult life. Sixty percent!

We must return to the fountain! If denominational or congregational leaderships choose not to return, please ask your Lord whether you should continue supporting the broken cisterns they offer (2 Timothy 3:5; 2 Peter 2:1). There are too many lives at stake to delay.

God bless you, and God bless our community.

Christians Have Only One Rabbi

"Don't ever let anyone call you 'Rabbi,' for you have only one teacher, and all of you are on the same level as brothers and sisters. And don't address anyone here on earth as 'Father,' for only God in heaven is your spiritual Father. And don't let anyone call you 'Master,' for there is only one master, the Messiah."

—Matthew 23:8–10 NLT

I love to teach the Word. It is a calling on my life, and God has empowered me in three significant ways.

First, God has given me a spiritual gift of teaching. All Christians are called to ministry and equipped with spiritual gifts that will, if used lovingly and faithfully, bless others (1 Corinthians 12:1–7, 13). Teaching God's Word is a calling and a gifting (Ephesians 4:11–12, Romans 12:7).

Second, God has given me a hunger to learn truth. We have always been invited to become lifelong learners of His Word (Psalms 1 and 119). The early Christians devoted themselves to the teaching of Jesus as shared by His apostles (Acts 2:42, Matthew 28:20). The Bible has strong words for those who are reluctant to keep learning (Hebrews 5:11—6:3). If I cease being a zealous learner, I will cease being an effective teacher.

Third, God has convinced me, sometimes painfully, that teaching God's Word is a grave responsibility and that I still have a lot to learn. The Bible says teachers will be held to a stricter judgment (James 3:1). I have no desire to share in the destiny of false teachers (2 Peter 2:1–19). Humility must remain my watchword (Psalm 25:9). I must remember and the people I teach must remember who I am and who I am not.

This leads us to the command Jesus gave His disciples in Matthew 23:8–10. Christians have only one rabbi, one father, and one master/teacher.

If those roles are filled by someone other than God—heavenly Father, Jesus Christ, and the Holy Spirit—then we are outside God's will and falling short of the incredible invitation God has for our life.

In the days of Jesus' earthly ministry, the Jewish people honored scribes—teachers of the law—and allowed these scribes to tell them what to believe about God's Word. The term *rabbi* meant "honored teacher" or "master," and people would become a rabbi's disciple in the hope of eventually becoming a rabbi themselves. The term used in Matthew 23:10 is translated into English as *teacher* (NKJ, NIV) and *master* (KJV, NLT), but with either translation, it carries the same connotation—a man who tells you what to believe and what to do.

Jesus commands us not to let any man or woman fill that role of rabbi in our life. The Holy Spirit has been sent as the spirit of truth: the means through which Christ will lead us into all truth (John 16:12–15). This fulfills the prophecy of Jeremiah 31:31–34 about the new covenant when God places His Word in each heart (Hebrew 8:7–13). Jesus invites all of us, weary and heavy laden, to come and learn from Him (Matthew 11:28–30).

Does this mean it is wrong to read the works of or listen to teachers, preachers, pastors, prophets, and apostles? Are we supposed to just go into a closet and wrestle with Scripture on our own? Obviously not, for God calls men and women to such roles in the church.

But what it does mean is that we are never supposed to elevate those people beyond the level of brother or sister in Christ (Matthew 23:8). I am never supposed to let any man or women, or group of people, supplant the One to whom I am disciple.

Through God's grace, I came across a seventeenth-century statement made by John Robinson, a Pilgrim pastor speaking to his congregation on the eve of their departure to the American colonies. He told them they would never rise above the one they chose as their guide to truth. If they chose Luther, they would not exceed what God let Luther see. If they chose Calvin, they would not exceed what God revealed to Calvin.

As the pastor of a Methodist church, I could talk about what John Wesley taught. All denominations trace their doctrines to the spiritual understanding of a particular man or small group. Unfortunately, many still seek to dictate what "their people" should or should not believe. My

Catholic friends are even encouraged to call a man Father. Somewhere along the line, we cross the line and disobey what Jesus commanded.

I am not asking us to leave our denominations, nor am I suggesting we ignore correction (2 Timothy 3:16–17, Romans 15:14). I am suggesting this: Only your Rabboni Jesus knows it all (John 20:16). Don't let anyone else set the ceiling on what He will reveal to you or do through you.

God bless you, and God bless our community.

Reflections on Marriage, Family, and Community

My Father, please make me an Adam of love

who would never partake of that tree,

and make my wife Eve, who,

not tricked by the serpent,

abides in Your garden with me;

where we tend to Your creatures

and nurture Your plants,

and give birth by becoming one flesh.

The children are Yours!

It's a marriage of three—

love of God, man and woman that mesh.

So God created man in his own image, in the image of God he created him; male and female he created them. And God blessed them. And God said to them, "Be fruitful and multiply and fill the earth and subdue it." (Genesis 1:27–28)

"Therefore a man shall leave his father and mother and hold fast to his wife, and the two shall become one flesh." This mystery is profound, and I am saying that it refers to Christ and the church. However, let each one of you love his wife as himself, and let the wife see that she respects her husband. (Ephesians 5:31–33)

Love Your Loved Ones
with God's Love

So now I am giving you a new commandment: Love each other.
Just as I have loved you, you should love each other.
—John 13:34 NLT

I love my wife, Christie. Throughout the thirty-five years I have known her, I have loved her. But I have not always loved her well.

For the first nineteen years, I had an excuse for not loving Christie well. I was not a Christian. I loved her with my love: human love. Our relationship began in romantic love, what the Greeks called *eros*. As we shared more of the fun and challenge of life, it quickly grew into the love of friendship, *philia* in the Greek.

It also drifted, with more time and responsibilities together, into the love called *storge* by the Greeks. This is the love of familiarity. There is an old saying about familiarity: "Familiarity breeds contempt."

What this means in a marriage or other close relationship is that we begin to take someone for granted. We keep a record of past wrongs we can pull out whenever there is conflict. We become more impatient with perceived faults in our "loved one" that get in the way of our doing what we want to do when we want to do it. Sound familiar?

Storge love is self-centered. Over time, it begins to influence our eros love and philia love, making them more self-centered. We focus on our own happiness or unhappiness rather than the happiness of our loved one or happiness as a couple. Yet we often blame our "loved one" when we are not happy. Sound familiar?

In 1991, the Lord saved me and introduced me to God's love, agape love: unconditional love. The transformation God began in me that day triggered a transformation in all of my relationships, including my marriage. Focus on self was replaced with focus on Christ and others.

I began after a few years to describe my marriage to others as a combination of eros and philia saturated by agape—the best of human love led by God's love—the way a marriage should be. What I didn't realize is how persistent self-centered storge love can be.

About nine months ago, the Holy Spirit moved in a fresh, powerful way in our home. Since then, Christie and I have drawn much closer in our ministry together. We pray at length together every day. In the midst of this increased spiritual intimacy, however, disturbing irritations began to emerge. I could not figure out what the problem was until my other best friend, Sparky, was compelled by the Lord to courageously speak truth in love to me.

I was the problem, and the problem had been going on much longer than I thought. The increased intimacy and time together over the previous several months had simply made it more disruptive—something that could no longer be glossed over.

I loved Christie with selfless agape love and healthy eros and philia love much of the time. But I often drifted back into self-centered storge attitudes, openly displaying my irritation with Christie's weak points (punctuality and clutter, for example) rather than loving her unconditionally for the wonderful, not-yet-perfect person she is. I sometimes disguised my criticism with humor, belittling Christie to our adult children and members of our congregation, the very people I am supposed to be teaching about Christlikeness.

I was in sin—grievous, totally unacceptable sin. My sin was an obstacle to the fullness of ministry to which Christie and I are called together. But most important, my sin was hurting the one person other than God I love most in this world—my beautiful Christie.

God brought me to truth and repentance. He and Christie have both forgiven me. God will help me as I find little ways to show my agape/philia/eros love to Christie every day—to practice what I preach!

And God led me to share this painful, wonderful lesson here because many of you have fallen into the same trap I did.

The Great Commandment tells us to love our neighbor as we love ourselves. But at John 13:34, Jesus made it clear that all Christian disciples must obey a new commandment in our love for each other. We must love each other not just as we love ourselves, but in the same way He has loved us—unconditionally, selflessly in serving, sacrificially.

In a patriarchal culture where women were second-class citizens, Paul drove this point home for husbands: love your wives like Christ loves His church (Ephesians 5:25). Today this is a reminder for all of us that agape love must start at home, or we will never get it right anywhere. Love your loved ones with God's love!

God bless you, and God bless our community.

Divorce Is a Preventable Disease

[Jesus] answered, "Have you not read that He who created them from the beginning made them male and female, and said, 'Therefore a man shall leave his father and his mother and hold fast to his wife, and they shall become one flesh'? So they are no longer two but one flesh. What therefore God has joined together, let not man separate."

—Matthew 19:4–6)

Marriage is in trouble in America. We all know that.

What too many fail to realize, however, is that the trouble began long before the national controversy over homosexual marriage. It began long before the modern tendency to live together without marriage and even intentionally have children outside marriage.

The core problem of marriage in our nation is divorce. Over 40 percent of our marriages end in divorce. And despite the strong scriptural language against divorce, this failure rate applies to marriages of professing Christians as much as it does to nonbelievers.

Bad marriages lead to divorce. As each succeeding generation becomes more scarred by bad marriages and divorce than the one before, the respect our culture has for the institution of marriage diminishes. The fundamental building block of human society crumbles. Our culture becomes dysfunctional and unhealthy. And then anything can happen.

Folks, it doesn't have to be this way. We don't have to resign ourselves to this decline. Divorce is a preventable disease. Bad marriages can be healed.

Let me touch on several key points:

- Premarital counseling is a must. Many of the points set forth below can be initially covered in high-quality premarital counseling. It prepares. It eliminates unpleasant surprises.
- Communication is a skill we can all improve. Most conflicts arise out of simple misunderstanding. Good communication produces understanding. The most important tip: Let understanding what your spouse is saying be more important to you than having your spouse understand what you are saying. Listen!
- Conflict is inevitable. How you resolve conflict makes all the difference. Solve the problem and protect the relationship. Avoidance, confrontation, and appeasement are poor methods. Collaboration (teamwork to solve the problem) and compromise are both good methods.
- Share your expectations and your dreams. Encourage each other.
- Be quick to apologize and sure to forgive. Do not go to bed angry and give the Devil a foothold (Ephesians 4:26–32). Do not keep a record of wrongs to bring back up in the next conflict (1 Corinthians 13:5).
- Recognize that the fundamental problem in marriage or any relationship, including our relationship with God, is selfishness. "What's in it for me?" we ask. For a Christian, loving service to your spouse, children (if you have them), other family members, community, and human society is as important as the blessings you receive in your marriage. In fact, the greatest blessing is to be a blessing (Acts 20:25).
- Men—loving your wife means more than just providing, protecting, and sex. We must show our beloved every day how we cherish her (Ephesians 5:25–33).
- Women—your husbands want and need your respect even more than they need your love (Ephesians 5:33). If wives consistently communicate respect, most husbands will do everything in their power to live up to it.
- We live in a world where we will face troubles with health, work, finances, other relationships, and so on. These are often stressors

on our marriage. How we respond to them as a couple reveals the strengths and weaknesses in our marriage. Solve the outside problems as they come, but also use those times of struggle to celebrate your strengths and address your weaknesses so you can grow as a couple.

- We all bring "baggage" into our marriage, including fears, frustrations, and disappointments from our life before marriage. You don't have to live with this baggage, and your spouse shouldn't have to live with it either. Seek healing and the divinely empowered freedom to let the past go.

- Get help when you need it. Marriage is wonderful but hard. When your car engine is missing, you take it to a mechanic. When the two of you are struggling and a solution doesn't come quickly, seek the wisdom of a gifted pastor, a biblically grounded marriage counselor, or a godly Christian couple.

- Pray together every day. According to a 1997 Gallup poll by the National Association of Marriage Enhancement, Christian couples who pray together daily have a divorce rate of less than 1 percent. I consider this the most profound statistic on the planet. Living together in God's presence is how two people become the threefold cord not easily broken (Ecclesiastes 4:12). Spiritual intimacy can be the most incredible marital intimacy of all!

We can heal marriage in America if we choose. Will you do your part? God bless you, and God bless our community.

The Devil's Strategy:
Divide and Conquer

"If a kingdom is divided against itself, that kingdom cannot stand. And if a house is divided against itself, that house will not be able to stand."

—Mark 3:24–25

"What therefore God has joined together, let not man [or devil] separate."

—Mark 10:9

To loosely quote something I heard Tony Evans say several years ago at a Promise Keepers gathering, "If the Devil can destroy the marriage, he can destroy the family. If he can destroy families, he can destroy the neighborhood. If he can destroy neighborhoods, he can destroy the city. If he can destroy cities, he can destroy the nations and the world."

We all recognize the tragic state of marriage and family in America today. Long before the most recent controversy over homosexual marriage, we were already dealing with the devastations of a 40 to 50 percent divorce rate. Each divorce means a broken home. Broken homes are a primary cause of poverty, crime, and mental illness—the Devil's delights.

People enter the relationship of marriage because they love each other and deeply desire to go through life together. So how does "together" become "apart"? I believe that in many marriages, the biggest problem is the inability of couples to handle conflict in a godly manner.

I am, among other things, a mediator. Mediation is a process that helps people settle conflicts. Since 1998, I have received hundreds of hours of training, and mediated more than two thousand cases. Most involved marriage and family. As a result, I have some insights to share.

We must first understand what marital conflict is: a marriage faced with a problem where the couple disagrees on how to solve the problem. If there is no problem, there is no conflict. If there is a problem but the couple is in agreement on the solution, there is no conflict.

Second, we must recognize that every marriage is going to have conflict, because every marriage will have problems and we are not always going initially agree on the best solution. The question is not whether you have conflict. It is how you deal with it when it comes.

People can take five basic approaches to deal with conflict:

- Avoiding—People who are very uncomfortable with conflict will often withdraw rather than deal with it. "I don't want to talk about it." They show no regard for the problem, because they refuse to address it. They show little regard for the relationship, because they leave it mired in an unresolved problem.

- Confrontation—Unfortunately this is the most popular approach, used not only in many marriages but in modern politics. Each party competes vigorously to get his or her way, ready to outlast, out-argue, out-yell, out-intimidate, or even out-shoot the other. There is significant regard for solving the problem, as long as it's "my way." But teamwork and relationship are sacrificed every time.

- Appeasement—Sometimes one party wants peace at any price. "Whatever you want, dear." Unlike the confronter, the relationship is of overriding importance to them, but they can fall into traps of unspoken resentment and perceived martyrdom. They also show little regard for the problem, because they fail to contribute to the solution.

- Compromise—This approach gives regard to both the relationship and the problem. Everybody gives a little and gets a little. Although it doesn't always lead to the best solution, it can be a very efficient way to deal with smaller problems (where we're going to eat, what we're going to watch) because it doesn't take a lot of time or energy.

- Collaboration—This approach demonstrates high interest in both the relationship and the problem. We are a team. As a team, we have a problem. We are not the problem. The problem is the problem. We will bring together our respective gifts and strengths and work together until we have consensus on the best solution available.

Avoiding, confrontation, and appeasement are the Devil's way. Only compromise and collaboration are godly.

The key word here is *team*. It takes teamwork to address marital conflict just as it takes teamwork to parent, build a home, keep the bills paid, and watch each other's back. If you let the Devil divide the team, it won't be long before you are dividing everything else in divorce court.

Please, if you are married and reading this column, take the time with your spouse to examine how you are dealing with your marital conflict. And if you need to change, change! Don't let the Devil divide and conquer your family.

Remember, if we can build up our marriages, we can build up our neighborhoods ... and cities ... and our nation ... and the world.

God bless you, and God bless our community.

Mary Had a Spiritual Mother

At that time Mary got ready and hurried to a town in the hill country of Judea, where she entered Zechariah's home and greeted Elizabeth. When Elizabeth heard Mary's greeting, the baby leaped in her womb, and Elizabeth was filled with the Holy Spirit. In a loud voice she exclaimed: "Blessed are you among women, and blessed is the child you will bear!"

—Luke 1:39–42 NIV

Mary of Nazareth was a very young woman, probably fourteen to sixteen years old, when the angel Gabriel came to inform her she would be the mother of God's son.

She was also a small-town girl. Nazareth was a village in the Galilean hills far north of the sophisticated city life of Jerusalem.

We don't know much about Mary's parents—just that her father, Heli, was a descendant of King David. In fact, the whole village of Nazareth may have traced itself to David. *Nazareth* means "root" in Hebrew. Isaiah 11:1 prophesied that the Messiah would come from "the root of Jesse," who was David's father.

We do know Mary's parents raised a good girl. We know Mary was good because God picked her to be His Son's mother. She would nurture His childhood development.

We also know Mary was good because of how she responded to Gabriel's announcement. Once she got past the puzzlement of how a virgin could have a baby, her response was "I am the Lord's servant. May it be to me as you have said" (Luke 1:38). This sounds remarkably like what her son, Jesus, would declare thirty-three years later in the garden of Gethsemane: "Not my will but Thy will be done."

So what does a young, small-town, engaged-but- not-yet-married good girl do when she finds out she is pregnant?

Her fiancé was a gentle man, but it was an arranged marriage. The only thing she knew for sure about Joseph was he didn't expect to marry a pregnant bride.

And although she loved her hometown, she knew how they would react to her pregnancy. Glances and gossip behind her back—even hostility. Remember, Nazareth is the hometown that tried to throw their hometown boy Jesus off a cliff (Luke 4:29).

Mary needed counsel. Mary needed a spiritual mother. So she hurried to visit her relative Elizabeth.

Why did Mary go to Elizabeth? I can think of several reasons:

1. Mary had hometown issues and needed someone outside that home environment to help her think things through.
2. Elizabeth was an older woman with the wisdom that life experience can bring.
3. Elizabeth was a devout and godly woman, "upright in the sight of the Lord" (Luke 1:6). She knew God and had access to God's wisdom.
4. Elizabeth had dealt with the hardship of social stigma herself. She had spent her life childless and barren in a culture in which a woman's most valued purpose was childbearing.
5. Elizabeth had six months earlier experienced her own miracle from God. God had granted her heart's desire for a child in her old age. Elizabeth didn't know just God's word. She knew God's power and presence!
6. The Holy Spirit had overshadowed Mary in bringing about the conception of Jesus. The decision to go to Elizabeth was probably Spirit-led.

So Mary hurried south to Judea. When she arrived, Elizabeth was filled with the Holy Spirit and cried out her joy for what God had done in Mary. "Blessed are you among women!" What a tremendous affirmation for this young, pregnant single woman to hear! What a confirmation that Mary had come to the right person.

Two women: one pregnant long after her time had passed and one pregnant before her time had come. One old, one young, both lovers of God who wanted His will for their lives, and both loving and caring for each other.

The Bible doesn't tell us anything about how Elizabeth and Mary interacted during the three months Mary stayed in Judea. But I am confident they prayed and worshipped the Lord together every day. Elizabeth shared with this young woman all the wisdom she had earned in her long life, and gave a listening ear to all the ideas and questions that poured forth from Mary.

When Mary returned home, she was three months pregnant and showing, but she was now prepared to deal with the reactions of her fiancé, family, and community. And she knew that no matter how they reacted, she had a friend she could turn to.

The story speaks for itself. Our young people, including those just young in the Lord, desperately need spiritual mothers and fathers. We must stop separating the generations and start connecting them.

God bless you, and God bless our community.

God Is Good All the Time

Moses said, "Please show me your glory." And He [God] said,
"I will make all my goodness pass before you and will proclaim
before you my name 'The Lord.'"

—Exodus 33:18–19

First person says, "God is good!"
Second person says, "All the time!"
First person: "All the time!"
Second person: "God is good!"

I hope by now that many of you have heard and participated in this wonderful proclamation-response about the goodness of God. I first heard it at Asbury Seminary in 1995 during a message by seminary president Maxie Dunham.

Maxie told us how during the suppressive years of communism in Eastern Europe when church services were forbidden, Christians would quietly use these simple, profound words to encourage each other on the street and in the workplace. We celebrated with Maxie that our Christian brothers and sisters in Eastern Europe were no longer under communist suppression and no longer required to be quiet or cautious about their faith.

We also committed not to be quiet ourselves in proclaiming the truth about God and His goodness. Since that time, I have proclaimed, "God is good" and invited the response, "All the time" whenever I had the opportunity—in the churches I pastor, on spiritual retreats like Emmaus and Kairos, and wherever Christians gather together.

I would like to take the opportunity in this column to proclaim the goodness of God, and I would particularly like to focus on the glorious truth that God's goodness is "all the time."

My mother, Mary M. Tweed, passed away in the early morning hours of Tuesday, January 8, 2008, after a wonderful and fruitful life of almost eighty-seven years. She, Dad, my sister, Janet, and I found out during the Christmas holidays that the cancer first found and treated three years earlier had returned. It was not treatable, and progressed rapidly.

Mom was a wonderful woman in every way: a loving and steadfast wife to her beloved Mac for sixty-four years; a terrific mom; an adoring grandmother and great-grandmother; an incredible homemaker; and a woman who served her country in three wars (World War II, Korea, and Vietnam) by holding down the fort at home while her husband was overseas in combat. She was an intelligent, beautiful, sweet, modest, and gracious person blessed with remarkable physical health for the first eighty-four years of her life. God is good.

Mom dealt courageously with her cancer surgery three years earlier and even more courageously with the chemotherapy her body did not tolerate well. Although she never fully recovered the youthful vitality of her first eighty-four years, she always did what she could. God is good.

When we learned of the cancer's return, my mom remarked that some people are given the opportunity of knowing when they will die. She did not fear death, because she knew God and His Son Jesus Christ. God is good.

On Christmas afternoon, Mom and Dad came to our home for a Christmas family meal. All of her presents had been saved back from Christmas morning. She was, without ever seeking to be, the "queen for a day" in a gathering with her husband, children, grandchildren, and great-grandchildren. God is good.

Mom's physicians connected us with Wellmont Hospice. In a time when there is so much controversy about our nation's health care system, the development of hospice care is a triumph and tremendous blessing. Hospice services empowered Mom to remain at home with compassionate and effective nursing care when needed and with a primary emphasis on care by her own family. Mom remarked toward the end, "Hospice would be a good place to work." She and my family are eternally grateful to the hospice nurses who came to our home, instructed us in pain medications and breathing treatments, and answered our questions over the phone at all hours. God is good.

Being the primary caregivers for Mom during the last few weeks was not always easy for Dad, Janet, and me, but it was at all times an honor and a privilege. Dad and Janet were there the whole time. They were both amazing. I was able to be with Mom the last three overnights. I was holding her hand when she took her last breath. Her suffering was minimal. She never became confused or incoherent, and always recognized our faces and voices. The tender smiles she shared even at the end are etched in our hearts. God is good.

Finally, and most important, I know where Mom is. She is in heaven. She is healed and happy and waiting for us to join her, because God is good all the time and God is good for all time. Forever (Psalm 100:5)!

"Taste and see that the Lord is good; blessed is the man who takes refuge in him" (Psalm 34:8 NIV).

God bless you, and God bless our community.

Women are the Key to the Next Great Awakening

The Lord gives the word [of power]; the women who bear and publish [the news] are a great host.

—Psalm 68:11 AB

God created mankind in His image, both male and female, to have lordship under His lordship on the earth. The woman He called man's *helper*, a term of honor God often used for Himself (Exodus 18:4; Psalm 54:4). The two were clothed in glory.

Then sin came. The serpent tempted woman, the "rookie" in paradise, who then tempted the man who loved her. Now they would be clothed in animal skins rather than glory.

Now, exiled into a harsh world, woman would have to carry children in her womb longer so they could survive after birth. Labor and delivery would be more painful. And woman would find herself married not to godly man but to fallen man: men who seek not just dominion over the earth but over her. Since they carried weapons while the women carried babies, men would succeed in lording over women even while they fought to lord over each other (Genesis 3:16, 4:8).

And so it has been ever since. The Taliban attitude toward women is as old as sin itself.

Once God entered covenant with the Hebrew people, He began to reveal how wrong it was to treat woman like man now treated her. Honor your mother, He commanded. Honor marriage! Treasure and praise a godly wife (Proverbs 31:10–31)!

God chose women like Miriam and Huldah to prophesy His word. He chose Esther, made a queen "for such a time as this," to be a savior of His people. And He chose Deborah to judge all of Israel. If it was not within God's will for a woman to preach, teach, or lead, these things could never have occurred.

Then Jesus came. God chose both a special man and woman to rear His Son, and both a male and female prophet to declare this baby the Christ (Luke 4:25–38). From the outset of His ministry, Jesus was followed by both men and women, with the women proving more faithful when the crisis of the cross arrived.

Jesus personally revealed His divine identity to both a prestigious man and a marginalized woman (John 3, 4). He invited women to do what no other rabbi had ever permitted: sit at His feet and learn (Luke 10:39). And when He rose from the dead, Jesus told those faithful women first, and had them tell the men (Matthew 28:9–10; John 20:1–18)!

Perhaps nothing demonstrates man's sinful tendency to lord it over women more than this. The men did not believe the women Jesus sent (Mark 16:11). Jesus rebuked them for that (verse 14).

As for the church, Jesus told all His disciples they would be His witnesses in the world, and to wait for power from on high. As prophesied by Joel, the Holy Spirit was poured down at Pentecost on 120 men and women, and they were all filled with God! Sons and daughters! Male servants and maidservants of the Lord!

In the years that follow Pentecost, despite continued male domination in the general culture, Chloe and Lydia headed households that hosted home churches. The four daughters of Philip prophesied. Phoebe was recognized as a deacon. Priscilla and her husband, Aquila, became Paul's beloved coworkers in the gospel and together taught a powerful preacher, Apollos, the fullness of that gospel (Acts 18:26). Another married couple, Andronicus and Junia, were called "outstanding among the apostles" (Romans 16:7).

If women cannot preach, teach, or lead in the church, these things could not occur. So what happened? How did so much of the church come to later believe women were still second-class citizens? Where did we lose the great truth that says, "There is no longer male or female, for you are all one in Christ Jesus … heirs according to promise" (Galatians 3:28–29)?

As could be expected, the newfound freedoms of women in Christ led to some "rookie" mistakes, particularly when it came to marriage. Christian marriage is the core of the Christian family, which is the core of Christian community, and the Lord does not want divisive marriage any more than He wants a divided church. So God clarified through Paul that in areas where they could not reach agreement, the wife should respect and submit to the husband (Ephesians 5:22–33).

Note: The wife was called to submit, not to obey as a child obeys a parent or a servant his master. And a husband is to cherish his wife like Aquila and Andronicus, drawing out her splendor rather than quenching it. A husband's lordship of his wife is not that of sinful man, who lords over people, but of godly man like Christ, who sacrifices and serves (Matthew 20:25–28).

Paul also addressed situations in church meetings where some wives were speaking out in ways that seemed disrespectful to their husbands. He told them to address those matters at home (1 Corinthians 14:33–36; 1 Timothy 2:11–15).

Note: The Greek word for *wife* also means "woman," but Paul consistently used different Greek words for *man* and *husband* and also used different words for *male* and *female*. It is clear from this that Paul was asking *wives*, not *women*, to be silent rather than teach or assert authority over their husband. Paul had already specifically honored the right of women to pray and prophesy in church meetings (1 Corinthians 11:5).

Unfortunately, the church did not prove over time to be immune from Greek culture or the Roman Empire, both of which were still ruled by sinful men. The church regressed to an Old Testament model of priests and people, rather than a royal priesthood of believers. Only men were appointed. Then when the New Testament was translated into Latin, Paul's words were changed. Women, not wives, were told to "be silent." And so it has been ever since.

I could share some very woman-demeaning quotations from respected theologians such as Augustine and Thomas Aquinas, and even unsupportable efforts made to change Junia's name to that of a male and purge the female reference in Psalm 68:11.

I could discuss the grave error of thinking the only way to give women equality is to declare these misunderstood Scriptures no longer authoritative, thus "throwing out the baby with the bathwater."

Instead I will simply point out how John Wesley empowered women to preach and pray in the First Great Awakening, and how Charles Finney did the same in the Second Great Awakening, and how both women and men led the Azusa Street Revival, and how glorious the gifts and callings of Anne Graham Lotz, Mother Teresa, Beth Moore, Joyce Meyer, Kay Arthur, Heidi Baker, and countless other sisters in Christ are.

Satan broke up the male-female team in the garden. Jesus fixed it. If we want another Great Awakening, we must embrace what Jesus did.

God bless you, and God bless our community.

God Bless America,
Land That I Love

"[I]f my people who are called by my name humble themselves, and pray and seek my face and turn from their wicked ways, then I will hear from heaven and will forgive their sin and heal their land."
—2 Chronicles 7:14

"God bless America, land that I love ..."

Loving and Holy Father, I come before you today in the name of Jesus Christ, your only begotten Son and my Savior King. I ask you to bless the United States of America.

I know you are the true God of all nations, not just America. You desire all nations to follow Jesus and be blessed. I join you in that desire. May your kingdom come and your will be done throughout the earth as it is in heaven.

Today, however, I pray specifically for America. I love America. It is the land where I was born and raised, the land where I live in freedom with my family, the land where I came to know Jesus and received your Holy Spirit.

We in America have declared that our inalienable rights to life, liberty, and the pursuit of happiness come from you, God. We have declared ourselves "one nation under God." We have declared, "In God we trust." Father, hold us to our declarations! God, bless America.

"Stand beside her, and guide her through the night with a light from above."

Please do not depart from us, Lord, in these days of great need. Be faithful even though we have been unfaithful. Dark times are upon us. We desperately need your truth and wisdom so we can make right choices.

There is much hatred in the world. Those who hate have easy access to weapons of destruction, even mass destruction. Guide America's decisions on how we respond to this hatred. Enable us to be as innocent as doves but as wise as serpents. Empower us to overcome evil with good.

There is much financial fear in America, Lord. You have allowed our faith in our money to be severely shaken. You have revealed how easily we can be controlled by greed at every level of society. Help us to learn from this, God, that we might put our faith in you and you alone.

Teach us how to love our neighbor rather than money and the stuff it buys so we will share with each other—not as a government-mandated redistribution of wealth but because we truly care for each other. Show us how to be grateful and good stewards of the bountiful blessings you continue to bestow upon us.

Lord, there is much political division in America. Even among those who have submitted their life to Jesus, there is heated and often hateful debate. There is sin in both political parties, and it is hard to discern the balance of truth because our political process is dominated by manipulative marketing strategies aimed at persuading, not informing. Father, you see beyond words and into the heart. You can never be manipulated. Please protect us from the deceptions of both sides. Do not let us lean on our own understanding. Do what only you can do, Lord, to make sure our elected leaders are people after your own heart.

"from the mountains, to the prairies, to the oceans, white with foam ..."

Father, you have blessed America with a wonderfully diverse geography and climate. Thank you for white beaches, amber waves of grain, and majestic purple mountains. Thank you even more for filling our nation with people of such amazing diversity, each one created by you in your image.

Help us to become again a united nation. Rescue us from those who would divide us on the basis of race, cultural background, creed, age, gender, economic status, and other forms of "them versus us." We know a house divided will fall. For our sake and the sake of our children, keep us from falling. Restore in us a sincere respect for one another, even when we disagree. Give us an awareness of how much you love and value everyone.

"God bless America, my home sweet home."

Thank you, my Father, for making America my home on earth. Thank you for all the other people who share this home with me, particularly in this beloved Kingsport area.

My deepest and most heartfelt prayer, God, is that you will continue to make America your home. I cannot bear the bitter thought of where America will be if by the unrepentant sin of your people, we lose your presence. So I ask, sweet Holy Spirit, that you stay right here by us, filling us with your love. Convict us. Transform us. Lead us into our nation's destiny for your glory.

God, bless America, land that you love.

Let's Get Disdain out of Our Politics

At the outset of this column, please consider the following Scriptures:

1. "I urge you, first of all, to pray for all people. As you make your requests, plead for God's mercy upon them, and give thanks. Pray this way for kings and all others who are in authority, so that we can live in peace and quietness, in godliness and dignity" (1 Timothy 2:1–2 NLT).
2. "Don't speak evil against each other, my dear brothers and sisters. If you criticize each other and condemn each other, then you are criticizing and condemning God's law. But you are not a judge who can decide whether the law is right or wrong. Your job is to obey it. God alone, who made the law, can rightly judge among us. He alone has the power to save or to destroy. So what right do you have to condemn your neighbor?" (James 4:11 NLT).
3. "But I say, if you are angry with someone, you are subject to judgment! If you call someone an idiot, you are in danger of being brought before the high council. And if you curse someone, you are in danger of the fires of hell" (Matthew 5:22 NLT).

My heartfelt prayers this fall are, first, that the church will have greater impact on our nation's politics, and second, that our politics will have diminished impact on the church.

By *church*, I mean every Christian believer in our nation—Republican, Democrat, and Independent—not institutional lobby groups. By *impact*, I mean the process of our politics, not just the outcome of elections.

The disdain with which our political parties publicly treat each other has intensified in recent years because election experts tell them "negative" works more powerfully than "positive" in affecting public opinion. We the people are saturated with this disdain through the Internet and twenty-four-hour-a-day media coverage. "Da Stain" (pardon the pun!) has horribly discolored the way we view the nation and each other.

Why would we ever tolerate the demonizing of our nation's president, let alone participate in it? Over the years, I have witnessed people, including friends, belittling Presidents Clinton, Bush, and Obama in front of children. How do we then teach our children and youth to respect our government, their parents, teachers, and others in authority?

Why would we ever condone the derision of any presidential candidate? In every case, there are tens of millions of Americans who support that person. When you mock the candidate, you mock the millions of people behind the candidate. Is it any wonder the United States seems so Un-united? Are we surprised to see our nation's enemies encouraged by our internal strife?

Arrogance of opinion may be a sign of strength by worldly values, but for Christians, it is sin. We are called to humility, and although we are also called to seek and speak truth, we are to speak the truth in love, not judgment (Ephesians 4:15).

There are many important issues of Christian faith in our political debate, including right to life, marriage, poverty, greed, health care, environment, racism, sexism, the world AIDS crisis, wars of aggression, and wars of protection. Neither party's platform addresses all of these to my satisfaction, so I prioritize. And I look to where the platform differences are most striking. My resulting list—right to life, marriage, and national security—seems right and righteous to me, but some other Christians reach different conclusions.

I have intelligent, good-hearted friends who support the ticket I do not support. How does the Word of God say I am to treat them? How does my respect for our democratic process say I am to treat anyone whose vote disagrees with mine? As a Christian and as an American citizen, how am I to treat the person who wins an election if I voted for the person who lost?

We are warned as God's people that we reap what we sow (Galatians 6:7). I urge us to start sowing daily prayer for all of our candidates and both political parties. I urge us to start sowing love and respect for the American electorate, both the people we agree with and those we disagree with. I urge us to be mindful of the problems we face and thankful for the bountiful blessings our nation enjoys.

I also urge us to stop being part of the problem. As each of us takes "da stain" out of our own heart, we will begin removing disdain from a political process that has, since 1776, helped make our country the great nation it is.

Finally, I urge us all to pray God will pick the winners based on what He wants. "In God we trust."

God bless you, and God bless our community.

Serve This Country Like
Our Veterans Served

"If anyone would be first, he must be last of all and servant of all."
—Mark 9:35b

On Tuesday as our nation celebrated Veterans Day, my father and I attended the dedication of the new Kingsport Veterans Memorial at J. Fred Johnson Park.

It is a beautiful memorial honoring those from our area who have served in the United States armed forces. Particular focus is given those who died for their country in World War I, World War II, the Korean Conflict, the Vietnam War, and the Afghanistan/Iraq War. But the pathways to those memorials for the dead are lined with the names of men and women who served but did not die in combat.

There is powerful truth in this. Those who serve, willing to risk their lives, are giving their lives whether they die or not.

The dedication ceremony was well done, but I spent most of my time watching the veterans in the crowd. Some were in uniform. Many, like my dad, were wearing commemorative hats or jackets with decals identifying their combat units. They were remembering.

Mac Tweed was one of the few there to serve in three of those five wars. Born on a mountain farm in Madison County, North Carolina, he enlisted in the US Marine Corps soon after Pearl Harbor. The farm boy became a combat pilot, flying B-25s in World War II, troop transports in Korea, and helicopters in Vietnam. He served thirty-two years and retired as a colonel. His helicopter squadron, Tweed's Tigers, remains one of the Corps' most honored military units.

My dad chose a military career to serve his country and provide for his family. He did not hate his "enemies." To the contrary, he continues to have great respect for the people of Japan, China, and Vietnam. They were men and women fighting for their country and families, just like him.

It is war my dad hates—war and the things that cause war such as greed and coldheartedness. Although my dad does not always explain things the same way his preacher son does, he recognizes that our battle is not against flesh and blood but against the spiritual powers of evil in this world (Ephesians 6:12).

My dad and his fellow veterans served their country under both conservative Republican and liberal Democratic presidents. They served in both unavoidable wars and controversial wars, and they served in peace. They served together: male and female; white, black, and brown; northerners and southerners; city and rural; poor and rich; Baptist, Methodist, Catholic, Jewish, and every other faith.

These veterans remember with whom they served and who they served. They know that in serving their country, they were serving every American, not just those with whom they agreed. In fact, because our nation's foundational principles recognize that every person on earth is "created equal," with God-given rights to "life, liberty and the pursuit of happiness," these veterans really served not just their own country but all people God wants to be free.

There is incredible contrast between what I saw this Tuesday on Veterans Day and what I saw last Tuesday on Election Day.

Frankly, the greatest gift God gave the church during this presidential election process is the revelation of what is in our hearts. Far too many Christians on both "sides" have been divisive, condemning, and self-seeking. Our words and behavior have poisoned the spiritual atmosphere around us. Everyone has to breathe it, as if we were unleashing weapons of mass destruction behind our own lines and on friendly forces.

We must change our ways, fellow Christians, and start serving like our veterans have served. Lay down the weapons Satan uses. The Lord has given us godly weapons to use, particularly love and prayer (2 Corinthians 10:4).

Stop mocking and cursing our elected and appointed leaders, and start praying for them every day. On those issues where a leader's heart is in harmony with God's heart, pray for even greater wisdom. On those issues where a leader's heart may contend with God's heart, pray for repentance. Saul was Christianity's most bitter enemy, but when they prayed for him, God turned his heart around and he became Paul, one of the greatest servants of Christ the world has ever known.

Above all things, fellow Christians, we must start giving heart service rather than just lip service to the Lord's commandment that we humbly love the people with whom we disagree. This is not something we get to vote for or against. And just as it was for those veterans I saw Tuesday, it must be love in both word and deed.

God bless you, and God bless our community.

Freedom and Independence Are Not the Same

So Jesus said to the Jews who had believed in him, "If you abide in my word, you are truly my disciples, and you will know the truth, and the truth will set you free."

—John 8:31–32

Now the Lord is the Spirit, and where the Spirit of the Lord is, there is freedom.

—2 Corinthians 3:17

Americans love to talk about freedom. Our Declaration of Independence declares freedom ("liberty") to be our God-given right. Our Constitution's stated purpose is to secure the blessing of liberty for ourselves and our posterity. Our national anthem sings of "the land of the free." One of our favorite patriotic declarations is Patrick Henry's "Give me liberty or give me death."

This national focus on freedom has sometimes been used to justify our involvement in wars to support people seeking freedom from tyranny. Our most recent examples are Iraq, Afghanistan, and Libya.

How have those efforts worked out? Saddam Hussein and Omar Kaddafi were killed. The Taliban was dislodged. All three nations made initial moves, with our help, toward a democratic form of government and the freedoms they hoped democracy would secure. All three nations are now in chaos.

The crucial lesson to be learned: freedom and independence are not the same. Too often, we learn this lesson the hard way.

At the political level, learning this lesson the hard way means we learn democracy is not enough. In the absence of principles of faith and morality that undergirded our nation in its birth, democracy simply replaces one form of tyranny with others—greed, corruption, the desire of the majority to control minorities, and the desire of the few to manipulate the many.

At the individual level, many of us have learned this lesson the hard way, particularly youth who rebel against parental authority and run away. Through independence from their parents, they seek freedom—the right to do what they want to do when they want to do it. Instead, they almost always find bondage to drugs, poverty, and a life of prostitution or other crime motivated by that poverty.

At the ultimate level, the level that engages all humanity, this lesson was learned the hard way by our earliest ancestors, Adam and Eve. They were tempted to independence from God's authority, deciding on their own what was good and evil, and led all of us into the worst tyrannies of all: Satan, sin, and death (Genesis 3; 1 John 5:19; Romans 6:16–23).

God our Creator sent Jesus Christ to set men free (Luke 4:17–21; Psalm 146:7), so it is essential that we understand what freedom really is.

Freedom is both freedom from things and freedom to do things. But it is not freedom from authority or freedom to do whatever we want whenever we want. Although created in the image of God, we were never created to be God. Instead, we were created to live in intimacy with the Lord under His loving, wise, and benevolent authority. We will never know freedom until we begin living as we were designed to live.

Jesus revealed this truth in His teachings and His life. The Son of God became one of us, emptied of His divinity, but remained in intimate communion with His Father through the Holy Spirit. He and the Father were "one" even while He walked this earth (John 10:30).

Likewise, Jesus prayed we would become "one" with Him (John 17:21–23). The Holy Spirit was sent to live in us even as He lived in Jesus (John 14:15–20, 16:7–15).

Jesus was also totally submitted to the authority of His Father, even when the Father's will called for Him to do the most difficult task anyone has ever done. Jesus became "last of all and servant of all," and so the Father exalted Him to "first of all," the name above every name (Philippians 2:5–11; Mark 9:33–37).

Likewise, as disciples of Jesus, we are to abide in His word, learning and obeying all His teachings as we humbly walk like He walked into "the freedom of the glory of the children of God" (Matthew 28:20; 1 John 2:3–6; Romans 8:16–21).

The Scriptures at the outset of this column summarize this narrow path to true freedom (Matthew 7:13–14). Learn and obey God's Word—all of it! Be filled, led, and empowered by God's Spirit (Ephesians 5:18; Romans 8:14; Acts 1:4–8)! Worship the Lord in spirit and truth (John 4:23–24)!

We can experience freedom from sin, death, separation from God, fear and anxiety, anger and bitterness, no hope and low hope, deceptions and foolish decisions, loneliness, addictions, poverty, lack of significant purpose, and striving.

We can experience freedom to intimacy with God, trusting obedience, everlasting life, loving and forgiving community, wisdom and understanding, awesome purpose with eternal significance, peace, authority and power over evil, joy, provision, rest, and unlimited hope in an unlimited God.

And as we walk this glorious path of freedom in our own lives, we will reveal that path to others, including our youth and our nation, both of whom are heading in the wrong direction.

God bless you, and God bless our community.

Reflections on Revival
and the Kingdom Coming

My Father, please make me a flower ... a songbird ...

a beaver ... a tiger ... a tree ...

for reflecting Your Beauty,

for singing Your Praise,

for work, war, or waiting on Thee.

I give You my life,

You give my life back,

perfect freedom for those who obey.

Use me! I thirst

for the rightness, the truth

that comes when I am what You say.

"Pray then like this: 'Our Father in heaven, hallowed be your name. Your kingdom come, your will be done, on earth as it is in heaven.'" (Matthew 6:9–10)

The Kingdom of God Is Still Near

From that time on Jesus began to preach, "Repent, for the kingdom of heaven is near."

—Matthew 4:17 NIV

Jesus talked about the kingdom of God all the time. Why don't we?

The phrases *kingdom of God* and *kingdom of heaven* occur almost a hundred times in the New Testament. Jesus was sent to proclaim the good news that the kingdom of God is near (Matthew 4:17, 23; Luke 4:43). The kingdom was the topic of the majority of His parables (for example, Matthew 13, 18:1, 20:1, 22:1, 25:1). The kingdom is what He sent His disciples to proclaim (Matthew 10:7–8; Luke 10:1–11).

During the forty days after the resurrection, our risen Lord walked the earth and taught about the kingdom of God (Acts 1:3). The preaching of Paul, the apostle to the Gentile world, is summarized as preaching the kingdom of God (Acts 28:23, 31). The end of the age will not come until the "gospel of the kingdom" is preached to the whole world (Matthew 24:14).

So why do we hear so little about the kingdom in today's church? Why are so few of us living in the reality of the kingdom and witnessing to it?

One reason is that the priorities of the kingdom have far too often given way to the priorities of "kingdoms" of the church. "I go to church." "Join my church." "I'm a [fill in your denomination]." "Our church believes ..."

The kingdom of God has only one King, Jesus Christ, so the kingdom cannot be divided. And since Jesus has all authority in heaven and earth, the kingdom cannot be controlled by man or successfully opposed by Satan (Matthew 28:18).

History shows, on the other hand, that the church can be divided very easily by people who battle for institutional and doctrinal control of her.

Once it is divided, Satan is able to prevail where he otherwise could not prevail (Matthew 16:18; Luke 11:17). It is a scheme of Satan to keep our focus away from the kingdom and instead on our church differences.

A second reason we don't focus on the kingdom is that we don't really understand it. Many of us tend to think of the kingdom as the place where Christians go when we die, or as something Jesus will initiate at the second coming. But that is not the good news Jesus and His apostles preached.

It is true that the final fulfillment of the kingdom will not take place until every enemy of God is destroyed (1 Corinthians 15:22–28). But it is also true that we are already receiving an unshakable kingdom now (Hebrews 12:28). Paul declared that we have been rescued from the dominion of darkness and brought into the kingdom of the Son (Colossians 1:13). We have, as a royal priesthood, been made the expression of His kingdom on earth (Revelation 1:6; 1 Peter 2:9).

Jesus said the kingdom had "come upon" people as they received healing and deliverance through either His own ministry or the ministry of His disciples (Matthew 12:28; Luke 10:9). The authority of the King manifested in their lives. Likewise, the kingdom manifests today in and through the life of every Christian who honors the Lordship of the King and has His Spirit within them (Matthew 7:21; Luke 17:20–21). When we gather together in one accord in His name, Jesus is among us (Matthew 18:18–20). And wherever the King is, the kingdom is.

The kingdom of God is about godly lives led by His Holy Word and the Holy Spirit (Romans 14:17; 1 Thessalonians 2:11–13). The kingdom is also about power, not just talk (1 Corinthians 4:20). When King Jesus said the keys to the kingdom would be given to us, He was talking about the power and authority to drive out the Devil and spread the kingdom, bringing healing to a broken world (Matthew 16:18–19, 28:18–20; John 12:31).

As always, with power and authority comes responsibility. We can help people enter the kingdom of God or, like the religious leaders of old, shut the door and keep them out (Matthew 23:13). The tragic truth is that in much of the church today, King Jesus himself is outside, knocking to be let back in (Revelation 3:14–21). When will we stop letting the enemy's schemes, shallow teaching, and the worries of this world choke the knowledge of the kingdom (Matthew 13:19–22)?

It will take forceful men and women to restore the preeminence of the kingdom of God in our Christian community (Matthew 11:12). Many in the church will resist change even when it is good for them (Luke 5:36–39). The good news is that the kingdom of God is still near. The King of Glory still wants to come in (Psalm 24)! And wherever the King comes, His kingdom comes on earth as it is in heaven (Matthew 6:10).

God bless you, and God bless our community.

Kingdom Problems Require Kingdom Solutions

"But seek first the kingdom of God and His righteousness, and all these things will be added to you."

—Matthew 6:33

The ability to identify and solve problems is vitally important in every field of human endeavor. We sometimes call it "critical thinking," and no step is more critical than the first one: fully identifying the problem.

Failure to accurately and fully identify a problem will inevitably lead to a wrong or inadequate solution.

As an example, you have pain in your abdomen. The proper definition of the problem is "Something is wrong within my body and causing pain." You seek out the source of the "dis-ease," find the cancer, and initiate plans to cure it.

However, if you simply define the problem as "I have pain," your solution can be pain medication. The problem you defined—the pain—will go away, but the cancer will kill you.

My friends, even the life-or-death issue of cancer is less important than the "everlasting life" issue of our relationship with God. Yet tragically, the church has failed in this most critical area to fully identify the real problems. As a result, we live inadequate lives, witness to an inadequate solution, and have too little influence on the world.

To correctly understand our problems, we must think from a kingdom of God perspective. This is, after all, the gospel Jesus proclaimed (Mark 1:14–15; Acts 1:3).

Simply put, the kingdom of God is the wise, benevolent rule of a loving God over those who trust, obey, and depend upon Him. Both heaven and earth were created as expressions of this kingdom. God chose to dwell in heaven amidst angels under His authority, and chose mankind to dwell on earth under His authority. It was all "very good" (Genesis 1:31).

But then the problem arose: a decision by some to come out from under the Lord's authority and rule on their own. This problem is best understood in kingdom terms as "rebellion."

Rebellion first arose in heaven as Satan led many angels to defy God (Revelation 12). Rebellion then arose on earth as mankind was tempted by that same prince of rebels to "be like God" and decide on their own what would be good and evil (Genesis 3).

The root problem of rebellion immediately led to other problems. Mankind's rebellion would not really mean "self-rule" but, instead, coming under the rule of the prince of rebels (1 John 5:19). Our "flesh," having tasted independence from God, would seek to remain independent—hence, the biblical concept of the "old self" (Romans 6:6). And independence from God's rule also separated us from the benefits of His rule: wisdom, protection, authority, and provision, including the provision of life itself. The consequences of sin include death (Romans 6:23).

Rebellion in heaven was a problem soon resolved. The rebellious angels were thrown out and are destined for everlasting punishment at the time all rebellion will be judged (Luke 10:18; Matthew 25:41).

God's love for mankind, however, prevents Him from treating the rebellion on earth in the same way. For us, His solution must restore the kingdom on earth while allowing the preservation of our lives, which means reconciling us to Him in the trusting, obedient, and dependent relationship we were created to have. To do this, God's solution had to address both the rebellion and the offshoot problems created from it. And so His solution came: Jesus Christ!

Jesus revealed in His life and teaching the incredible love of God, but those who preach "all we need is love" fail to recognize both the importance of God's other scriptural commandments and how the evil of our sins separates us from God. Rebellion continues.

Jesus paid the price for our sins on the cross and rose in victory over death. But those who simply preach our need to accept God's forgiveness of sinners fail to honor His command that we live lives of trusting obedience—lives that, to overcome our "flesh," must depend on the power of the Holy Spirit (Acts 1:3–8). Otherwise, sin and Satan continue to assert control.

The Lord sent the Holy Spirit to baptize, empower, and lead those who trust in Him. But if that power is preoccupied with our own prosperity rather than loving, sacrificial service to God and others, we are catering to our "flesh" and not His Spirit (Galatians 5:13–17). We fail to empower the life God wants (1 John 2:3–6). We will not see evil dislodged and the kingdom restored around us.

Kingdom problems require kingdom solutions. Know God's love. Receive God's forgiveness. Receive God's Holy Spirit. But most of all, receive God's Lordship over all your life. Then go help others do the same.

Jesus put it this way: "Thy kingdom come. Thy will be done, On earth as it is in heaven." (Matthew 6:10 NAS)

God bless you, and God bless our community.

Take Your Position in the Kingdom of God

See to it that you do not refuse Him who speaks. If they did not escape when they refused him who warned them on earth, how much less will we, if we turn away from Him who warns us from heaven? At that time His voice shook the earth, but now He has promised, "Once more I will shake not only the earth but also the heavens." The words "once more" indicate the removing of what can be shaken—that is, created things—so that what cannot be shaken may remain. Therefore, since we are receiving a kingdom that cannot be shaken, let us be thankful, and so worship God acceptably with reverence and awe, for our God is a consuming fire.
—Hebrews 12:25–29 NIV

God's words leap off this page of Hebrews: "We are receiving a kingdom!"

We don't have to wait until we die. We don't have to wait for judgment day. We can be receiving the kingdom of God now!

This is not what we normally hear in our churches, is it? Dr. Myles Munroe offers an excellent explanation: most churches preach the gospel of Jesus Christ, not the gospel Jesus Christ preached.

Jesus preached, "Repent, for the kingdom of heaven is at hand" (Matthew 3:2). "…The kingdom of God has come upon you" (Matthew 12:28). "…The kingdom of God is within you" (Luke 17:21 NIV). "…Seek first the kingdom of God and His righteousness…" (Matthew 6:33 NKJ).

Jesus declared, "…This gospel of the kingdom will be preached in the whole world for a witness to all the nations…" (Matthew 24:14 NASB). During the forty days between His resurrection and His ascension, Jesus spoke to His disciples about the kingdom. Then He sent them out in power to preach and witness (Acts 1:3, 8).

Paul also preached the kingdom (Acts 28:31). And for Paul as well, the kingdom was not talk but power (1 Corinthians 4:20). So why are we not proclaiming and receiving the kingdom now?

The kingdom of God is the kingdom of light in the darkness, and neither sickness nor demonic oppression can stand against it (Colossians 1:12–13; Acts 5:12–16). The king of this kingdom has all authority in heaven and earth, and He delegates His authority to those who wholly submit to His rule and represent Him in the earth (Matthew 28:18; 2 Corinthians 5:20; Mark 16:15–20).

The kingdom is righteousness, peace, and joy in the indwelling presence and power of the Holy Spirit (Romans 14:17). This is the kingdom life we are offered in this broken world, and the life we are to offer others.

How do we receive this kingdom? We need to understand the Greek word our English Bibles translate as *we are receiving*. The word is *paralambano*, and in Hebrews 12:28 it is used in the present active tense. This means it is something that is happening and ongoing, something that has begun and is in progress but is not yet complete.

Paralambano is not a passive word. The primary meaning of *lambano* is "to take, grasp, seize, or acquire." *Para* indicates "alongside" or "in the presence of." In Greek culture, *paralambano* usually meant "to take to oneself, to take over an office or take a position, or to take someone with you."

In other words, if we want to receive the kingdom of God, we must actively take our position in that kingdom. We must recognize and embrace our identity, ability, and responsibility in Christ the King: sons and daughters of our heavenly Father who are indwelt by the Holy Spirit; a royal priesthood of believers who set self-centered agendas aside and follow our King, humbly loving and serving people while boldly standing against evil.

Dear friends, Hebrews 12 speaks of a divine shaking. That shaking is upon us. I do not know how long it will last or how soon it will intensify. But I know this shaking will not stop until God has accomplished His purpose in it. And I know this worldwide shaking will affect every facet and social structure of human life.

The church will be shaken early and vigorously because the Lord needs a faithful, righteous church to represent His kingdom in this hour. Cultural and "religious" Christianity will not survive. Those in the church who are not receiving the kingdom will be shaken out because it is only the kingdom that cannot be shaken.

In your prayer time after reading this column, I urge you to search your heart and take your position in the kingdom. I urge you this Sunday in your congregations to stop "church as usual" and take your position in the kingdom.

"Lift up your heads, O gates, And be lifted up, O ancient doors, That the King of glory may come in!" (Psalm 24:7).

God bless you, and God bless our community.

Ask What You Can Do
for His Kingdom

"Thus says the Lord of hosts, 'If you will walk in My ways, and if you will perform My service, then you will also govern My house and also have charge of My courts, and I will grant you free access among these who are standing here.'"

—Zechariah 3:7 NASB

In a season of political conflict both at home and abroad, we should remember something said in another time of national and international tension: "Ask not what your country can do for you—ask what you can do for your country."

John Kennedy, who spoke these words at his 1961 presidential inauguration, was a Democrat, but these historic words were inspirational to Democrats, Republicans, and everyone else. They were words of selflessness spoken to an increasingly selfish culture—words of giving and serving spoken into a culture too focused on getting and then getting away.

We still need to hear those words today. Christians need to hear them more than anyone. They apply to our patriotism, but they apply even more to our faith.

We ask God for things all the time. "God, please get me out of this jam!" "God, please bring down these absurd gas prices!" "God, please heal my friend."

God wants us to ask Him. The Bible encourages, "Ask and it will be given to you" (Matthew 7:7). The Bible admonishes: "You do not have because you do not ask" (James 4:2). For a Christian, asking God means a child is asking their Father, and our heavenly Father loves to give to His children (Matthew 7:11).

So why do we experience so many occasions when God doesn't give us what we ask for? Why can't we tap into the fullness of Christ's promise: "My Father will give you whatever you ask in my name" (John 16:23)?

What many fail to understand is although God's love is absolutely unconditional, God's promises are conditional. To receive everything we ask of God in prayer, Jesus imposes these conditions:

1. "Have faith in God ... do not doubt in your heart but believe what you are saying will happen" (Mark 11:22–24; Matthew 21:22).
2. "Have faith in me and do what I have been doing" (John 14:12–14).
3. "Remain in me by obeying my commandment to love one another as I have loved you, and by bearing fruit that will last" (John 15:7–16).

These conditions can be summarized in a single sentence: when you are doing what God asks of you, then God will do whatever you ask of Him.

You see, God's offer is actually much better than President Kennedy's. God wants us to ask Him for things. But He doesn't want the cart before the horse. First He wants us to ask what we can do for Him, and do it. It is His kingdom that needs to come on the earth, not ours!

And at least in general terms the Lord has already said what He wants us to do. Believe in Him. Trust Him and everything He says. Live out that trust by obeying His command to love and serve. You can ask God for anything that will empower that kind of life, which means you can love and serve in His power, not just your own (Zechariah 4:6).

I see many Christians who are faithful. They love unconditionally and serve sacrificially. But their faith is smaller than their faithfulness. They have not been taught to believe in the manifestations of God's power— miracles, healings, and extraordinary answers to prayer. They do good, but not nearly as much good as they could do.

I see other Christians with great faith in God's readiness to perform awesome supernatural works. They pray boldly. But often their faithfulness is smaller than their faith. Their teaching has focused on their own experiences and prosperity—what they can get more of than what they can give. Some think faith in God means faith in whatever prayer they are praying ("name it and claim it"), when faith in God really means praying what God wants you to pray. They see manifestations of God's power, but not nearly what they could see.

Zechariah 3:7 prophetically says that if we live like Jesus and serve His purposes, then we will receive all the power, authority, and heavenly help we ask for. This brings great faithfulness and great faith together, which is the way it should be. *Faith* and *faithfulness* are, after all, a single word, not different words, in the biblical languages of Greek and Hebrew. They need to be one word in our lives as well.

Ask God what you can do for His kingdom, and then ask for all He can do for you.

God bless you, and God bless our community.

It Is Time to Fan Our Own Flame

For this reason I remind you to fan into flame the gift of God, which is in you through the laying on of my hands. For God did not give us a spirit of timidity, but a spirit of power, of love and of self-discipline."

—2 Timothy 1:6–7

For the typical American, fireplaces and campfires have become recreational. But for most of human history, they were daily necessities that provided light, warmth, and the ability to cook food.

And for most of that history, including biblical times, there were no matches. If you had to start a fire from scratch, you faced the laborious process of working with flint or friction. Whenever possible, you would avoid that work by preserving some embers from a fire that could be fanned back into flame when fire was needed again.

The apostle Paul and his protégé Timothy both spent a lot of time around campfires and fireplaces as they traveled throughout the Roman Empire, spreading the gospel of Jesus Christ. In his last known letter, written from prison in Rome shortly before his execution, Paul used this daily shared experience to illustrate for Timothy an essential truth about Christian life and ministry. You need to fan the gift of God within you into flame!

There are three things we must understand about this essential truth.

First, every Christian has the gift of God within them. What is this gift of God?

The Greek word used by Paul for "gift" is *charisma*—a word he used in 1 Corinthians 12 and Romans 12 while describing the gifts of the Holy Spirit given to each believer. But Paul also uses *charisma* to more generally describe the free gift of eternal life we have received through the Spirit of life within us (Romans 6:23, 8:9).

To determine whether Paul is reminding Timothy of a particular spiritual gift or the overall gift of the Holy Spirit, we should look to the next sentence in his letter where he describes the gift as "a spirit of power, love and self-discipline." This clarifies that Paul is talking about the gift of the Holy Spirit, not just a spiritual gift through the Holy Spirit. It is the gift of "God within you."

Second, this gift of "God within us" must be fanned into flame.

An ember will not in itself provide the light, warmth, or cooking heat we need. The power of fire is within the ember, but that power is not released until the ember becomes flame.

Likewise, the infinite power of God is available to Christians through the Holy Spirit, but having divine power available and releasing that power are not the same thing. Just like with the ember, we must fan into flame the gift of "God within us" before His light will shine and His power will go forth.

Third, you (I repeat—you!) have the primary responsibility for fanning into flame the gift of "God within you."

This is where the rubber meets the road. Christians are to be self-motivated in both their spiritual growth and their service to God. And for the most part, we are not. We look for a preacher to fire us up with stimulating sermons and a praise team or choir to ignite our souls with their talent and enthusiasm. But most of us don't spend significant time in personal study and prayer, and most don't engage in personal praise and worship apart from those times we sing along in a worship service.

Many of us will agree to serve our local church when asked, but how many seek out their pastor to ask how they can grow in ministry, finding new ways to serve the Lord?

Sports teams hire coaches that can motivate, but they also expect self-motivated players. Employers expect self-motivated workers. And both teachers and parents know how frustrating it is when students have no self-motivation. Why do we so easily accept the absence of self-motivation in the church?

The even more perplexing question is this: why would people who truly believe in God as heavenly Father, eternal life-giving Savior, and

Holy Spirit not make it their first priority in life to grow closer to God and serve Him well?

Without the power of God, we cannot fulfill our mission as the church (Acts 1:4–8). That power will not be released unless our congregations become self-motivated Christians. Until then, we are a team without self-motivated players. In every other endeavor of life, we call such teams "losers."

Friends, it is time to fan our own flames and see God's glorious love and power blaze forth.

God bless you, and God bless our community.

God Cares How Much We Care

For to us a child is born, to us a Son is given. ... Of the increase of His government and of peace there will be no end. ... The zeal of the Lord of hosts will do this.

—Isaiah 9:6–7

In the temple He found those who were selling oxen and sheep and pigeons, and the money-changers sitting there. And making a whip of cords, He drove them all out of the temple. ... His disciples remembered that it was written, "Zeal for your house will consume me."

—John 2:14–15, 17; see also Psalm 69:9

Do not be slothful in zeal, be fervent in spirit, serve the Lord.

—Romans 12:11

The three Scriptures set forth above all speak of zeal: the zeal of Father God for His plan to redeem the world through Jesus, the zeal of Jesus to purify God's household of worship and prayer, and our calling as Christians to share in that zeal of the Father and Jesus as we serve them.

So how are we doing? How would you rate your level of zeal in worshipping and serving the Lord? How would you rate the zeal of the congregation or faith group to which you belong?

Merriam-Webster Dictionary Online defines zeal as "a strong feeling of interest and enthusiasm that makes someone very eager or determined to do something." *YourDictionary.com* adds, "… having passionate energy for a belief or purpose." These are both good definitions of zeal, and we have all observed and experienced it somewhere.

Many people express their zeal for sports. The University of Tennessee's Neyland Stadium and Bristol Motor Speedway are just two of the sports venues where we see crowds of people filled with zeal.

Others channel their zeal into social causes or politics, music, travel, or even shopping sprees.

Zeal feels good most of the time, and it is an incredible motivator for both the ones who have it and the ones who get touched by it. That is why sports teams like to play home games and why performers, both in entertainment and politics, like to play before responsive crowds.

As for the church, well, David said, "For a day in your courts is better than a thousand elsewhere" (Psalm 84:10). How many of us say that? Paul called everything else in his life "rubbish" compared with the wonder of his relationship with and service for Jesus Christ (Philippians 3:8). How many of us feel that way?

Very shortly after I came back to the Lord in 1991, I attended a worship service at the church where I was a member. In the midst of the calm and polite atmosphere of that service, I felt an almost uncontrollable desire to stand up and shout, "Hey, friends, let's wake up! This is Jesus we are talking about!"

I had such zeal, but at least in that setting, the other people in the congregation did not. And since that time, I have been in many Christian gatherings where "they did not."

On the one hand, this lack of zeal in the church has caused me great concern because of what the risen Lord said to the churches of Ephesus, Sardis, and Laodicea (Revelation 2:1–7, 3:1–6, 14–22). Jesus has strong rebuke for churches that have lost their passion and sense of priority. They represent Him, after all, so how much the church cares will reflect to the world how much the Lord cares. A poor representation of Jesus by the church has caused many people to turn away, not come.

On the other hand, I have great empathy for the lack of zeal among Christians because I have "been there, done that." My faith as a child and youth was without zeal because I didn't know better. And although my return to faith involved great zeal, I have experienced times when it was quenched through both weariness and discouragement.

The enemy uses the cares and desires of this world to choke our zeal (Mark 4:19). He also uses times of little progress to discourage us and plant seeds of confusion about who we are and why we are here (Proverbs 13:12). It is in discerning these enemy strategies that we can find the answer to the problem—God's presence and God's purpose.

God invites us into His presence through worship and prayer so we can be refreshed and reenergized by His touch (Acts 3:20). If you have ever felt His touch, you know the truth of this. And if you haven't felt His touch in a long time, you know how the zeal from that refreshing can fade.

God also invites us into His purpose: to restore God's kingdom on the earth by bringing His healing love, truth, and goodness to the people around us. What we do for the least of these, we do for Him (Matthew 25:31–46)! Every Christian who has stepped into one of God's mission fields as a life priority can tell you about the zeal that fills your heart and transforms your soul.

God cares how much you care. It is the merciful who receive mercy, the hungry and thirsty who get filled, the sowers who reap, and the ones who draw near to God who have God draw near to them.

Seek God's presence. Embrace God's purpose. Let the zeal of the Lord fill your heart, and watch what happens!

God bless you, and God bless our community.

God Is Willing to Heal Us

A man with leprosy came and knelt before Him and said, "Lord, if you are willing, you can make me clean." Jesus reached out His hand and touched the man. "I am willing," He said. "Be clean!" Immediately he was cured of his leprosy.

—Matthew 8:2–3 NIV

We are a people preoccupied with the desire to be healthy. It shows up, like our other priorities, in what we talk about and where we spend our time and money. The cost of health care is a national crisis. Most of our TV shows are sponsored by pharmaceutical companies advertising pills to improve our physical, emotional, and sexual well-being. Some of us read the nutritional labels on food packaging more often than we read the Bible—which leads me to my next point.

Why isn't the church coming forth aggressively to address this need people have for healing? Why do so few churches have healing services or invite people up for healing prayer during Sunday morning worship and other gatherings?

The ministry of Jesus on earth was preaching, teaching *and* healing (Matthew 4:23). He said, "As the Father has sent me, even so I am sending you" (John 20:21). He promised we would do even greater things than He had done (John 14:12). And to top it off, God's Word gives this commands and promises:

"Is anyone among you sick? Let him call for the elders of the church, and let them pray over him, anointing him with oil in the name of the Lord; and the prayer offered in faith will restore the one who is sick, and the Lord will raise him up" (James 5:14–15).

"And these signs will accompany those who believe: ... they will lay their hands on the sick, and they will recover" (Mark 16:17–18).

Why are we so reluctant to seek God rather than pills for our healing? God created and sustains the universe, so we know He has the power to heal. The only question is whether He is willing to use that power. And Matthew 8:2–3 is just one example of hundreds in Scripture that give us the answer to that question. God loves us! He is willing to heal us! He wants to make us whole, and He is waiting for us to believe in His love and ask.

My ministry has been holding a Tuesday night healing service for several years now. We have seen, among other wonderful things, people instantly healed of asthma, migraines, staph infections, bronchitis, and sciatic back pain. We have seen anxieties and depression lifted and addictions broken. Please let me share a few of the things we have learned.

First, we must break free of the "Nazareth syndrome"—the attitude that you know by your past experience with Jesus what He will and won't do (Mark 6:1–6). Everything is possible for those who believe, but the skepticism taught by the world has invaded the church, and it limits what Jesus will do. Pray as we have prayed, "Help my unbelief!" (Mark 9:23–24).

Second, we must truly care about the people we pray for. Faith without love is nothing (1 Corinthians 13:2). Compassion motivated the healing ministry of Jesus (Matthew 14:14). We need more than a church prayer list. We need the fervent effective prayer described in James 5, which has its foundation in a passionate love of people and hatred of the evil that oppresses people.

Third, do not blame God for sickness. It is true that God may occasionally allow suffering to test our faith (Job) or keep us humble (Paul's thorn in the flesh). But read Acts 10:38. God is not going around giving people cancer. God is on our side in wanting to heal all who are oppressed by the Devil. And like Jesus, we have been anointed with the Holy Spirit and power to do just that.

Fourth, ask God to help you diagnose the real problems as you pray. Doctors tell us anxiety, depression, loneliness, and bitterness are at the root of 80 percent of their patients' "medical" problems. Who are better equipped than God and His people to deal with these problems of the heart? Who else has the power to deliver people from demonic attack? We must encourage our weary and heavy-laden people to bring their pain to Jesus.

Finally, we must trust God even when His apparent answer to our prayers for healing is "No." What He may be saying is "Wait" or even, "I have a better idea." We can always be assured that the Lord wants the very best for us, so ask the Holy Spirit to help you discern and pray what God wants prayed (Romans 8:26).

Praise God for the prayer and healing ministries we already have in some of our hospitals and congregations. Please, let's build on and multiply those. The need is so great, and our loving, healing God is so willing!

God bless you, and God bless our community.

An Enemy Too Long Ignored

Be sober-minded; be watchful. Your adversary the devil prowls around like a roaring lion, seeking someone to devour. Resist him, firm in your faith, knowing that the same kinds of suffering are being experienced by your brotherhood throughout the world.

—1 Peter 5:8–9

There are many "who's to blame" debates being aired in this election year. One divisive effort seeks to determine who was most responsible for ignoring the threat of al-Qaeda and Osama bin Laden until 9/11, when it was too late. The correct answer appears to be "Virtually all of us."

We have learned a crucial lesson the hard way. Ignoring a dangerous enemy can lead to disaster. And what the Christian community must do is apply that "lesson learned" where it will do the most good. We need to embrace our responsibility to stand against Satan, his demonic servants, and his evil works in our community, nation, and world.

A majority of mainline Christians do not seem to believe in Satan or demons anymore. This is despite the fact that Satan (a name meaning "adversary") is referenced more than fifty times in Scripture. The Devil (a word meaning "accuser") is referenced more than thirty times. Demons, who are also described as unclean or evil spirits, are referenced more than a hundred times. The Bible says Jesus came to destroy the works of the Devil (1 John 3:8). If we cannot believe what the Bible says about Satan, why believe what it says about Jesus?

Most evangelical Christians believe in Satan, but many seem to limit their actions on that belief to those times they blame him for a sin they committed—like Flip Wilson's Geraldine character exclaiming, "The

Devil made me do it!" Please remember—God didn't accept that excuse when Eve gave it (Genesis 3:13)

Charismatic Christians believe in Satan, and some actively stand in prayer against his efforts. Praise God for that! Even in these congregations, however, there can be a tendency to focus on joyful songs of "stomping the Devil under our feet." Jesus made it clear to His disciples this was not a party matter (Luke 10:17–20). Our joy is in our salvation, and our stand against the Evil One is for the serious business of freeing others to the deliverance we have.

Here are some key scriptural points to consider:

First, Satan and his demonic servants have been disarmed and condemned by the triumph of Jesus on the cross (Colossians 2:13–15; John 16:8–11). The evil one will be driven out (John 12:31–32). However, that time is not yet come, and the Devil continues to seek our destruction (1 Peter 5:8–9).

Second, Satan has blinded the minds of unbelievers so that they cannot see the truth about Jesus (2 Corinthians 4:4). Our prayers and loving witness can help them escape this trap, but they are currently captive to his will (2 Timothy 2:24–26). The apostle John says, "The whole world is under the control of the evil one" (1 John 5:19).

Third, Satan's chief remaining weapon is the lie—the opposite of Jesus, who is truth. He tempts us to ungodly decisions, making the ungodly seem good, attractive, or effective (Matthew 4:1–11; Genesis 3:4–5; 2 Corinthians 11:13–14, 2 Thessalonians 2:9). He defies grace by falsely accusing us and leading us to self-condemnation or condemnation of our neighbor (Revelation 12:9–10; Zechariah 3:1–4). He is the father of lies (John 8:43–44) because he knows the truth will set us free (John 8:32).

Fourth, we are to stand against Satan's schemes (Ephesians 6:11–12). Anointed with the Holy Spirit, Jesus walked this earth "doing good and healing all who were under the power of the devil" (Acts 10:36–38). Anointed by that same Holy Spirit, we are to walk just like Jesus walked (1 John 2:6). As the Father sent Jesus, so He sends us (John 20:21).

Fifth, there is one essential precondition to successfully resisting the Devil and watching him flee. Our lives must be submitted to the Lord (James 4:7).

My suggestion is that we all start together with the basics. In the Lord's Prayer, Jesus emphasized our need to pray, "Deliver us from the evil one" (Matthew 6:13 NIV). Jesus prayed himself that the Father would protect us from the evil one (John 17:15), and Paul promised that the Lord would respond faithfully to such prayers from us (2 Thessalonians 3:1).

Can we not all commit to pray every day that the Lord will protect our children and schools from the evil one and his schemes? Pray that God will protect our marriages and families, neighborhoods, spiritual leaders, troops, and civil servants. Pray a wall of fire around our city that Satan cannot penetrate (Zechariah 2:5). And then pray that this wall of fire will cause Satan's veil of blindness over the lost to go up in flames so they can see Jesus!

The Lord is waiting to hear such prayers from His people, and He will honor them.

God bless you, and God bless our community.

We Must Learn to Cast
Out Demons

"And these signs will accompany those who believe: in my name they will cast out demons."

—Mark 16:17

This column may cause some of you to believe that Doug Tweed has finally "gone off the deep end." But what I say here needs to be said.

Demons are real. They are neither myth nor fairy tale. They are not primitive explanations for what we now call mental illness. And they are not a problem we can afford to keep ignoring.

Six years ago, I wrote a column titled "An Enemy Too Long Ignored." That column, reviewable on our website, addressed the importance of acknowledging the existence of Satan and forces of darkness. The emphasis was on our need to pray daily for the protection of our families, neighborhoods, and leaders.

Today I want to address more specifically how we can help people who are oppressed by demons, because it is not just a matter of whether demons are real. It is a matter of what demons really do. They oppress people's lives. Jesus came to free and heal those who are oppressed by evil (Luke 4:17–21; Acts 10:38; 1 John 3:8).

The Bible makes reference to demons, who are also called unclean or evil spirits, more than a hundred times. Anyone familiar with Scripture remembers how often Jesus delivered demonized people. He empowered his disciples to do likewise (Matthew 10:1; Luke 10:17–19). And as set forth in Mark 16:17, Jesus said the believers who followed (you and me) would

227

also deliver people from demonic oppression through the authority and power of His name.

Yet how many churches in our region have deliverance ministries? How many of our preachers and teachers even speak of demons, the difficulties they cause, and how we can be set free?

There is not enough space in this column to comprehensively address the issue of demons. Three "tried and true" books on the subject are *Deliverance from Evil Spirits* by Francis MacNutt, *Pigs in the Parlor* by Frank and Ida Mae Hammond, and *They Shall Expel Demons* by Derek Prince. Here, because my wife, Christie, and I have been involved in deliverance ministry for several years, I offer some basic things we have learned.

Demons can oppress or possess. Oppression is an evil influence or interference. Possession, which is far less common, is control. Christians cannot be possessed, because the Holy Spirit is within them, but Christians can definitely be oppressed.

Not all illness is caused by demons. There are spirits of infirmity that cause physical disorders (Luke 11:11–13). But many physical problems are simply physical, and Jesus and the disciples moved in both healing ministry and deliverance ministry.

Likewise, mental illness can be the result of life's traumas, particularly in childhood, or chemical imbalances and other neurological disorders. But demons can aggravate those conditions, and can independently cause depression, anxiety, obsession, confusion, nightmares, and delusion. It is crucial in every situation to seek spiritual discernment about whether demonic oppression is part of the problem. God has provided some Christians with the gift of discernment of spirits, along with words of wisdom and knowledge, for that very purpose (1 Corinthians 12:8–10).

Demons look for a way in—a foothold such as unforgiveness, involvement with the occult, pornography, or severe trauma. Once they find and use that opening, they do not leave on their own. Secular caregivers have no ability to deal with them, and medications can only dull your awareness of them, not free you.

Mere belief in Jesus will not guarantee your ability to cast out demons (Matthew 17:14–20; Acts 19:13–16). Some demons are relatively weak, but others are powerful and resistant. They often work in teams. Strong faith and spiritual maturity are, along with a biblical understanding of deliverance ministry, very important.

At the same time, we must understand that all demons, including Satan, are subject to the authority of Jesus. When the church knows what she is doing, the gates of hell cannot prevail against us (Matthew 16:18).

Finally, demons that have been cast out can return (Luke 11:25). It is essential that the person delivered from oppression also be shown how to close the foothold that allowed the oppression in the first place. The goal is not simply to get rid of evil. It is to displace evil with good, dark with light, and lie with truth. We must both deliver and disciple.

Demonic influence is behind most if not all of the insane shootings in our schools and workplaces. It also is behind the inability of many people to break free from emotional struggles such as depression, fear, or addiction. It is time for the church to rise up and do what only we can do to solve those problems.

God bless you, and God bless our community.

The Lord Will Shake Things Up

At that time His voice shook the earth, but now He has promised,
"Yet once more I will shake not only the earth but also the heavens."
This phrase, "Yet once more," indicates the removal of things that
are shaken- that is, things that have been made- in order that the
things that cannot be shaken may remain.

—Hebrews 12:26–27

We have frequently focused in this column on our need to change.

As examples, on June 15, 2007, I submitted "We Need the Folk who Rock the Boat." On October 6, 2006, I submitted "You May Need to Tear Down to Build Up." Both of those columns emphasized the importance of change, despite the cost and pain it may bring, and the value of those people in our midst who are willing to be agents for change.

Those columns also acknowledged our stubborn resistance to change, particularly in the church. Jesus pointed out at the end of His parable on fresh wine and old wineskins: "And no one after drinking old wine desires new, for he says, 'The old is good'" (Luke 5:36–39).

Jesus Christ, the King of Kings, is "making all things new" (Revelation 21:5), and He constantly calls all people, Christian and pre-Christian, to repentance—a change of mind and change of direction. But the great majority of us do not have ears to hear or eyes to see, so God often has to shake things up Himself.

The flood in Noah's day and the Tower of Babel both reveal basic truth about a God who intervenes when things get totally out of hand. Anyone who doubts the loving nature of the Lord in this needs to read 1 Peter 3 and 4, where we are told that Jesus took the gospel to those killed in the flood.

The Old Testament people of God experienced "shake-ups" from Jehovah many times. When they drifted away from the Lord, He removed His hand of protection so they would experience oppression, awaken to their need for Him, and cry out. When they became too resistant to those wake-up calls, God orchestrated the events that led to destruction of the temple and seventy years of exile.

And for those who believe these "shake-ups" no longer apply after the cross, please remember the Lord's Great Commission for His disciples to go out into the world (Matthew 28:18–20, Acts 1:8). They received the Holy Spirit, but they didn't go! It took an outbreak of persecution, divine visitation, angelic dreams, and rooftop visions to tear the Jewish Christians loose from their distrust of Gentiles and initiate the evangelism of the earth by which you and I received eternal life (Acts 8:1–4, 9:15, 10).

So, what about today? We are living two thousand years after the time Jesus walked the earth. If a thousand years is like a day to God (2 Peter 3:8), then we are beginning the third day.

According to Barna Group, Ranier Group, and other polls available on the Internet, the Christian percentage of the world population is now in decline for the first time. Forty-eight percent of the people in the European Union do not even believe in a personal God. Three out of four indicate that religion is not important to their life.

In the United States, where the majority of people still profess Christianity, 80 percent of our youth and young adults are projected to be disengaged from any organized religion by age twenty-nine.

Our culture worships money and fame, not God. We depend upon science and technology: our own wisdom and strength. Our politics are polarized, not united, and manipulative rather than transparent. Our media celebrates sex, controversy, and violence.

The family structure is shattered. Less than half our children are raised in one home by their biological parents. There is both an aggressive push for homosexual marriage and a decreased interest in marriage between men and women.

And lest we forget, one of every five pregnancies in the world is terminated by abortion—the deliberate taking of defenseless human life.

Folks, these are systemic problems that are gaining momentum. They cannot be "tweaked" into a state of repair. Major overhaul is the only answer, but the forces in control will not willingly submit to such costly and painful change. So expect a shaking from the God who loves us and will not forsake us.

Economic upheaval can dislodge our love of money. Forces of nature can reveal the limits and dangers of our technology. Desperate times can bring even sharply divided groups together.

And most important, God's shaking can cause the people called by His name to humble themselves, turn from their self-oriented, partially engaged, lukewarm ways, and pray (2 Chronicles 7:14; Revelation 3:14–22).

God bless you, and God bless our community.

God Will Lead Us into Righteousness

He leads me in paths of righteousness for His name's sake.

—Psalm 23:3b

The path of the righteous is level; you make level the way of the righteous. In the path of your judgments, O Lord, we wait for you ... For when your judgments are in the earth, the inhabitants of the world learn righteousness. If favor is shown to the wicked, he does not learn righteousness.

—Isaiah 26:7–10

We have all heard this phrase at least once in our life: *We can do this the easy way or the hard way.*

It's not a phrase we like to hear. It is always applied to a choice we have not wanted to make. The person speaking is, in a nutshell, saying we will take that path whether we like it or not. All we can choose is how painful the process will be.

Friends, the Lord intends to restore righteousness to the earth (Isaiah 61:11; 2 Peter 3:13). And His Scriptures clearly say, "We can do this the easy way or the hard way."

Every Christian is thrilled to declare God is love. But we often gloss over the truth that God is also the righteous one who calls His people to righteousness (Acts 22:14; Matthew 6:33). The term *righteous* appears in Scripture more than six hundred times. Yet most of us would struggle to define it.

Righteousness is about right rather than wrong, good rather than evil. It is the opposite of "sin." And it can never mean "self-righteousness," because we are not capable of being right, good, or sin-free on our own (Romans 3:9–23).

The righteousness we must have is, in fact, not our own. It is "the righteousness of God" we receive "through faith in Jesus Christ" (Romans 3:22). But be careful how you understand this! The righteous live by faith (Romans 1:17). The righteous are doers of the Word, not just hearers (Romans 2:13).

Put another way, the righteous truly trust Jesus. We are not required to be stumble-free. But we have decided that our heavenly Father and His Word determine what is right and wrong, not us. We want to follow Jesus, not just get a ticket to heaven. We seek through God's Holy Spirit to love God and neighbor.

The Lord has declared that He will judge the world in righteousness (Psalm 96:13). He is not limiting this to a final judgment day. Just as He brought judgments on Egypt, Israel, and other nations in Scripture, the Lord continues to bring judgments upon people and nations today (1 Chronicles 16:14).

God doesn't do this because His wrath has replaced His love. He does it in His love because He knows righteousness, not sin, is best for every person and every nation. "Righteousness exalts a nation, but sin is a disgrace to any people" (Proverbs 14:34).

Those who know their shepherd's voice can be led obediently in paths of righteousness (Psalm 23:3). This is the easy way, led by the One who is the Way (John 14:6). When we stray, we receive our Father's loving discipline, which may be painful at first but soon restores both righteousness and our peace in Christ (Hebrews 12:11).

However, as set forth in Isaiah 26, there is also a hard way to learn righteousness. It is the only way the wicked will learn: the judgments of God. The wicked may or may not want a Savior, but they don't want a Lord. They want to decide for themselves what is right and wrong. Since God loves them, He will do everything He can to turn them around.

Judgments are coming. Where they produce righteousness, they will be worth it. Imagine a system of business and finance (including health care) where everyone embraces the Golden Rule, or a political system led by people known for their honesty and humility. Imagine a sexually righteous nation where marriage is a divine covenant between man and woman, and there is chastity outside marriage. No broken homes. No abortions of unwanted children. No sexually transmitted disease.

Can a nation struggling with wickedness learn righteousness? Consider Haiti.

Despite the media's saturation-level coverage of the January 12, 2010, earthquake, hardly any reported what happened on February 12. In a nation known not just for extreme poverty but for widespread corruption and voodoo witchcraft, Haitian President Préval called for his people to come together for three days of fasting and prayer. More than a million people showed up, twelve hours a day for three days, in the name of Jesus! What a step into righteousness!

Now ask yourself what it will take to bring our nation (or community) to a similar turnaround. Remember—one way or the other, easy or hard, God will lead us into righteousness.

God bless you, and God bless our community.

The River of Revival
Runs through Us

Then the angel showed me the river of the water of life, bright as crystal, flowing from the throne of God and of the Lamb through the middle of the street of the city; also, on either side of the river, the tree of life with its twelve kinds of fruit, yielding its fruit each month. The leaves of the tree were for the healing of the nations.
—Revelation 22:1–2

My heart cries out for revival in the church! We need a sustained move of God so that His presence, power, purity, and purpose can wash away our worldliness and replace it with His holy love.

In revival, religious practices give way to close, open fellowship with God and each other. Corporate management gives way to Spirit-leadership. Instead of looking for a church that pleases us, we become people that seek only to please God.

As we come out from under the baskets of our sanctuaries, Christ's light shines brightly through us into the darkness of our communities, and the light wins (Matthew 5:14–16).

There have been wonderful times of revival in our nation's history: the First Great Awakening (eighteenth century), the Second Great Awakening (nineteenth century), the Azusa Street and Charismatic revivals (twentieth century), and others. All came at times of dramatic need in our nation, and all had, at least for a time, a powerful positive effect on both the church and the nation.

The Bible also gives us pictures of revival. Rediscovery of God's Word led to revival in the time of King Josiah (2 Kings 22–23). Openness to the outpouring of the Holy Spirit brought incredible revival during the early years of the Christian church (Acts 2–5).

And in both the Old and New Testaments, God shared a beautiful vision of revival as a river (Ezekiel 47; Revelation 22:1–2). This river of life flows out from the throne and temple of God, bringing purity, nourishment, healing, and abundant life wherever it goes. Jeremiah 2:13 helps us understand that this river of revival, this fount of every blessing, is God Himself.

What can we do to bring this river of revival to our region? The Lord spoke this question into my spirit: "How does God make a natural river?" I looked it up.

Rivers are birthed in the high country by small trickles of water on the ground's surface. These trickles are called rills. During some seasons of the year, rills can be created from above by rainfall and snowfall, but year-round, they are primarily created by underground springs that burst to the surface.

As the rills flow downhill, they begin to join together, forming brooks. As brooks flow together, streams are created that in turn flow together and create a river. Eventually, you have a river system, with a main river fed by all its tributaries.

The river of revival is formed the same way. There is living water that flows from above. I think of the stairway to heaven at Bethel, with angels ascending and descending (Genesis 28:12–13). But the main source of living water for this revival will pour from springs of the earth: you and me.

The Hebrew name *Adam* means "man" but is closely related to the Hebrew word *Adamah*, which means "ground." We were made from the ground (Genesis 2:7). And Jesus declares that from the innermost being of those who believe in Him "will flow streams of living water" (John 7:38). These streams are, in fact, the Spirit of the Living God (John 7:39)!

Brothers and sisters in Christ, we can be the rills of revival. So, "Let's get rill!" Let's deal with the things in our life that obstruct the flow of God through us: unbelief, pride, and selfishness, unforgiveness, worldly priorities, and the like. God can pour out through us in prayer, worship, witness, and simple acts of obedient love.

Churches of Kingsport, let our rills, brooks, and streams run together so the river will form. For too long, we have let the enemy divert, dam, and divide us with legalism, materialism, elitism, and denominationalism.

Why can't our spiritual leaders come together in a citywide ministerial or church association so we can network in ministry together, matching resources to needs? Why can't we have citywide worship services and prayer meetings in our conference centers and stadiums? Why can't we have an ongoing citywide network of continuous prayer for our city that is supported by the thousands of people in our collective congregations?

As our streams come together, I believe God will add divine waters from above—raining down His Holy Spirit. Remember—it doesn't rain much in the desert, but it rains all the time in the Amazon Basin.

If we say we can't do this because our doctrines are different, I respond that unless we demonstrate unconditional love among ourselves, our doctrines means nothing (1 Corinthians 13:2). And if we feel we're just too busy with what we are already doing, I respond, "'Martha, Martha … only one thing is needed'" (Luke 10:41–42). We need God. The many hurting people of our region need God.

And God is just waiting for His people to let Him flow out through them.

God bless you, and God bless our community.

Visions of What Revival Will Bring

"And it shall come to pass afterward, that I will pour out my Spirit on all flesh; your sons and your daughters shall prophesy, your old men shall dream dreams, and your young men shall see visions."
—Joel 2:28; Acts 2:17

There are Christians scattered throughout the Kingsport area who are praying every day for revival. I am one of them, and I am grateful for every one of them, because we desperately need revival. We need a spiritual awakening in the church that will open the door to what only God can do: community healing and transformation (2 Chronicles 7:14).

Please understand. I love Kingsport and the surrounding region. I share your gratitude for all the blessings we have here.

But for those with eyes to see, there is also darkness everywhere. Our lives have all been touched by divorce, addiction, abuse, rejection, depression, anxiety, confusion, "and the list goes on." We have many people in bondage to poverty and many others in bondage to pornography or other sexual brokenness. We have thousands of people who do not know Jesus.

God can deliver us from these things. God can deliver our loved ones and our neighbors. We need revival!

Five years ago, I asked God to show me what revival would look like. He gave me a series of six short "visions" in rapid succession.

Vision number one was a picture of the cloud of God over a reverently praying congregation. The cloud represents God's presence. We need to become a house of prayer (Isaiah 56:7).

Vision two showed three women praying for another woman at a prayer rail. There was a spirit of community and assurance among all four. As the

239

prayer concluded, there were hugs of appreciation and a sense of "He has heard and will answer."

The church is not about "clergy" who minister while "laypeople" observe and receive. All Christians, male and female, are part of a royal priesthood, and we can all minister with each other in great faith and with great effectiveness (1 Peter 2:9; 1 Corinthians 12:1–27).

Vision number three was a person standing tall and straight in a "heavenly place," a limitless and timeless place that I knew to be before the throne of God. The person was connected and aware of where he was and with whom he was.

Revival includes personal revival—the tremendous intimacy each individual Christian is invited to have with God (Ephesians 2:6; Hebrews 10:19–23).

Vision four was a picture of four faces together like petals on a flower. All the faces looked the same, except one was bigger, as if I were seeing three children and an adult, or a father, mother, and two children. They were all laughing.

Revival will bring restoration of families, the building blocks of both community and the church. God will turn the hearts of fathers to their children and the hearts of children to their fathers (Malachi 4:6). There will be joy!

Vision number five showed a person, with other people behind him, standing in the light before an immense, intimidating darkness. The person in front and the people behind him began to grow. As they grew, the light grew. The darkness receded, faded, and withdrew.

A friend of mine saw this as a picture of Isaiah 60:1–5. A spiritually awakened church will prevail against the forces of darkness (Matthew 16:18; John 1:5–9).

Vision number six was a street scene of downtown Kingsport, with people whistling hymns on their way to work, and stopping to visit, laugh, and pray with each other.

Revival is not a religious thing. It is a life thing (Acts 2:42–47).

These six short visions may speak to your heart in ways they did not speak to mine. You may have your own visions. The key is that God has a vision. God wants to bring revival, Spirit awakening, to His people so they can be a light shining with the brilliance of His glory (Matthew 5:14).

And He wants to bring revival so we, His children, can have life abundant—life in the kingdom—life filled every day with His Holy Spirit, righteousness, peace, and joy (Romans 14:17).

So, what is God waiting for? I can't say I have anything like a complete answer for that. His ways are not my ways.

But I believe, to some degree, that God is waiting for us to want what He wants (Psalm 37:4). God is waiting on us to return to our first love: loving Him with all our being (Revelation 2:4; Mark 12:30). God is waiting for us to see our childlike need for Him in every aspect of life and community (Mark 10:14–15; Revelation 3:17).

And God is waiting for enough of us to ask for revival. "If my people pray ..."

Will you join those who are praying for revival? Will you join those who know how desperately we need Him now?

God bless you, and God bless our community.

Imagine God's Kingdom
in our Community

Asked by the Pharisees when the kingdom of God would come, He replied to them by saying, "The kingdom of God does not come with signs to be observed or with visible display. Nor will people say, 'Look! Here it is!' Or, 'See. It is there!' For behold, the kingdom of God is within you [in your hearts] and among you [surrounding you]."

—Luke 17:20–21 AB

In our Sunday night teaching service at Friends of the King Ministries, we have been discussing foundational truths.

What is the gospel of the kingdom of God? Who is Jesus Christ? Who is the Holy Spirit? Who are we once we become disciples of Jesus? What does it mean to know God as our Father?

All of these questions are absolutely crucial to our understanding of reality. And our studies of Scripture reveal many facets of truth to each one—facets not in terms of different points of view, but in the sense of a beautifully cut diamond. Jesus is Lamb of God and Lion of Judah, suffering servant and King of Kings, Son of God and Son of Man, the one who hung on the cross, and the risen one revealed in Revelation 1 with a face that shines like the sun. Wow!

Last week, we examined what the Lord's Prayer says about the kingdom of God. Our prayer is not that we go to heaven, but that the kingdom of God comes to earth. The kingdom exists wherever the rightful rule of King Jesus is honored, embraced, and established. We asked ourselves, "What would the kingdom look like if it was down here in our greater Kingsport/ Gate City/Tri-Cities community?"

In other words, can we imagine (visualize) the outcome of what we pray for?

The answers we came up with were, in my opinion, breathtaking.

Everyone in the community would know what it is to love and be loved, both by God and neighbor. Everyone would be valued.

There would be no pride and self-centeredness, no more people trying to force their own agendas onto others. Our humility would empower the selfless nature of our love, including our healthy love of ourselves and our appreciation of what God made when He made "me" and "you."

There would be no unbelief. Our trust and faith in God would match His flawless trustworthiness and faithfulness. Through our great faith, the Lord would work miracles and move mountains.

We would grow daily in truth, wisdom, and understanding as, led by the spirit of truth, we meditated daily on God's Word. We would be set free from the countless lies of Satan that have been imposed upon us.

Hope would abound. No one would suffer from despair, depression, cynicism, or low expectations. Disappointments, if they occurred, would heal quickly.

We would all find God's kingdom purposes for our lives on earth: no more aimlessness and no more focus on being great at unimportant things.

Everyone would know the peace of God. There would be no fear, and no more dissension or division, because we would all live together in God's perfect love.

Marriage would be a sacred institution of God joining a man and woman together for the rest of their lives. Broken homes and broken children would be no more.

Sex would be a sacred element of marriage. As a result, after one generation, sexually transmitted diseases would be no more.

There would be no poverty. Those who have would share with those who need.

Each man, woman, boy, and girl would walk in joy with the Lord throughout every day. And our community's prayers for the rest of the world would bear much fruit.

At the end of that Sunday night meeting, I was gripped by the awareness that this "imagining" we had done is absolutely achievable! This isn't false hope. This is what God wants for us.

Isn't there at least one person in our community who could draw so close to God that these kingdom realities could become his or her lifestyle? Of course there is.

And if one person could do it, could not two, or a family, or small group of friends, or a congregation, or many congregations? God is for us. Who can stand against us?

Perhaps the greatest lie imposed upon the church is the lie of low expectations. The Lord would never ask us to pray for something He is not ready to do. He told us the kingdom was among us and within us. He told us to pray for His kingdom to come here just like it is in heaven. Do we believe Him or not?

I urge us all to pray, "Thy kingdom come ..." with faith, deep desire, and eager expectancy. Imagine!

God bless you, and God bless our community.

Heaven and Earth Come Together

Then I saw a new heaven and a new earth, for the first heaven and the first earth had passed away, and the sea was no more. And I saw the holy city, New Jerusalem, coming down out of heaven from God, prepared as a bride adorned for her husband. And I heard a loud voice from the throne saying, "Behold, the dwelling place of God is with man. He will dwell with them, and they will be his people, and God himself will be with them as their God."

—Revelation 21:1–3

The most widely held misconception among Christians today is the idea that we leave this earth and go to heaven when we die, to live there forever. As the old hymn goes, "Some glad morning when this life is o'er, I'll fly away, to a home on God's celestial shore."

The truth revealed in Revelation 21 and other Scripture is that there will be both a new heaven and a new earth (Isaiah 65:17; 2 Peter 3:13). Even more amazing, this new heaven and new earth will come together.

In other words, we don't leave earth forever to go to heaven. Instead, God and heaven come "down to earth" to be with us. Our eternal destiny is to live with God and each other in a divinely vibrant experience of both physical and spiritual reality. Butterflies, flowers, trees, birds, angels, and heavenly mansions ... wow!

The Greek word for *new* used here is *kainos*, a word that goes beyond the concept of something restored to its original state. *Kainos* means "new and improved." Yes, the existing heaven is good, and God declared the earth as first created to be good (Genesis 1). But the "new" heaven and earth will be the perfected versions of their predecessors, just as we will be the perfected versions of ourselves.

A crucial part of this perfecting is the "coming together." For us, being completed includes our need to come together with God (John 17). The word *baptized* means "immersed" or "saturated." We must be baptized in God's Holy Spirit (Matthew 3:11; Acts 1:5–8). The bride and the Bridegroom marry.

Likewise, heaven and earth will not be perfected until they come together as the dwelling place of God and His people. The prophet Habakkuk envisioned, "[T]he earth will be filled with the knowledge of the glory of the Lord as the waters cover the sea" (Habakkuk 2:14). What I see described here is all the earth being baptized in God's presence. Again ... wow!

Our eternal future is more exciting than we can imagine, friends, but I am also excited about how heaven and earth can come together for us in the "here and now."

It has happened before, the first time being the garden of Eden (Genesis 2). God planted that garden on the earth for His beloved Adam and Eve, but He also put the heavenly Tree of Life in the garden's center, and the Lord of heaven walked there (Genesis 3:8). Heaven touched earth.

It happened again in the Holy of Holies (Exodus 25:8, 22). God chose this small room containing the ark of the covenant as the place where His glory would reside among and speak to Israel—the place heaven touched earth for them.

It happened gloriously in Mary's womb. A child was conceived by the Holy Spirit—Son of God and Son of Man. The heavenly Word was emptied into the earth-bound form of humanity (Philippians 2:6–8). Then as a man on earth, Jesus was filled with heaven through the Holy Spirit (Colossians 1:19).

Heaven walked the earth wherever Jesus went. The truth of God's love was revealed, the sick were healed, and the demonically oppressed were set free.

Finally, Christ died for our sins, rose in victory, and ascended to the Father with all authority in ... heaven and earth together (Matthew 28:18)! The veil in the temple was torn down. The Holy Spirit was poured out into our earth-bound bodies. The Holy of Holies was now available on earth to everyone who knows Jesus as Lord (Hebrews 10:19–22).

Heaven and earth came together in a house of 120 people on Pentecost (Acts 2:1–4). Where those heaven-filled disciples walked, the truth of God's love was revealed, the sick were healed, and the demonically oppressed were set free. And everything that happened for them is available to you and me.

It is time. It is time for all of Christ's disciples to be immersed in God's Spirit and enter the Holy of Holies. When we come together to pray, worship, and serve with that desire and expectancy, it will happen. We can lay down our watches and orders of worship because our Lord will truly be among us (Matthew 18:20).

Heaven and earth will come gloriously together. And things will never be the same.

God bless you, and God bless our community.

Reflections on Intimacy with God Through the Holy Spirit

My Father, please make me whatever You will,

I ask it with all of my heart!

Let me move toward the oneness

that Christ prayed we'd have

where no one can tell us apart.

Let me speak of Your wonder

to all that You love,

of a Vastness far more than I know—

power bound by no rules

but Your wisdom and grace,

our faithlessness, our only foe.

"I do not ask for these only, but also for those who will believe in me through their word, that they may all be one, just as you, Father, are in me, and I in you, that they also may be in us, so that the world may believe that you have sent me. The glory that you have given me I have given to them, that they may be one even as we are one, I in them and you in me, that they may become perfectly one, so that the world may know that you sent me and loved them even as you loved me." (John 17:20–23)

Christ Prayed for Intimacy
with You and Me

"I do not ask for these only, but also for those who will believe in me through their word, that they may all be one, just as you, Father, are in me, and I in you, that they also may be in us, so that the world may believe that you have sent me. The glory that you have given me I have given to them, that they may be one even as we are one, I in them and you in me, that they may become perfectly one, so that the world may know that you sent me and loved them even as you loved me.

—John 17:20–23

On Easter Sunday, our sanctuaries will be filled with people celebrating the resurrection of Jesus Christ. Even the most casual Christian likes to remember how Jesus defeated death for Himself, for us, and for our loved ones (1 Corinthians 15:55–57).

As for today, "Good" Friday, most of those people will be winding up the workweek and looking forward to some weekend recreation. A much smaller number will gather to solemnly celebrate the crucifixion: the death that made the defeat of death possible.

Why did Jesus go to the cross? Was it just to provide people with a ticket to heaven, or were there other purposes?

This is a question I addressed at Easter 2008 in my column titled "Christ Died So He Could Live Through Us." There I spoke of how the grain of wheat fell to the ground so that it might bear much fruit. Christ came in one body so He could live and minister through many bodies—Christ in you and me, the hope of glory—part of God's plan to restore the kingdom of God on earth as it is in heaven.

It was a good column, and worth reading again, but it wasn't good enough. It didn't tell the whole story. As Paul Harvey would say, it is time to hear the rest of the story.

People who pray are especially likely to pray when they are about to face a serious challenge. They will pray for God's help and for the outcome from this challenge that is their heart's desire.

Jesus was a man who prayed, and He prayed before He went to the cross. The gospels of Matthew, Mark, and Luke describe one of those prayer times in Gethsemane, when Jesus asked if there were any other way. This shows us how great the challenge of the cross was—the greatest challenge ever faced by anyone anywhere.

The gospel of John doesn't describe the Gethsemane prayer time, but instead sets forth the prayer of Jesus just before He went to that garden. It is the prayer of John 17, and we should each read it carefully and reverently today.

It is a prophetic prayer, because Jesus embraces within it both things that had occurred and things that were about to occur. It is an intercessory prayer because Christ prays for His disciples and the believers who would come after them, including you and me. It is a revelation prayer because it shows us the outcome our Lord desired with all His heart to see happen as a result of His crucifixion.

Jesus prayed that we would become one with Him in the same way that He was one with the Father. This was and is His heart's desire.

You will not appreciate the weight and wonder of this prayer until you reflect on the oneness Jesus shared with His Father. Jesus was filled with all the fullness of God (Colossians 1:19)! He said and did only what His Father directed (John 5:19, 12:49). The Father and Son knew each other completely (Luke 10:22). The oneness between the Father and the Son is so perfect that we embrace the Christian doctrine of the Trinity to describe it: three persons, one God.

The English word that best describes such oneness is *intimacy*. The Lord wants the same perfect intimacy with us that He has with His Father. This is what eternal life really is: intimacy with Jesus and the Father (John 17:3).

The cross, by eliminating the barrier of sin, allowed Christ to give us the "glory" the Father gave Him. This "glory" is the Holy Spirit, who empowers intimacy with God, because through the Holy Spirit, both the Son and the Father can dwell in us even as we dwell in Christ (John 14:23).

And this intimacy is for now. Jesus prayed for intimacy while the world is still lost and we still live in it, not after we die or He returns. It is when the lost see our intimacy with God that they will know God sent Jesus and loves them (John 17:23).

Intimacy with the Lord is intimacy of heart, mind, soul, and strength (Mark 12:30). We experience His love and love Him back. We renew our minds by embracing the mind of Christ. We tap into God's power and provision with peace and joy as we do His will (Matthew 6:33; Romans 14:17). In oneness with Him, we can also walk in oneness with each other.

My friends, are we doing all we can do to help Jesus achieve His heart's desire for deep, daily intimacy with us? If not, wouldn't this Good Friday be a "good" day to start?

God bless you, and God bless our community.

God's Most Important
Gift to Us Is Himself

Then the Lord said to Aaron, "You shall have no inheritance in their land, nor own any portion among them; I am your portion and your inheritance among the sons of Israel."

—Numbers 18:20 NASB

Several years ago, I received a word from the Lord through a dear friend, the Reverend Geraldine Swagerty of Full Gospel Mission. By "a word from the Lord," I mean a message given by God at a particular time to a particular person or people. The word I received was the verse set forth above, Numbers 18:20. At the time, I thought I understood what this word to me meant.

By then I had been the pastor of St. Mark House of Prayer for about five years. It was and still is a wonderful congregation, and being there was and still is a great blessing. Many lives have been changed, including mine. But St. Mark was (and still is) a small congregation. After an initial growth surge from less than fifteen to about thirty, we stopped increasing in attendance. Because I had experienced much competitive success in my "former life" as a trial attorney, it was hard to avoid feelings of frustration and failure.

In this word from the Lord, I thought I heard God saying, "It's okay, Doug. I know there are obstacles to growth at St. Mark. You are a white pastor of a mostly black congregation of a mostly white denomination in a church-saturated, mostly black neighborhood. You will not 'inherit' the attendance growth and perceived success some of your minister colleagues are experiencing, but you will receive Me. I am your portion."

Looking back now, I am embarrassed to see what a childish, self-centered spin I was putting on God's Word. It felt good to hear I wasn't failing God. It felt great to hear God was offering me such an intimate relationship with Him—perhaps a relationship more intimate than those experienced by the "more successful" pastors. I even had the audacity to feel on occasion I was making some kind of humble sacrifice, giving up trappings of success for this closeness with God.

What a silly fool I was! God, forgive me! Thank God, He has.

You will be relieved to know I am now older and at least a little wiser. God helped me reexamine what He was saying in Numbers 18:20. It is, in fact, a word for me, for you and for all Christians. God says, "I am your portion." This is the heart of our inheritance. This is the great gift, the one essential gift, the gift that brings along with it every other gift. God gives us Himself.

Here is how God "connected the dots" for me between Christians and Numbers 18:20.

In the Old Testament, God offered Himself to all of Israel, inviting them to be a kingdom of priests (Exodus 19:3–6). However, priests of God must talk with God, and the people were afraid to talk with God (Exodus 20:19). So Moses' brother Aaron and his family were set apart by God to become His priests (Exodus 29:44).

When the Hebrew people finally entered the Promised Land, God directed Joshua to divide the land among the twelve tribes. But the priests did not get land. They received something much better. They received God as their portion.

Today Christians live under the new covenant in Jesus Christ (Luke 22:20). God still has priests under the new covenant, but this priesthood is not Aaron's family. Instead, all Christians are part of the royal priesthood of God (1 Peter 2:9). And because we are His priests, God is "our portion."

God offers Himself to us as Father, perfect in His loving protection and provision for His children.

God offers Himself to us as Jesus—our Savior, eldest brother, best friend, and loving, righteous King.

God offers Himself to us as the Holy Spirit, the very presence of God poured into our lives to empower, comfort, heal, teach, and transform us. Through the Holy Spirit, the Father and Son can live in us (John 14:23).

Because I am finally beginning to understand what God was saying to me years ago, I no longer seek the blessings God can give me. I seek God, knowing that as I receive the gift of Him in my life, all the other things I need will follow (Lamentations 3:21–25; Matthew 6:33).

I no longer try to succeed for God. I simply seek God, knowing He is able to do through me far more than I could ever ask or imagine (Ephesians 3:20–21). And I try to give to others the gift of God I am receiving.

I hope I have done that today.

God bless you, and God bless our community.

Jesus Says, "Come And See."

The next day John again was standing with two of his disciples, and as he watched Jesus walk by, he exclaimed, "Look, here is the Lamb of God!" The two disciples heard him say this, and they followed Jesus. When Jesus turned and saw them following, He said to them, "What are you looking for?" They said to Him, "Rabbi" (which translated means Teacher), "where are you staying?" He said to them, 'Come and see."

—John 1:35–39 NRSV

No biblical story better describes the present need of the church in America.

Andrew and John were hungry for a move of God. Their nation was birthed as a nation under God. Their history included times when the nation conquered its enemies and was known for its wealth and wisdom. But those days were gone. The nation had moved further and further from God. Now enemies prevailed and people were in bondage. There had not been a prophet in Israel for four hundred years.

Then came John the Baptist, the greatest preacher anyone had ever heard. Bold in both appearance and attitude, he had a powerful two-part message.

The first part was "Repent!" Turn away from your sin and back to God. Stop the greed, deceit and sexual immorality. If you are a nation under God, start acting in a godly manner.

It was a word desperately needed to deal with how far the culture had fallen. Ring a bell?

The second part was "The kingdom of God is near," a word also desperately needed to deal with how far the people's hope had fallen.

The Lord was coming in power to restore God's rule in the land. Finally righteousness could prevail.

Strong words of both conviction and hope! Thousands upon thousands came to the Jordan River to be baptized, including Andrew and John, who became two of the Baptist's disciples.

Then another man showed up at the river: Jesus from Nazareth. He came to be baptized by John, and after Jesus left, John declared to the people who this Jesus was: "I'm not fit to tie His shoes. When He was baptized, heaven opened. God called Him the beloved Son. The Holy Spirit landed on Him like a dove. This is the Messiah, the Lamb of God who takes away the sins of the world. He will baptize not with water, but with Holy Spirit and fire."

The next day John the Baptist directed the attention of Andrew and John toward Jesus in a way that clearly said, "Go follow Him." The two young men left the Baptist and became the first two people to go to Jesus. As they did so, Jesus turned and asked them a simple but profound question: "What are you looking for?"

This is a question all of us need to be asking ourselves. What are we looking for in our lives, our relationship with God, and our communities of faith?

Remember what Andrew and John already had with the Baptist: a great preacher who spoke of the Father, Son, and Holy Spirit; who preached the need to repent, be baptized, and live a moral, honest life; who taught there would be a judgment day, but that Jesus is the Savior who can cleanse us from our sins.

Doesn't that sound exactly like what most people look for in our Bible-believing churches today? Yet Andrew and John left that because they wanted and needed more. Do you want more? Isn't it clear our nation needs more?

Andrew and John responded to Jesus with their own question: "Where are you staying?" This simple question was also profound. The Greek word for *staying* is *meno*, which means "stay," "abide," or "remain." Although it could certainly include where Jesus slept, it went far beyond that, because Jesus remained at all times in the presence and rule of His heavenly Father. He therefore "stayed" in the kingdom of God wherever He went.

When Jesus responded, "Come and see," He wasn't just talking about His room at the Motel 6. He was going to show them the kingdom of God moving on the earth, healing the sick, delivering the demonized, raising the dead, stopping the storm, walking on water, and teaching both who God really is and who mankind is designed to be.

Andrew and John would "come and see" all of that. Then three years later, soon after the Lamb of God paid the price for our sins, they would, along with 118 other disciples, "come and see" what John the Baptist had promised in the very beginning. In an upper room on Pentecost, they were all baptized in the Holy Spirit—immersed in the abiding presence and power of God. Now it was their turn to be the kingdom of God moving on the earth, healing, delivering, and revealing to the world who God really is and who we are designed to be.

Church, regardless of your denomination, it is time to leave the Baptist. It is time to come into the baptism of the Holy Spirit and see the kingdom move on this earth again. Only then can righteousness prevail.

God bless you, and God bless our community.

I Am Glad Jesus Left

"Nevertheless, I tell you the truth: it is to your advantage that I go away, for if I do not go away, the Helper will not come to you. But if I go, I will send Him to you."

—John 16:7

Jesus Christ walked this earth for thirty-three years. Only three years of that time were dedicated to His Spirit-led, Spirit-empowered ministry of proclaiming the kingdom of God and demonstrating its might (Matthew 4:1; Acts 10:38).

It doesn't seem like much time for our Savior to be among us. But I am really glad He left.

Please don't get me wrong. Like you, I have imagined how wonderful it would be to walk with Jesus those three years, hear Him preach, and observe firsthand those incredible miracles. Equally wonderful would be those times when He took us to some quiet place, spoke face-to-face, and led us in prayer.

I have empathy for the initial dismay of the first disciples when Jesus announced His departure. He said it was to their advantage He was leaving, but they wouldn't understand until fifty days later on Pentecost. That is when they learned that having Christ with you on the inside is even better than having Christ with you on the outside.

On that first Pentecost after the ascension of Jesus, God poured His Spirit into 120 disciples of Jesus, and they became more than just disciples. They became the first fruits of the "Ecclesia" ("Assembly," "Church") of Christ the King (Acts 1:5 and 2; Ephesians 1:16–23).

That day they became Spirit-led, Spirit-empowered men and women, just like their Master, who would do the works He did (Acts 1:8; Romans

8:14; John 14:12). They became sons and daughters of God, born of His Spirit, who would follow in the footsteps of their firstborn brother Jesus (John 3:3–8; Romans 8:29). And they became the beginning of the "hope of glory" for all creation, because Christ now lived in them (Colossians 1:27)!

I am personally glad Jesus left, because in 1991, when I cried out in desperation for God's help, He poured the Holy Spirit into me. The finger of God went through me, imparting a revelation that God is everything He says He is, Jesus did exactly what He says He did, and the Bible is precisely what it describes itself to be (John 14:26, 15:26). My life was transformed.

I am glad Jesus left, because a year later, while on a mission trip, the Holy Spirit filled me with a revelation of how much God loves all of us despite our brokenness (Ephesians 3:17–19). His love will never give up.

I am glad because when I worship the Lord in song or prayer, the Holy Spirit pours love into my heart that I can passionately and reverently pour out to my Lord (Romans 5:5; 1 John 4:19). I am learning what it means to worship in spirit and truth (John 4:23–24).

I am glad because if Jesus still walked the earth, He might be in Kingsport with me today and in Russia with someone else tomorrow. But because His Spirit is in me, I can always be connected to Jesus, like a branch on the Vine (Romans 8:9; John 15). I am still a work in progress, with many bad habits yet to shed, but I can have conversations with Jesus every day in my heart.

I am glad because the Holy Spirit is the Spirit of the Father. My heavenly Father abides in me as well as in His Son (Matthew 10:20; John 14:23). Twice I have heard God call me "son" and joyfully wept at the reality that I am His beloved child.

I am glad because through Holy Spirit, Jesus Himself is my teacher (Matthew 23:8–10; John 16:13–15). When I prayerfully read Scripture, He gives me deeper understanding and helps me connect the dots.

I am glad because the Holy Spirit has birthed a marital intimacy with my wife, Christie, that we could never have mustered on our own (Malachi 2:14–15). I am glad because we have been enabled to lay hands on people and see them healed of diseases and demonic oppression (Mark 16:15–20). And yes, we are blessed to pray and speak in the languages of the Spirit as well.

There will come a joyful day when I will see Jesus face-to-face. Then Christ will be both inside me and outside me (1 John 3:2). Until then, I am glad to have experienced, like many others, the baptism of the Holy Spirit that is the reality of Pentecost for all who seek it.

If you have not yet received this incredible blessing of Spirit baptism, and many haven't, ask the Lord for it now (Acts 8:14–17, 19:1–7). Jesus wants us all to be glad He left.

God bless you, and God bless our community.

The Lord Will Walk with You and Talk with You

When Enoch had lived 65 years, he fathered Methuselah. Enoch walked with God after he fathered Methuselah 300 years and had other sons and daughters. Thus all the days of Enoch were 365 years. Enoch walked with God, and he was not, for God took him.

—Genesis 5:21–24

We are told at Colossians 3:16 that the Word of God can dwell in us richly as we sing psalms, hymns, and spiritual songs. Unfortunately, we often sing the truth better than we live it.

Consider these lines from "He Lives," the great Easter hymn: "Christ Jesus lives today! He walks with me and talks with me along life's narrow way."

Then consider this verse from "In the Garden": "And He walks with me, and He talks with me, and He tells me I am His own."

Now ask yourself these questions: *How frequently during this last week was I consciously aware of my Lord's presence with me? How many times did I hear Him speak to me? How often was my heart touched with the wondrous truth that I am His beloved?*

More and more Christians are awakening to the fact that Christianity is a relationship, not a religion. But for almost all of us, the day-to-day experience of that relationship remains elusive.

We have our moments of prayer when we talk to God. We have those times when good things happen and we thank Him for His blessings. Some experience His presence in congregational praise and worship, and most are stirred at least occasionally by a sunrise or a baby's smile.

At the other end of life's spectrum, walking through the dark valleys, we reach out to God because we need strength, comfort, or hope. Those of us who never turned to God before will do so when we have nowhere else to turn. And He is always faithful about responding, even if it is not in the way we might choose.

But what I am talking about, and what those hymns are talking about, is much more than just an awareness of God at the high and low points of life. Walking with God is about a life in constant companionship and partnership with God. It is a life continually aware of God's incredible love for you, His profound purpose for you, and His powerful presence with you.

Just imagine what such a life would be like! Attitudes, thought patterns, and behaviors would improve dramatically. God's wisdom and assurance would always be right there for you. Depression, loneliness, and fear would have no place to latch on. And your ongoing awareness of His love would make it much easier for you to love God back, and to love everyone He loves.

Well, friends, the "good news" is that this life of loving companionship and partnership with God is exactly what He wants for each of us. Most churches are not teaching it, but Jesus Christ prayed we would walk in "oneness" with Him just like He walked the earth in oneness with the Father (John 17). He promised to be with us always (Matthew 28:20). Through the Holy Spirit, He is faithful to that promise (John 16:12–15). He lives in us and we live in Him (John 15).

Even the Old Testament reveals God's desire for us to walk with Him (Micah 6:8). And a guy named Enoch, six generations out from Adam, did just that. Enoch's trusting companionship with God pleased God so much, He didn't let death touch Enoch (Hebrews 11:5).

If Enoch can walk with God, how much more empowered are we to walk with God, having received Christ as Lord and God's Holy Spirit within us?

Frankly, there is only one obstacle that stands between me and such a wondrous God-filled life: me. If I don't believe I can receive it, I won't. If I believe but don't seek it with my whole heart, I won't find it (Jeremiah 29:13).

King David, a man after God's own heart, provides the key focus: "I have set the Lord always before me; because He is at my right hand, I shall not be shaken" (Psalm 16:8). God is constantly aware of us. David resolved to be constantly aware of Him.

Let's resolve together to discipline our daily lives against the distractions the world throws at us. Like Brother Lawrence's great devotional book written centuries ago, we should be "practicing the presence of God" all the time.

As you and I learn to set the Lord constantly before us, He will walk with us and talk with us. We will bask in His love. Spiritually awakened, we will be empowered to awaken others.

More than our lives will change. The church will change, and this world will change.

God bless you, and God bless our community.

Sanctification Is an Inside Job

Now may the God of peace himself sanctify you completely, and may your whole spirit and soul and body be kept blameless at the coming of our Lord Jesus Christ. He who calls you is faithful; He will surely do it.

—1 Thessalonians 5:23–24

Sanctification is a fancy word—a theological word— so it is not often used when we discuss how to integrate our faith into our daily lives. This is a tragic mistake, because sanctification is exactly what God wants for His children (Leviticus 20:8; 1 Thessalonians 4:1–8).

The Hebrew word for *sanctify* is *qadash*. The Greek word is *hagiazo*. Both simply mean "to make holy." We are to be holy just as our heavenly Father is holy, and the church is to be a holy nation (1 Peter 1:14–16, 2:9).

For a detailed discussion of holiness, see my column titled "Holiness Is What We Need" published March 4, 2011, in this newspaper [the *Kingsport Times-News*] and on our website. *Holiness* means to be separated from this world and its evil, and joined to God and His goodness. It is the concept of being set apart, devoted, and consecrated, coupled with the concepts of godly character, moral purity, and closeness to the Lord.

Sanctification starts when we are born again (John 3:3–7). However, this is only the beginning of the sanctification process. God is not satisfied to simply cover our sins in the sacrifice of Jesus. He wants to transform us from glory to glory until we actually become like Jesus (2 Corinthians 3:18).

Sanctification is the goal of discipleship. It is becoming right spirits, restored souls, and pure hearts. It is reestablishing the image and likeness of God in us so we can become the light of the world and salt of the earth we are called to be. And most of us are failing to progress in it because we do not adequately understand how it works.

Sanctification is not human effort to be good or do good. Sanctification is an inside job.

Consider this diagram of a human life. At the center of our being is our heart. This is not where our emotions are. Instead, it is the site of our will and our desires: what we want to happen and what we choose to do. Our heart is the location of our character.

Inside our heart is our human spirit, which was designed to be connected with God's Spirit. Until we are born again, our human spirit is dormant and ineffective.

Surrounding our heart is our soul, which is made up of several components: (1) our mind, including our intellect, memories, and imagination; (2) our emotions, which are triggered by the signals that come from our mind; and (3) our personality, which is the interaction between our mind and our emotions.

Surrounding our soul is our body, with its needs and appetites. And outside our body is the world—everything and everyone else.

When we live independent of God, we necessarily live from the outside in. All of our information about what is true, good, and important comes from the world through our body's senses and into our mind. Since the world is still dominated by the father of lies, we receive a great deal of deception. This corrupts our mind and emotions and thereby, what we desire and choose in our hearts.

When we are born again, however, we receive the Holy Spirit. This does far more than just seal our salvation. Our human spirit actually becomes one with the Holy Spirit (1 Corinthians 6:17). Our spirit is now awakened and right!

The Holy Spirit connects us to Jesus like a branch to a vine, Christ abiding in us as we abide in Him (John 15:1–5). Now, for the first time, we have the option to live from the inside out!

We can invite the spirit of truth within us to renew our minds as we study God's Word, displacing the world's lies with the truth that sets us free. We can invite the spirit of grace to heal our memories and emotions as we learn to forgive ourselves and others. We can invite the spirit of love to cast out all our fears as we pray and trust in God's answers.

We can invite the spirit of righteousness to transform the desires of our heart and the spirit of wisdom to lead us in our choices. As we trust and obey, we are partnering with the Spirit of the Lord to "work out our salvation"—this incredible sanctification process—with reverence and eager expectation (Philippians 2:12–13). The result is a transformed character of love, joy, peace, patience, kindness, goodness, faithfulness, gentleness, and self-control (Galatians 5:22–23).

My friends, the Holy Spirit wants to do an inside job on all of us. And that is very good news!

God bless you, and God bless our community.

God Sent His Spirit to Lead
Us, Not Just Help Us

"When He [the Holy Spirit] comes, He will convict the world of guilt in regard to sin and righteousness and judgment: in regard to sin, because men do not believe in Me; in regard to righteousness, because I am going to the Father, where you can see Me no longer; and in regard to judgment, because the prince of this world now stands condemned."

—John 16:8–11 NIV

Those who are led by the Spirit of God are sons [and daughters] of God.

—Romans 8:14 NIV

I was asked a great question a few weeks ago. What issue(s) do I see as most vital for the church in the United States today?

Questions can be powerful. The right question at the right time can determine the outcome of a legal trial, medical treatment, or presidential election. The right question, coupled with the right answer, can send an individual or group in the direction they must to go to fulfill their true purpose.

For me, the most vital issue for the church today is our understanding of the Holy Spirit's mission on earth. In each of the three major wings of the church—evangelical, mainline, and charismatic—we do not seem to adequately understand how the mission of the church is intertwined with the mission of the Holy Spirit.

John 16:8–11 tells us why the Holy Spirit has been poured into the church—to convict the world of sin, righteousness, and judgment. This is the Holy Spirit's ministry, not simply the ministry of Christians as witnessing ambassadors for Christ. And just as Jesus Christ accomplished what He was sent here to do, so the Holy Spirit will accomplish what the Spirit was sent here to do. God does not fail (Isaiah 46:8–10)!

The challenge for the Holy Spirit is that He must accomplish more of His purpose in the church before He can effectively accomplish it through the church. The church struggles with unbelief, quenching the Holy Spirit just like the skepticism in Nazareth quenched Jesus' ability to do miracles (1 Thessalonians 5:15; Matthew 13:58). And we grieve the Spirit with our lack of love for one another (Ephesians 4:30–32).

An even more pervasive problem may simply be our attitude. The words we have always focused on concerning the Holy Spirit are *power, comfort, strength, fruit, gifts, seal, helper, presence,* or *one who stands beside you.* These words give us the impression that God has sent the Holy Spirit to assist and encourage us in our mission to the world.

Sounds good, but what happens, often without our conscious thought? The Holy Spirit becomes Tonto to our Lone Ranger, Robin to our Batman—our companion when we want help.

We forget the most important truth about the Holy Spirit. The Holy Spirit is not just sent by God. The Holy Spirit is God (1 Corinthians 12:3; 1 Thessalonians 4:8)! He's not here to help us in "our" ministry. We are here to serve Him in His mission—to convince the world of the truth. It is plainly stated in Romans 8:14. The Holy Spirit leads. We must follow.

For those who may protest that Jesus is head of the church, not the Holy Spirit, remember, the Holy Spirit is called not just the "Spirit of God" but the "Spirit of Christ" (Romans 8:9). Also remember that when Jesus walked the earth, the Holy Spirit led Him (Matthew 4:1). God, the Holy Spirit, was with Jesus, intimately connecting Jesus with His Father so Jesus could do and say exactly what His Father wanted Him to do and say. (Acts 10:38; John 5:19–20, 12:49).

Likewise, the Holy Spirit is with us, intimately connecting us with Jesus, so we can do and say exactly what Jesus wants us to do and say (John 16:12–15). There is only one God: Father, Son, and Holy Spirit, so to be led by the Holy Spirit or by Christ is the same thing.

The glorious Father and glorious Son are in heaven. They didn't just send back a book. They didn't just send power. God, the glorious Holy Spirit, has poured His person into us! He will lead us in His mission every day if we will just trust and listen. Then the tide will truly turn on this earth.

The world will see judgment demonstrated as the condemned powers of darkness fail before the authority and power of the Spirit-led sons and daughters of God. The world will be persuaded about and convicted of sin by the Spirit-given testimony of the Bible and the church. The world will recognize righteousness in a loving, Spirit-filled and transformed family called "Christ-ians."

Let's do all we can to hasten that day (2 Peter 3:12). Think of life as a wonderful dance with the Lord, and let the Holy Spirit lead!

God bless you, and God bless our community.

Start Unwrapping Those
Unopened Gifts

"If you then, who are evil, know how to give good gifts to your children, how much more will your Father who is in heaven give good things to those who ask Him!"

—Matthew 7:11

We all know what it is like to receive gifts. In fact, there are many times in our lives, such as Christmas, birthdays, weddings, and anniversaries, when we expect to receive gifts, nicely wrapped in decorative paper and ribbon.

And we always open those gifts, don't we? In fact, the idea of leaving a gift unopened is so unusual, it grabs our attention. The church has, for this reason, often used the image of the unopened gift to help nonbelievers understand salvation by grace.

Jesus is the Son of God. By His death on the cross, He paid the price of sin for everyone in the world. A restored relationship of eternal life with God is thus offered to each of us as a gift. We open that gift by trusting Jesus as our Savior and Lord (John 3:16–21; Ephesians 2:4–9). Amen!

Every Christian has opened the gift of salvation in Jesus Christ. Why have so many of us failed to open and use the other priceless gifts our loving God provides?

There are the gifts of prayer and Scripture that we unwrap but then often leave in the box. For those who believe the Bible is the divinely inspired written Word of our Creator, what can be the excuse for not studying it every day? Why do the majority of us fail to pursue the intimate time with God that can come only in regular extended prayer?

There are also two priceless gifts that, for many Christians, never even get unwrapped.

The first of these unwrapped gifts is the glorious role of servant. The essence of the Christian life is the opportunity to serve our Lord and others (Mark 9:35–37). We are all called to ministry as His royal priesthood (1 Peter 2:9; Ephesians 4:12). We witness to the world around us by becoming the light of the world—doing the good works we were created in Christ to do while giving God the glory for it (Matthew 5:14–16; Ephesians 2:10). We wash feet (John 13:1–17)!

But for too many Christians in our culture, the focus is self-centered. They "go to church," and sometimes they don't even do that. They may be believers, but they are not disciples (Mark 8:34–38). The body of Christ is weakened by the failure of these members to do their part (Romans 12:4–6). Even more tragically, because they do not walk as Jesus walked, they never really get to know Him (1 John 2:3–6).

The second and more controversial group of unwrapped gifts is described by the biblical Greek word *charismata*. It is a word our Bibles translate in English to mean "spiritual gifts." However, *charis* means "grace," and a more literal translation of *charismata* would be "the results of grace." The topic is addressed in Romans 12, Ephesians 4, and, most comprehensively, 1 Corinthians 12–14.

Grace and truth came to the world through Jesus Christ (John 1:17). So do the results of grace and truth. When the resurrected Christ gave His followers the task of witnessing His truth to the world, He commanded them to wait until they received power He would send from heaven (Luke 24:48; Acts 1:8). Ten days later, the Holy Spirit arrived and these "results of grace" we call the spiritual gifts manifested.

The book of Acts is saturated with this evidence of God's presence and power in His people. The church grew like wildfire! All Christians receive these spiritual gifts (1 Corinthians 12:7). Why do so many Christians in our culture today fail to embrace them or even believe in them?

I have researched the various justifications many mainline and evangelical theologians use to deny or distrust the gifts of the Spirit. Put plainly, you cannot believe in the Bible and at the same time reject the existence or importance of these "charismata." God's Word says He does not want us to be ignorant about them (1 Corinthians 12:1). He tells us to eagerly desire them (1 Corinthians 14:1).

Scripture never suggests there will come a time when the spiritual gifts lose their importance, at least not until the second coming of Christ. And if your concern is about how often spiritual gifts have been abused in the past, please recognize that preaching and pastoring have also been abused in the church. You don't throw out the baby with the bathwater! You must not bury these spiritual talents (Matthew 25:14–30).

Outside the United States and Europe, the church is experiencing explosive growth amidst manifestations of God's presence and power through spiritual gifts. Why not here? I know it can happen, but only if we begin to unwrap and make use of all the divine gifts God has provided to us. Prayerfully read God's Word on both the "charismata" and the role of servant. Then trust and obey.

God bless you, and God bless our community.

Partner in Life with the Holy Spirit

His divine power has granted to us all things that pertain to life and godliness, through the knowledge of Him who called us to his own glory and excellence, by which He has granted to us his precious and very great promises, so that through them you may become partakers of the divine nature.

—2 Peter 1:3–4

Early in his walk with Jesus, before he was filled with the Holy Spirit, Peter spoke with concern about all he had given up to follow Jesus (Mark 10:28). Near the end of his earthly walk, in his final letter to the church, a Spirit-filled Peter spoke instead about all he had received because he knew Jesus—everything needed for a life of godliness.

This life of godliness is described in both of Peter's letters. It is the life of people chosen by God for His own possession: people set apart by God to proclaim and demonstrate the excellence of our glorious Savior King (1 Peter 2:9). It is not a life free of persecution, but it is a life of love, faith, joy, and fruitfulness with a rich and everlasting reward (1 Peter 1:8; 2 Peter 1:8–11).

When Peter speaks of God's precious and great promises that bring about this life, I think of how all the promises of God are "Yes" in Jesus Christ (2 Corinthians 1:20). And I know Peter was thinking in particular of the great "promise of the Father": the Holy Spirit who would come upon them, saturate ("baptize") them, and provide them the power to witness for Jesus and His kingdom throughout the earth (Acts 1:2–8).

This brings us to Peter's most extraordinary statement of all—our ability to become "partakers of the divine nature."

By *nature* (Greek word: *phusis*), Peter is referring to the essential character and qualities of someone or something. Mankind is designed in the image and likeness of God, but our separation from God by sin brought us under the influence of the prince of rebels, Satan, and caused us to be "by nature" children of wrath rather than children of God (Ephesians 2:1–3). Now we are invited through Christ to reconciliation with God and the restoration of our original design.

Paul calls this "alive together with Christ" (Ephesians 2:5). Peter calls this "partakers of the divine nature." And the key to grasping what both men are describing comes in an understanding of the Greek word *koinonos*, traditionally translated since the time of King James as *partaker*.

Many of you are familiar with the Greek term *koinonia*, used in Scripture to describe the close mutual relationship or "fellowship" among the early Christians (Acts 2:42). The term has also been translated as *partnership* in the gospel (Philippians 1:5).

Koinonos is the word used to describe someone who is in "koinonia": a person who lives in fellowship and partners in purpose with another. The term was used to describe Peter's partnership with James and John in the fishing business (Luke 5:10). Peter uses it in his letter to describe a partnership much more profound.

Partaker is an old English word for one who participates or shares in something. Although not inaccurate, it doesn't catch the fullness of what Peter is describing—our ability to become godly as we live in loving fellowship with God and partner in His kingdom purposes for the earth.

Think of all the Scriptures that affirm this awesome truth. Through the Holy Spirit, our fellowship is with the Father and the Son, and made complete when it is also with each other (1 John 1:3; John 14–16; 1 Corinthians 1:9; 2 Corinthians 13:14).

Jesus prayed we would be one with Him (John 17:20–23). As we join with Christ, the Holy Spirit, who is also called the Spirit of Christ, becomes one with our spirit (Romans 8:9; 1 Corinthians 6:17).

Christ is the head, and we are His body, called through the Holy Spirit to "grow up into Him in every way" (Ephesians 4:15–16; John 16:13–15). Apart from Him, we can do nothing, but in a life of partnership with our Lord, we bear much fruit (John 15:5).

God's purpose is to reconcile all things to Christ. This ministry of reconciliation, which involves convicting the world of sin, righteousness, and judgment, has been given to both the Holy Spirit and to us (John 16:7–11; 2 Corinthians 5:18–20). If we partner with Him, the Holy Spirit will speak through us, pray through us, and move in love and power through us in ways beyond our ability to ask or imagine (Ephesians 3:20–21).

Christ called the Holy Spirit the *Paraclete*, Greek for "one who comes alongside" (John 14:16). Sounds like partnership to me! Scripture also calls the Holy Spirit the spirit of truth, grace, life, glory, wisdom and understanding, strategy and might, and knowledge (intimacy) and fear (reverence) of the Lord (John 16:13; Hebrews 10:29; Romans 8:2; 1 Peter 4:14; Isaiah 11:2). What a partner in life to have!

Scripture cautions us to "test the spirit" with the Word of God because both false spirits and our own flesh will seek to mislead us (1 John 4:1; Galatians 5:16–24). When we do that, and learn to partner or "walk by the Spirit," we begin to experience lives filled with righteousness, peace, and joy (Galatians 5:25; Romans 14:17). Marriages, families, friendships, workplaces, and communities are transformed.

Even more important, when we partner in life with the Holy Spirit, we start becoming the answer to the prayer of Jesus that we be one with Him and each other. Then this broken world will finally begin to realize that God sent Jesus and that God loves them (John 17:22–23).

God bless you, and God bless our community.

Reflections on Prayer

My Father, please make me a moon in the darkness!

Please make me a star in Your sky!

Please make me the salt of Your world that preserves!

Please make me a love that won't die!

Please make me Your temple!

Please make me Your priest!

Please make me a man who will pray

every night, every day, for the rest of my life,

for those who don't choose to obey.

Rejoice always, pray without ceasing, give thanks in all circumstances; for this is the will of God in Christ Jesus for you. (1 Thessalonians 5:16–18)

Enter into the Presence of the Lord

I have set the Lord always before me; because He is at my right hand, I shall not be shaken. Therefore my heart is glad, and my whole being rejoices; my flesh also dwells secure. For you will not abandon my soul to Sheol, or let your holy one see corruption. You make known to me the path of life; in your presence there is fullness of joy; at your right hand are pleasures forevermore.

—Psalm 16:8–11; see also Acts 2:25–28

David was a shepherd, warrior, psalmist, and king. Far more important, David was described by God Himself as a man after God's heart (Acts 13:22). Why did the Lord say that about him?

I believe David was a man after God's heart because what David was "after," more than anything else in his life, was to be in God's presence. David adored God. God delighted in manifesting His presence to David because David delighted in Him (Psalm 37:4).

Many of us have sung the praise chorus David wrote about the presence of the Lord: "One day in your courts is better than a thousand elsewhere" (Psalm 84:10). But are we at all like David? Do we practice what we sing?

Is the manifest presence of God what we are after when we gather for a worship service, congregational prayer time, or personal time of devotion? Do we set the Lord's presence before us each morning, looking to be aware throughout the day that He is at our right hand?

The tragic truth is that many church-attending Christians have never experienced the presence of the Lord. And for many others, the experience of His presence has never gone beyond an initial conversion experience or an awareness of God's presence during musical praise and worship. Yes,

285

God is enthroned on the praises of His people (Psalm 22:3). But to truly enter His presence goes beyond entering His gates with thanksgiving and His courts with praise (Psalm 100:4).

I have learned that we enter God's presence most completely in the stillness, not the noise. The Lord responds to the reverent adoration of a worshipping heart, to humble focus on Him rather than self, and to a deep or desperate longing for His embrace.

When we enter God's presence in such stillness, we can receive His peace and enter His rest. We can experience a sense of timelessness—a glimpse of eternity. We can hear His "small, still voice" (1 Kings 19:12). We may even experience the heaviness of His glory or a powerful impartation from what I can only describe as the finger of God.

And always in His presence, we will know in our innermost being the wondrous reality of God's perfect love for you and me.

Perhaps the apostle John captured it best: "My fellowship is with the Father and with His Son Jesus Christ" (1 John 1:3). To enter the presence of the Lord is to fellowship with the eternal Creator as His child and to fellowship with our Savior Jesus, the King of Kings, as His devout disciple. When you can have such divine fellowship, my friends, where else would you ever want to be?!

Christie and I have been taught, by the grace of God, how to enter the presence of the Lord both at home and with others. Please let me share just two of the things we have learned.

First, God does not like to be put "on the clock." Entering His presence is not the "fast food" process we expect in the rest of our busy lives. One-hour worship services, two-minute prayers, and fifteen-minute daily devotionals will not "get 'er done."

Second, thanksgiving and praise are, as suggested by Psalm 100, the best way to start and the best way to prepare our hearts. Hold back on those petitions and intercessions until after you have spent meaningful time in the Lord's presence. Desire God more than the things God can do for you. Then, when you do make your requests, you will be able to pray more in harmony with God's will.

Those of us who gather at Friends of the King Ministries experience God's presence often. Whether you join us, join others, or focus on your time with God at home, the key is to begin entering the presence of the

Lord. The Father and the Son are searching for people who will live in their presence (Revelation 3:20–22). As John said, "Make our joy complete" (1 John 1:4).

God bless you, and God bless our community

The People of God Need to Encounter God

And Jesus cried out again with a loud voice, and yielded up His spirit. And behold, the veil of the temple was torn in two from top to bottom.

—Matthew 27:50–51

My preferred Merriam-Webster.com definitions for the word *encounter* are "to come upon face-to-face"; and "to come upon or experience, especially unexpectedly."

When you have an encounter with a person, that person has your focused attention. Whether the encounter is planned or by chance, it is intensely personal and you are instantly engaged. Encounters have an effect on you. They are not easily forgotten.

It is in this context that I say God's people today need to encounter God.

God has always pursued direct personal relationship, not religion. He walked and talked in the garden with Adam and Eve. He walked with Enoch in a relationship so wonderful that Enoch went to heaven without dying (Genesis 5:24). He visited Abraham at his home, wrestled with Jacob, and spent forty days on a mountain with Moses (twice!). God's ongoing intimate relationship with David inspired the greatest love songs (psalms) ever written.

Yet the best was yet to come. In the Old Testament, virtually every encounter with God was a "one-man show." But in the New Testament, there would be only one "one-man show"—Jesus—and He would open a way for all of us to encounter God—the greatest show on earth!

Remember, God did appear and speak to all His people on one occasion in the Old Testament at Mount Sinai, but they were not ready for it (Exodus 19:17–20:21). Therefore, when the tabernacle and later the temple were built, a special place to house the ark of the covenant was veiled and set apart called the Holy of Holies, or Most Holy Place.

The Holy of Holies was where God declared He would encounter His people, but because of the sins of the people, it would again be a "one-man show." The high priest alone could enter, and only once a year to atone for the people's sins that year (Leviticus 16).

But then came Jesus and everything changed. He died in atonement for all sins for all people for all time (1 John 2:2)! At the moment of His death, the veil that barred the rest of us from personally encountering God in the Holy of Holies was permanently torn down!

The writer of Hebrews says it well: "Since we have confidence to enter the Most Holy Place by the blood of Jesus ... let us draw near to God with a sincere heart in full assurance of faith" (Hebrews 10:19–22).

In other words, the door is wide open and the divine invitation has been issued. Let's go in!

Why are encounters with God so important? Let's start by recognizing that an encounter with the eternal Creator and Sustainer of the universe is the most incredible privilege imaginable. Think how excited we get at the chance to meet a sports hero, movie star, or world leader, and then multiply that by a trillion.

I've had several direct encounters with God since 1991. Not all of them were initially pleasant, particularly those dealing with conviction of sin. But every encounter was life empowering and life transforming. And every encounter deepened my desire for the next one. It is about knowing God, not just knowing about God (John 17:3).

Rest assured that I am nothing special, friends—just a Christian who knows he is a Spirit-filled child of His heavenly Father. Our Father has no desire to be an absentee dad or even an every-other-weekend dad. He wants to spend lots of time with His children. That is why it wrenches my heart to see so many Christians in so many congregations who do not have or even seek encounters with Him.

Gathering together for worship should be about much more than good fellowship, good music, and a good sermon. It should be a family encounter with God.

Personal devotional time should be about much more than an inspiring devotional book, a prayer list, and a welcomed few minutes of peace and quiet. It should be an encounter with God.

This Sunday is Pentecost Sunday—the anniversary of a day when 120 people had a breathtaking encounter with their God. It was their first such encounter, not their last. And it didn't just begin a tremendous change in them. It began a tremendous change in their city, their nation, and the world.

It is long past time we joined them. Seek to encounter the God who loves you more than you can imagine. He is waiting. Draw near to God and He will, I repeat, will draw near to you (James 4:8).

God bless you, and God bless our community.

Go to Your Tent of Meeting

Now Moses used to take the tent and pitch it outside the camp, far off from the camp, and he called it the tent of meeting. And everyone who sought the Lord would go out to the tent of meeting, which was outside the camp. Whenever Moses went out to the tent, all the people would rise up, and each would stand at his tent door, and watch Moses until he had gone into the tent. When Moses entered the tent, the pillar of cloud would descend and stand at the entrance of the tent, and the Lord would speak with Moses. And when all the people saw the pillar of cloud standing at the entrance of the tent, all the people would rise up and worship, each at his tent door. Thus the Lord used to speak to Moses face to face, as a man speaks to his friend.

—Exodus 33:7–11

It has been my great privilege over the last several months to prepare and teach a three-day curriculum on prayer titled "Lord, Teach Us to Pray."

Although much of the prayer conference relates to intercessory prayer, my favorite part is teaching about the effect of prayer on our intimate relationship with God. And my favorite part of teaching about intimacy in prayer concerns the Tent of Meeting.

What is prayer? It is more than just talking to God, or even hearing from God. It is being with God, and the opportunity to walk with God through life like Enoch (Genesis 5:18–24; Micah 6:8).

In a nutshell, prayer is paying attention to the God who is always paying attention to you. As you know, God never takes His eyes off us (Psalm 139:1–16; Matthew 10:29). God does not take vacations. He doesn't even blink. So every time we turn our attention to God, we are connected and together. We are in the fellowship of prayer even if we don't say, hear, or do anything.

Paul understood this when he boldly instructed us to "pray without ceasing" (1 Thessalonians 5:17). He knew the importance of vigilant intercession (Colossians 4:2). Yet like the apostle John, Paul knew his fellowship with the Lord was even more important than serving Him (1 John 1:3–4). Continuous prayer is continuous fellowship. As David sang, "I have set the Lord always before me; because He is at my right hand, I shall not be shaken" (Psalm 16:8).

I earnestly desire, like many of you, to walk in continuous fellowship with God, but I am a "work in progress," and the many distractions of this world are incessant. Our loving Lord will never disconnect from us (Hebrews 13:5). But whenever I let these distractions of the world take my attention off God, I disconnect myself. The longer I am disconnected, the more vulnerable I am to the schemes of the enemy (1 Peter 5:8–9). That is why the Tent of Meeting is so important.

Moses had many responsibilities in the camp of the Hebrew people. He needed to spend much time there, and I am sure he threw up many "prayer flares" to God as he went from problem to problem to problem.

Moses knew, however, that short prayer times in the midst of these camp distractions were not enough. So he pitched a tent far away from those distractions—the noise, the sin, even the simple cares of this world (Matthew 13:22). Moses went there frequently to seek the Lord, and look how the Lord responded! The manifest presence of God would come and meet with Moses "face to face." Moses loved God and shared His desire to see the people saved, so God and Moses met as friends (John 15:14–15).

The Tent of Meeting was not just for Moses, but for "everyone who sought the Lord." I have learned to go there daily. My very best times on this earth are there. I hear from God. I experience His indescribable presence and love. And my times there make it much easier for me to keep my attention on God when I walk back out into the world.

God wants daily Tent of Meeting times with all of us. All you have to do is give God some substantial, distraction-free time. Leave the camp of noise and daily cares, including your cell phones and computers. Pitch a spiritual tent. And eagerly await the One who loves you beyond measure.

Like with me, it may take a time or two to learn how. But the Lord is faithful. He will come. And it will change your life.

God bless you, and God bless our community.

"Thank You" Is More
Than Good Manners

Enter His gates with thanksgiving and His courts with praise; give thanks to Him and praise His name. For the Lord is good and His love endures forever; His faithfulness continues through all generations.

—Psalm 100:4–5 NIV

Thanksgiving may be my favorite holiday. I recognize it is not an official Christian holiday like Christmas and Easter, but we probably behave more like Christians on Thanksgiving than on any other day of the year.

It is easy to get sidetracked on those other holidays. Christmas, the day chosen to celebrate the birth of Jesus, finds most of us preoccupied with shopping for gifts, decorating houses, and a guy who comes down chimneys most homes today don't even have.

Then on Easter weekend, when we are invited to focus on the crucifixion and resurrection of Christ, far too many of us get distracted with chocolate bunnies, hiding eggs, and finding new outfits to wear.

Praise God for Thanksgiving, a day when we manage to stay on track with the reason for the season. We gather as family and friends and give thanks for family and friends. We take time out of our busy lives to gratefully remember our other blessings—all those things we take for granted most of the year.

We "feel good and eat good" on Thanksgiving. A lot of us even take naps we don't normally take. And it isn't because turkey contains tryptophan, the so-called "drowsy" drug. In actuality, turkey contains no greater quantity of tryptophan than other meats we consume.

The real reason so many of us feel good and even nap on Thanksgiving is the God-given power of gratitude. "Thank you" is more than good manners.

You remember how we learned as children to say, "Thank you." Our mothers, grandmothers, aunts, and older sisters constantly reminded us. "What do you say, Doug?" "Thank you." "You're welcome."

"Thank you" was something I first learned to say simply because I was supposed to say it. I appreciate that lesson in manners and wish more children today were taught it. But I appreciate even more the lessons I have since learned about thanksgiving from Bible passages such as Psalm 100, Psalm 136, and Philippians 4:4–7. These Scriptures help us see the four-step pattern of gratitude's power:

First step: We remember good things that have happened in our lives—blessings received and challenges met. This frees us from being completely stuck in our present problems and worries so we can begin to come before Him.

Second step: We thank God for those good things that have happened. In remembering that all good things come from God, we give Him the credit He deserves and clothe ourselves in an attitude of humility and dependence upon Him. Properly dressed, we enter His gates.

Third step: We remember God provided those good things because God is always good and He loves us with a perfect, never-ending love. This turns our focus from the good things of the past to the good God of our present and future—a God worthy of our continued praise and trust. We enter His courts.

Fourth step: Strengthened in our hope, we can begin to taste a divine peace and joy that comes in spite of our difficult circumstances. We can boldly and reverently come before God's throne, presenting our present burdens to Him with thanksgiving because we know we are still the sheep of His pasture. The Good Shepherd of yesterday, when we received past blessings and met past challenges, is the same Good Shepherd today, tomorrow, and forever.

Thanksgiving triggers four simple steps that cover a vast amount of territory because they take us from darkness to light. They take us from focusing on our self and our problems to focusing on God. Powerful!

The apostle Paul, who knew a lot about both blessings and hardships, said this: "Be thankful … Whatever you do, whether in word or deed, do it all in the name of the Lord Jesus, giving thanks to God the Father through Him" (Colossians 3:15–17).

What Paul was saying, I believe, is that every day should be a thanksgiving day for all of us. Whimsically, that will be good for me, because it gives me 365 favorite holidays each year. On a deeper and more sacred note, this will be good for all of us and all of those we love because sincerely saying "thank you" to God is more than good manners. Much more!

God bless you, and God bless our community.

We Need Some Desperate People to Pray

I cry to you, O Lord; I say, "You are my refuge, my portion in the land of the living." Listen to my cry, for I am in desperate need; rescue me from those who persecute me, for they are too strong for me. Set me free from my prison, that I may praise your name. Then the righteous will gather about me because of your goodness to me.
—Psalm 142:5–7

"If my people who are called by my name humble themselves and pray and seek my face ..."
—2 Chronicles 7:14

Many of you are familiar with the worship song "Breathe," which became popular when released in 2009 by Michael W. Smith.

The lyrics express awesome truths about God's Word spoken to us and His Holy presence living in us. Then, in the refrain, we are invited to sing, "I'm desperate for You."

I have sung that refrain many times, and watched as it moved hundreds of Christians into a sincerely worshipful attitude toward the Lord. It is a great song, very reminiscent of a song—Psalm 142—written by David, a man after God's own heart.

Unfortunately, what we sing in church can be very different from how we live and pray. The vast majority of Christians gathering in our region do not appear desperate at all, particularly in their prayer lives. Yet families and individuals are falling apart all around us, and our nation and world are doing likewise. What is going on?

I came back to the Lord in 1991 because I became desperate. I finally recognized that I was on the verge of losing everything I cared about, and finally understood that I was personally powerless to prevent that loss. When I cried out to God, He rescued me just like He did David.

The Hebrew people were Egyptian slaves for hundreds of years, but didn't cry out in desperation to God until the Egyptians began killing their baby boys. Then God rescued them (Exodus 1–2).

This pattern is repeated over and over in the book of Judges. God's people drift from God-reliance into self-reliance. They become vulnerable to persecution from neighboring nations. In desperation, they cry out to God and He faithfully rescues them. After a generation, they get comfortable, drift back into self-reliance, and repeat the steps.

In New Testament times, the church's response to persecution was always desperate prayer, and God's answers were powerful (Acts 4:23–31, 12:5–17, 14:19–20, 16:22–40). I am personally convinced that the conversion of Saul of Tarsus, who became Paul the apostle, was the result of such prayer.

The New Testament also tells of a church that is not desperate. The Lord has difficult words for the church in Laodicea: "Because you are lukewarm, and neither hot nor cold, I will spit you out of my mouth" (Revelation 3:16).

Why do we look today so much more like Laodicea than we do the praying church in Acts? Why are we not gathering desperately and often in these difficult, dangerous times to pray for ourselves, our neighbors, our nation, and our world?

America's farms are devastated by drought, the latest in a long series of natural disasters. Our economy and Europe's teeter on the brink of recession, and we do not have the resources for more stimulus and bailout.

There are more Mideast hot spots than ever before, with an increasing risk of nuclear and biochemical weapons falling into terrorist hands. Madmen are entering our schools, workplaces, and sanctuaries to kill.

And when a godly business owner expresses his belief that marriage is between man and woman, he faces persecution not just from homosexual lobby groups but from mayors of major American cities.

For those who will not feel desperate until disaster touches their own lives, I can only say that is not God's way. For everyone else, I have some blunt questions.

Just how bad does it have to get? Do you really believe your vote in November will solve these problems? Do you believe your church programs will solve these problems? Are you finally ready to recognize that we are on the verge of losing many things we deeply care about, and that we are personally powerless to prevent those losses?

A few people are gathering at Friends of the King Ministries every Sunday morning, 9:00 to 11:00 a.m., to earnestly pray for our churches as they meet. We cry out for spiritual awakening and an encounter with the living God.

A few are also gathering Friday night at 7:00 p.m. to pray for our city, region, nation, and world. And as described in my April 20 column, prayer groups are also forming in Hawkins County and Johnson City.

Whether you join one of these groups or form your own, we need some more desperate people to pray.

God bless you, and God bless our community.

We Must Learn to Pray Together

"If my people who are called by my name humble themselves, and pray and seek my face and turn from their wicked ways, then I will hear from heaven and will forgive their sin and heal their land."
—2 Chronicles 7:14

Since I began writing this newspaper column in 2006, I have addressed the topic of prayer several times. A terse summary of those columns might go like this: Prayer is essential for each of us if we really want God in our life. Prayer between husband and wife is essential if we really want God in our marriage. Community prayer is essential if we really want God in our community.

After years of laboring to develop support for the National Day of Prayer and our annual Kingsport Mayor's Prayer Breakfast, I was delighted two years ago to see Mayor Phillips merge the two events into a single, well-attended prayer event. Please support the Kingsport Mayor's Prayer Breakfast on Thursday morning, May 3, our 2012 National Day of Prayer. Likewise, support the Funfest Prayer Breakfast this summer.

Having said that, we need to recognize that one or two days of community prayer per year has the same effect on a community that attending church once or twice per year (Easter and Christmas) has on Christians. If that is all you do, it is better than nothing, but not at all what it could be. You reap what you sow (Galatians 6:7–9).

This explains my excitement over the wonderful community prayer movement emerging in Hawkins County. One thousand Christians gathered at Volunteer High School on March 31. Even more gathered at Cherokee High School in February. Smaller weekly prayer gatherings are increasing in number all over the county, very reminiscent of the grass-roots prayer movements that triggered the First and Second Great Awakenings—times of revival that rocked our nation in the eighteenth and nineteenth centuries. Go, Hawkins County! Go, God!

A few years ago, I was asked by the president of a ministerial alliance to present a plan for an ongoing multichurch prayer network. Here are the key elements of that plan:

1. Each congregation has a prayer team with a prayer coordinator chosen to be the team's servant leader. The team meets weekly for prayer. They stay in touch throughout the week by e-mail, Facebook, or other technology. They pray daily for their pastors and spiritual leadership, and for the ministries and other individual needs of that congregation. They also work with their pastors to get the entire congregation more engaged in prayer. Ultimately, every home could become a prayer center.

2. The prayer coordinators of the different congregations in the city meet monthly for prayer. They generally focus on community, national, and world concerns rather than individual prayer needs. They stay in touch throughout the month via technology, and are led by either a citywide prayer coordinator or a small leadership team. Each prayer coordinator reports to their prayer teams and their pastors after citywide meetings. This allows each congregational team to pray for communitywide issues as well as the needs of their congregation.

3. The prayer coordinator network can also organize periodic citywide prayer events. A web page could be maintained that allowed anyone to learn at any time about important prayer needs of the city.

I believe a prayer network could be initiated in our Kingsport region or any other region quickly and with minimal expense. But people have to be willing. The sad end to my presentation before the ministerial alliance is that all the pastors loved it and said they would support it. But when they left the meeting, they did nothing about it, even after they were prompted. They were sincere, but just too busy doing what they were already doing.

On the other hand, although I have not been directly involved in the Hawkins County prayer movement, I am confident these three things are going on.

First, some churches are looking beyond their four walls and coming together across denominational lines.

Second, this is happening because some pastors have "caught fire," broken free from their busyness, and are leading their people across those lines.

Third, a small group of humble men and women have made this kingdom prayer crusade their passion. These are the encouragers and facilitators who do the legwork, pray for the "pray-ors," and never give up.

Again, go, Hawkins County! Go, God! Increase the flame!

And for my city of Kingsport and other area communities, I pose this question: "Who will go for us?" (Isaiah 6:8). Who in our community is ready to take on this kingdom prayer crusade for God's glory?

God bless you, and God bless our community.

Turn On the Power of
Your Prayer Faucets

Are any among you suffering? They should keep on praying about it. And those who have reason to be thankful should continually sing praises to the Lord. Are any among you sick? They should call for the elders of the church and have them pray over them, anointing them with oil in the name of the Lord. And their prayer offered in faith will heal the sick, and the Lord will make them well. And anyone who has committed sins will be forgiven. Confess your sins to each other and pray for each other so that you may be healed. The earnest prayer of a righteous person has great power and wonderful results. Elijah was as human as we are, and yet when he prayed earnestly that no rain would fall, none fell for the next three and a half years! Then he prayed for rain, and down it poured. The grass turned green, and the crops began to grow again.

—James 5:13–18 NLT

The power of intercessory prayer is cumulative. It increases as we add to it and build it up. The Lord commanded us to "keep on asking," "keep on seeking," and "keep on knocking" (Matthew 7:7, with literal translation). James, half-brother of Jesus, expands upon that command in this fifth chapter of his letter to the church.

For me, the teaching of James brings forth the image of a prayer faucet. Just as a faucet's purpose is to provide running water for washing and nourishing, a prayer faucet provides living water to clean up our lives and help us grow. Using verses 13–18 of James 5 and looking at how a faucet functions, here are seven points that can help us better understand prayer:

1. The size of your faucet is the size of your faith. Verse 15 identifies faith as crucial to effective prayer. A person of great faith prays like a hot tub faucet (Matthew 8:5–13) whereas a person of little faith prays with a trickle (Matthew 17:20). Be encouraged: the more you exercise your faith in prayer, the more your faith (and faucet size) grows.

2. You keep the prayer pipes clean, and the living water free flowing, by getting your heart right with God before you begin your petitions. Verse 16 reveals confession and repentance to be the "Drano" of intercession. (See 2 Chronicles 7:14.)

3. The faucet won't work if it isn't plugged into the water source. Verse 14 directs us to pray in Jesus' name—under His direction for His glory consistent with His character to further His kingdom. Jesus promised that if we pray this way, He will do anything we ask (John 14:13–14)!

4. Get the object you wish to water with prayer under the spigot. Verse 14 says to pray "over" and anoint the person. Jesus laid hands on people and healed them one at a time (Luke 4:40). Be specific and personal in your prayers, guided by His Holy Spirit.

5. Turn the faucet all the way on. Verses 16–17 tell us that fervent prayer is effective prayer. This is prayer motivated by fervent love of people and by the love of good and hatred of evil (1 Peter 1:22, 4:8; Amos 5:15). God cares how much we care.

6. Keep that faucet running until the object of your prayer is fully watered. Verse 13 instructs us to be persevering in prayer and continuous in praise. Jesus spoke of the persistent widow (Luke 18:1–8) and the neighbor who came knocking on the door at midnight (Luke 11:5–8). And Daniel prayed twenty-one days before the angel came to give him a prophetic vision of his people's future (Daniel 10). It is important to remember that the angel had been trying to come to Daniel since day one. What if Daniel had quit praying earlier? Pray until you get an answer or direction from God.

7. Finally, recognize that multiple faucets can water much more rapidly and fully than a single faucet. Verse 14 calls for the elders to come, not just a representative. When we gather, two or three or a hundred, of one mind and accord in His name, things really begin to happen (Matthew 18:18–20, Leviticus 26:8)! Of course, I'd rather have three pure-piped, plugged-in, turned-all-the-way-on hot tub faucets than 1,000 trickles. But just think of the effect if we finally have a thousand hot tub faucets coming together in our community. We'll have prayer that changes not just our city, but the world!

My friends, let's all turn on our prayer faucets together, and see what happens!

God bless you, and God bless our community.

We Need More Watchmen on the Walls

On your walls, O Jerusalem, I have set watchmen; all the day and all the night they shall never be silent. You who put the Lord in remembrance, take no rest, and give Him no rest until He establishes Jerusalem and makes it a praise in the earth.

—Isaiah 62:6–7

Our nation's problem with illegal immigration has skyrocketed over the last several decades, for two fundamental reasons.

First, there are many Mexicans who want to work and provide for their families. Second, the United States has a woefully insufficient number of guards and walls protecting our southern border.

Our nation's problems have also skyrocketed over the last several decades in other areas: sexual immorality, divorce, unwed mothers, abortion, substance abuse, depression and anxiety disorders, school and other senseless shootings, teenage and military suicide, corporate and political corruption, church corruption, biblical illiteracy, new age and occult practices, and an ever-growing gap between rich and poor.

I am not suggesting illegal immigrants are the cause of these other escalating problems. To the contrary, hardworking illegal immigrants benefit our nation far more than citizens who can work and refuse to do so.

I am, however, suggesting that the two fundamental reasons for these horrible problems are very similar to the reasons we have so many illegal immigrants.

First, there are spiritual forces of evil that constantly cross the border from the heavenly places into our land (Ephesians 6:10–13). Their work is to kill, steal, and destroy (John 10:10).

Second, we have a woefully insufficient number of "watchmen on the walls" of our homes, communities, and nation to pray and guard against this evil.

If you do not have a biblical worldview, this column will be hard for you to accept. But the Bible describes reality whether you accept it or not, and Scripture makes it clear that our real struggles in life are, both individually and as a society, with these spiritual forces of evil. One of the Lord's most basic instructions in prayer was our need to pray for protection against this evil (Matthew 6:13, part of the Lord's Prayer).

As Christians, we have been provided divine weapons that can take authority over evil and destroy its strongholds (2 Corinthians 10:3–5; Luke 10:19; Matthew 16:19). Yet we continue to focus virtually all our time and energy on worldly solutions that will never be sufficient. It is "not by might, nor by power, but by My Spirit, says the Lord of Hosts" (Zechariah 4:6).

The prophetic words about watchmen at Isaiah 62:6–7 provide a divine strategy for restoring a city, nation, or society to health. They apply to Jerusalem. They apply to the church, identified in Scripture as New Jerusalem (Revelation 21:2). And they apply in principle to any land where God's people live, including our wonderful Kingsport/Gate City/Tri-Cities region (2 Chronicles 7:14; Ezekiel 22:30).

The Hebrew word for *watchman* is *shamar*, and it refers to more than just an observer or sentry. *Shamar* means "watchman, guard, gatekeeper, preserver, and protector." They watch. They ward. They keep the gates closed against the enemy, and, even more exciting, they have the ability to open the gate for the Lord (John 10:1–3; Psalm 24:7–10)!

The fundamental assignment of the spiritual watchmen is persevering prayer: taking no rest as they give the Lord no rest. The enemy does not take holidays (1 Peter 5:8–9).

My friends, we need watchmen on all the walls. We need watchmen for our homes and families; our neighborhoods, schools, and other public areas; our civic and spiritual leaders; our cities; and our nation.

These watchmen (and watchwomen, of course) need to be biblically trained in prayer and spiritual authority. They must be networked together so there are no breaches in the prayer wall (Nehemiah 3, 4). And there must be many, because numbers matter (Leviticus 26:7–8). The body of Christ has been functioning with too few doing all the work for far too long (Ephesians 4:11–16).

At Friends of the King Ministries, we have developed a three-session prayer training curriculum, "Lord, Teach Us to Pray," including a thirty-three-page prayer manual. The three sessions are "Pray Without Ceasing," "A House of Prayer for All Peoples," and "Watchmen on the Walls." We hope to offer this training at churches and other organizations throughout the region, and the need for prayer is so great, I can't even feel guilty about using this book to encourage you to give us a call.

The key, however, is not where you get your prayer training, but that you get it, that you find the walls God wants you to pray from, and that you get others involved with you. We need more watchmen on the walls, and we need them now.

God bless you, and God bless our community.

Join Us in a Declaration
for Our Land

Please customize this declaration for the community where you live, and then declare it in faith!

As residents and citizens of the "land" that encompasses the greater Kingsport area in Tennessee and the greater Gate City area in Virginia, and as ambassador citizens of the eternal kingdom of God, we hereby declare the following in the name of Jesus Christ, our King:

1. We love, revere, trust, and obey the one true God: Creator and Sustainer of all things, who is described in the Old and New Testaments of the Holy Bible, His God-breathed Scriptures. We bless and glorify God, who is and always was perfect in His majesty, holiness, power, wisdom, goodness, faithfulness, and unconditional love.

2. We love, revere, trust, and follow Jesus Christ, the only begotten Son of God, whose shed blood and death on the cross fully paid the price for all sins of all mankind for all time. Jesus is the way, the truth, and the life. He is resurrected from the dead and now sits at the right hand of His heavenly Father as King of Kings and Lord of Lords, with all authority in heaven and earth.

3. We rejoice that by the grace of God through our faith in Jesus Christ, we are forgiven of all our sins, reconciled to God, and recipients of His Holy Spirit. As God has forgiven our sins, so we forgive our enemies and all those who have sinned against us. We are saints born of God—His beloved children now and forever.

Christ lives in us, the hope of glory, and we are clothed in His righteousness!

4. We humbly and gladly submit our lives and our land to you and you alone, Lord, laying aside our selfish desires and agendas so we may fully embrace your plans and purposes for us. Teach us. Heal us. Deliver us. Refine us. Mature us. Unite us. Fill us with your Holy Spirit and your love, wisdom, understanding, and power. Lead us in all things by your Spirit, and grant us, male and female, the revelation of the sons of God.

5. We lift up our ancestors and all those who have preceded us in our land. We repent for ourselves and on their behalf for sins of pride, greed, violence, bigotry, lust, untruth, witchcraft, idolatry, unbelief, and all other shortcomings. Forgive them, heavenly Father, as you forgive us, because all of our sins were borne on the cross by Jesus.

6. We thank God for the saints who have preceded us in our land and earnestly join our prayers, Holy Father, to their prayer that your kingdom come and your will be done in our land as it is in heaven.

7. Our Lord Jesus became a curse for us on the cross. We therefore declare every curse on our land and its people to be broken and without further power. We ask for the release of all heavenly blessings that have been obstructed by those curses.

8. We lift up the lost in our land to you, Lord. You love them and died for their sins. As we were once blind and now see, so now we proclaim an end to the blindness the enemy has imposed upon them. We pray that their eyes, ears, and hearts will open to receive the wondrous gospel. Anoint our witness to them, heavenly Father, and draw them to your Son.

9. We stand against the powers, principalities, and forces of darkness in our land, declaring them disarmed and condemned by the power of the cross and the resurrection victory of Jesus. We revoke any permission ever given for their presence in our land and declare them unwanted trespassers to be removed by our Lord from our midst.

10. Come, King of Glory, Lord of Hosts with your heavenly host! Let our land become a resting place for your abiding presence and

glory on this earth. Let your righteousness and truth completely displace the forces of darkness and deceit that oppress us.

11. We declare our land to be part of the kingdom of God. We declare Gate City to be a spiritual gate between heaven and earth. We declare Kingsport to be a port of the King from which our Lord will send forth His people and His heavenly host.

12. O Lord our God, let us be loving cities of sanctuary in the days ahead as you begin to shake the earth and the heavens. Let us be a people of prayer joined in unceasing Spirit-led intercession for our nation, for Israel, and for the world. Above all, let us be a land of constant worship where you are honored, blessed, and enthroned in the praises of your people.

Declared and proclaimed this 30th day of September 2011, and every day thereafter!

Special Reflections

My Father!

My Jesus!

My Spirit!

My Life!

Please make me,

please make me, I pray,

to become all the things

I can be that will please You

on this and each following day.

All these things Jesus said to the crowds in parables; indeed, he said nothing to them without a parable. This was to fulfill what was spoken by the prophet: "I will open my mouth in parables; I will utter what has been hidden since the foundation of the world." (Matthew 13:34–35)

Otherland

Once upon a time, long, long ago and far, far, away, there was a small kingdom called Otherland.

Otherland was very much like you would want small kingdoms long ago and far away to be. There were rolling hills sloping gently down to lush valleys. There were forests and meadows, springs and ponds, and a few small rivers and lakes. There were farms, villages, and a couple of towns. Everyone traveled by foot, cart, or pony.

And although the people in Otherland were not perfect, almost all of them were nice. They obeyed the law, which was important in Otherland, where the laws were very firm but applied equally and justly to all. The law came from the king of Otherland, who lived in a castle on the kingdom's highest hill with his two children, Princess Beth and Prince Billy.

Beth and Billy were happy children. Their mother had died from an illness when they were babies, but their father, the king, had done everything he could to provide them with a loving home and wonderful things to do.

They had the run of the castle, with its lawns and gardens. They could swim in the castle moat, which was fed by cool underground springs. They could ride their ponies. They could play with any of the puppies and kittens born on the castle grounds, or fly kites from the highest castle tower. They could play make-believe with costumes from the royal wardrobe, and hide-and-seek in the secret passages within the castle walls.

In fact, there was really only one thing they were told they could not do. The king would not let them leave the castle on their own. Of course, being children who liked to do what they wanted to do, this gradually became the thing Billy and Beth wanted to do most of all.

So one morning, long before the sun came up, Beth and Billy sneaked out of their bedrooms. They had borrowed clothes from the servants' children so people in the town they were planning to visit would not recognize them. They had their allowance money, which they had been saving up for weeks. And as they saddled their ponies and slipped out the garden door of the back castle wall, they were far too excited to think about how worried their father would be when he found out they were missing.

Beth and Billy rode their ponies almost all day before reaching the town at the far end of the kingdom they had picked for their adventure. No one would know them there. The first place they visited when they arrived was the candy store, followed by the bakery with its doughnuts and brownies, and the toy store where they let you play with the toys as long as you wanted just so you could see if you wanted to buy one. They saw a double feature at the puppet theater, and laughed until their sides ached at the clown show.

Finally, while listening to the soft splashes of the town fountain where they had both waded and made wishes, they fell asleep in the town square.

When Billy and Beth awoke, their stomachs were hurting from all the candy and cake they had eaten the night before. But that was not the worst part. During the night, their ponies had wandered off or been taken away, and they could not find them anywhere. The rest of their money was in the saddlebags on those ponies, and so they had nothing with which to buy breakfast.

They searched for hours without success, seeing lunchtime pass without lunch. They were tired and hungry, but they could not simply ask for help, because then people would question them about who they were and where they had come from. Their father would find out, and they would be in even more trouble.

Beth and Billy didn't know what to do. When suppertime approached, their hunger was very strong. Remember, as a prince and princess, they had never really been hungry before. They made a decision they would never have thought they could make. They decided to steal two apples from the town fruit stand.

The storekeeper had gone inside to begin closing up. Everyone was heading home to eat supper, so no one was on the street. Billy and Beth sneaked over to the edge of the fruit stand, much more scared than when they had sneaked out of their bedrooms to begin this adventure. They did not realize that when experienced thieves wanted to steal apples, they did so during the busiest time of the day when everyone was on the street and there was so much going on, they would not be noticed. Billy and Beth were noticed.

It was the town sheriff himself. He was the storekeeper's brother and coming over for supper that evening. He came around the corner just in time to see Beth and Billy each grab an apple and run, and they ran right into his arms. Immediately, because the law is very firm in Otherland, he took them right to the judge.

Billy and Beth were guilty, and they did not try to make things worse by lying about it. They did try to explain: why they took the apples, who they were, where they were from. But the fact that they were not lying does not mean they were believed. They were thieves. Who can trust a thief? They were certainly not dressed like a prince or princess, and the whole town knew the king would never let his children go so far from the castle without a proper escort.

Besides, even if they were telling the truth, it would not change the punishment for what they did. In Otherland, the law was the law, applied equally and justly to all, whether you were a beggar or the child of a king. The punishment under the law for theft, a most serious crime, was to cut off the right hand of the thief.

And, just so, the judge pronounced sentence. Billy and Beth were sent to jail for the night. In the morning, their right hands would be cut off.

Beth and Billy did not sleep at all that night. They huddled in each other's arms, imagining as they cried what it would feel like to have your hand cut off … What would it be like to live the rest of their lives without their right hands?

When the jail door opened the next morning, their hearts jumped in fear even higher than their bodies jumped from the cot. The sheriff's voice was gruff, as unforgiving as it had been the night before. "Go on. You're free."

Maybe it was his tone, or their tiredness, or their shock, but they didn't understand what the sheriff was saying. "Get on out of here!" he barked, and this time they heard!

Billy and Beth rushed out of the jail. Their ponies were outside, and they did not even stop to question where the townspeople had found them. They jumped on those ponies and rode back toward the castle as fast as the ponies could run. It was only as they came within sight of the castle that they began to think about what their father, the king, was going to say. They had disobeyed. They had stolen, broken the law that their father had always told them was so important to the peace of the kingdom.

Then they saw their father. He was standing on the road in front of the castle. They stopped, but only for a second, because their father waved at them and called out, "Come on!"

Beth and Billy galloped their ponies to within a few feet of their father, jumping off before the ponies came to a full stop. They ran into their father's arms, and he hugged them and kissed them while they hugged him back as tightly as they could. All three just stood there for the longest time hugging, kissing, laughing, crying, and loving each other.

Then their father asked them if they were hungry. Billy and Beth had not eaten for two days. They hadn't even gotten a bite of the stolen apples. "Oh yes," they said, and their father told them to go on to the castle kitchen where the royal cook was waiting to fix them whatever they wanted.

Beth and Billy were so hungry and so excited as they ran off to the kitchen that they never noticed that their father was missing his right hand.

But the look on the king's face was one of pure joy. You see, his children were home!

The Deacon, the Child,
and the Slave

Once upon a time, long, long ago and far, far away, there was a village halfway up a mountain that bordered a narrow desert valley. The lord of this village had one child, a beautiful daughter, who under the traditions of the village would come to rule when her father died.

On his child's tenth birthday, the lord called for the village deacon, his most trusted servant and friend. The deacon was himself a person of great importance in the village, with enough wealth to have long since retired. But the deacon loved his lord and remained available, particularly for special occasions. This was a special occasion.

"Deacon," said the lord, "it is very important that my child receive instruction in leadership so that she will be prepared to rule this village when I am no longer here."

"Yes, Lord," said the deacon, bowing.

"On the far side of the desert valley is a great teacher who can offer my child these lessons in leadership," said the lord. "But I cannot take her there because of my duties. You are the one I trust to take her there safely."

"Yes, Lord," said the deacon. "How shall the child travel, Lord?"

"Our village has one pony. She will ride it," answered the lord.

"How shall I find this great teacher, Lord?" asked the deacon. The lord gave him a map.

"How shall we carry our supplies, Lord?" the deacon inquired.

"I will lend you my slave," said the lord. "He will carry the supplies for the journey."

And so it was. Early the next morning, the lord led his child out to the village square, where the deacon was waiting with the pony and the slave. The slave stooped so the child could climb on his back and onto the pony.

319

Then, after the slave secured the pack of supplies on his back, the deacon led them out of the village and down the mountain.

The party traveled without incident throughout that first day and into a second, but then they experienced an unexpected setback—a rockslide. As the slave and the deacon both sprang to protect the child, a rock shattered the slave's right leg.

"Leave me here, Deacon, so you and the child can continue your journey," the slave said through clenched teeth while the deacon bound his leg to a splint.

"No," said the deacon. "I cannot leave you to the danger of the wolves on this mountain, for you are the lord's slave. You will ride the pony. I will carry the supplies, and the child can walk."

And so it was. They continued their journey through the remainder of that day and into the next. Now it was the slave who rode while the deacon carried the pack of supplies and the child followed behind. Then, just as they were nearing the bottom of the mountain, there was a second mishap. This time it was the pony that stepped in a crevice and injured its leg. After the pony had been treated and released to return to the village, the deacon pondered what they could do. Finally, he spoke. "I will carry the slave. Our supplies are much lighter now, for we have completed more than half our journey. Child, you must try to carry them."

And so it was. After a quick glance at the map, the deacon led them to the bottom of the mountain and out onto the desert valley, the slave fixed on his back in the same fashion that the pack of supplies was now secured on the back of the child.

Three hours later, they lost the map. A sudden gust of wind caught the deacon by surprise while he was studying which way they should go. Disheartened, the deacon sat down and put his head in his hands, wondering how he could have failed his lord so badly.

Then the slave spoke. "Deacon, you may not know this, but I was raised in this desert valley. I believe that if you can continue to carry me, and the child can continue to carry the supplies, I can remember and tell you which way to go."

And so it was. Through the rest of that day and the next morning, the slave chose their path as the deacon carried him, and the child followed behind with the supplies. They had almost reached the far side of the desert valley, and then, they experienced yet another setback.

Again it was a sudden wind that caught them by surprise, but this time it was a huge and violent sandstorm. Both the deacon and the slave huddled over the child to protect her. When the storm finally subsided, the child was safe, but both the deacon and the slave were left blinded.

Tears of pain mixed with tears of dejection in the eyes of both men. They had come so far, and now there was no way to continue. It was then that the child spoke.

"Deacon, Slave, we have come so close to our goal because the two of you are so brave and so good. I believe that if you, Deacon, can continue to carry the slave, and if you, Slave, can continue to remember the way, then I can hold the deacon's hand and lead us."

And so it was. Once again, the party continued its journey. Now, instead of following at the rear, the child led them, holding the blind deacon's hand while the blind and crippled slave called out directions from the deacon's back. Three hours later, they reached the entrance of a tremendous cave.

The child described the cave entrance to the others. The deacon confirmed that it sounded like the place described on the map. The slave added that it sounded like the place of which his desert people spoke. The child approached the cave and called out, "Great teacher, are you there?"

Out from the cave came her father, the lord. "What have you learned, child?" he asked.

The child stood straight and tall as she answered, "I have learned that to be the deacon of the lord, or the child of the lord, or the slave of the lord, is all the same thing. We are all the lord's and the lord is ours, and that is what matters."

"You have learned well, my child," said the lord. Then he hugged his daughter, and healed his deacon and his slave, and they all went home.

(There are three Greek words in the New Testament that can be translated as *servant*. *Doulos* is often translated as *slave*. *Diakanos* is often translated as *deacon*. *Teknon* is usually translated as *child*. This story was inspired by Mark 9:33–37.)

Walkertown

Once upon a time, long, long ago and far, far away, there was a place called Walkertown.

Walkertown was about two-thirds of the way up the steepest, highest mountain you can imagine. Homes and shops were located wherever ledges in the contour of the mountain would allow. Narrow pathways were carved out of the mountain's side, as were the small terraced gardens and the small town square. And the people of Walkertown walked everywhere they went.

Walkertown was not a place where many new things occurred. The people tended their crops, livestock, and children, traded goods and an occasional yarn, and were generally content. There was really no other place to go or anything else to do.

Oh, there was a legend that at one time, there had been a bridge spanning the distance between Walkertown's mountain and the adjacent mountain, which was just as steep and nearly as high. The deep valley between the two mountains was overgrown and impassable, but the legend spoke of a village on that other mountain and how the people of the villages would cross the bridge and visit each other. It was even said that people of the two villages were related by many marriages that had taken place.

No one in Walkertown, however, had ever seen that village or that bridge. No one knew anyone who had seen that bridge, or even knew anyone who knew anyone who had ever seen it. It was a legend, and although it came up in conversation once in a while, people didn't think about it often. They were generally content with what they knew in their own lives. And of course, they walked everywhere they went.

There was one other legend. It described a lake at the top of Walkertown's mountain that was the most beautiful place you could imagine, with clear, still, deep blue waters surrounded by lush flower-laden meadows and vibrantly green forests. To hear of it was to yearn to go there, but no one in Walkertown had ever seen it. The mountainside above Walkertown was far too steep to climb. No one knew anyone who had ever seen the lake, or even knew anyone who knew anyone who had ever seen it. It was a legend, and it wasn't talked about often because the people were focused on the way things were. And as you already know, they walked everywhere they went.

Then came the day someone rang the town bell. Everyone in town walked very quickly toward the town square, because the town bell never rang except to call the annual town meeting, and it wasn't time for that! When they arrived at the square, they could see who had rung the bell: Billy and Beth, two young adults who had always been well liked and never caused any disruptions, at least before now. "What's this all about?" asked voices in the crowd. "Why did you ring the bell?" "What's wrong?"

Beth and Billy stepped forward, gesturing for the crowd to quiet. They then announced that they had decided to leave Walkertown—that they were going to attempt to climb down the mountain, cross the valley, and find the village of the legend.

"You can't do that!" "You'll be killed!" The whole population of Walkertown was aghast! "No one who has tried to even reach that valley has ever returned to tell the tale."

But the reaction of the townspeople could not change the minds of Billy and Beth. After handshakes and hugs with family and friends still clamoring for them to stay, they shouldered their packs and walked to the lower end of town. When the pathway ended, they kept going down the mountain and out of sight.

The people of Walkertown talked about Beth and Billy for weeks, wondering why they had left and what would happen to them. Over time, though, the talk began to die down and things began to return to normal. They tended their crops, their livestock, and their children, and as always, they walked everywhere they went.

But then the town bell rang again! "What is going on this time?" the townspeople asked while they hurried to the square. As each person arrived, they saw standing, right where they had stood before, none other than Billy and Beth.

"Are you all right?" "What happened to you?" The questions flooded toward the two young people. "Did you reach the valley?" "Did you find the village of the legend?"

Beth raised her hand for silence, assuring them their questions would be answered when everyone got there. After a few minutes, Billy stepped forward and spoke. "Beth and I are all right. Traveling down the mountain was very hard. It is steep everywhere, and as we came nearer to the valley, the mountainside was overgrown with thickets of briars and thorns. But we were committed to our task and kept going even though it would sometimes take a whole day to travel just a few yards."

"Then why are you back here?" cried out someone from the crowd."

Again Beth raised her hand. "We were determined to find the other village," she said. "But after four weeks, while we were still trying to reach the bottom of our mountain, we met someone. And he showed us something so wonderful, we knew we had to abandon our journey and return home to show you."

"You met someone?" The crowd buzzed in confusion. "Who could you meet on the side of the mountain?" "Where did he come from?" "What could someone show you that would be so important to us?"

Billy stepped forward without a word. He reached behind his head and lifted the black cloak on his back to the side. Then he spread his wings and rose up from the square into the air! Immediately, Beth reached behind her head, lifting aside her black cloak, and spread her wings, joining Billy in the air. They soared over the heads of the crowd, back and forth, laughing and calling out, "Come on! Pull your cloaks aside. You can do it, too!"

(You see, I had not yet described to you one thing about the people of Walkertown. They all wore long black cloaks hanging down from their shoulders and over their backs.)

Well, you may or may not be able to guess how the townspeople reacted when they saw what Beth and Billy were doing.

One group looked up and started yelling, "Come down from there!" "You'll kill yourselves!" "You must be crazy!" Then looking at each other, they said, "Well, I'm not going to just stand here and watch those fools kill themselves." And they grabbed the hands of their children and their grandchildren and walked off the square.

Another group looked up skeptically, saying, "This must be a trick." "They're using ropes or wires or something." "I can't believe they think we would fall for something like this." And shaking their heads, they grabbed the hands of their children and their grandchildren and walked off the square.

A third group reacted a little more deliberately. "Well, what will those young people think of next?" they said. "I don't know about you, Gertrude, but walking was good enough for my parents and good enough for my grandparents, and it's good enough for me." Taking the hands of their children and grandchildren, that is exactly what they did.

Beth and Billy folded their wings and gently landed on a deserted town square. "What are we to do?" they wondered. "Should we just leave? Perhaps go try to find that other village?" No, they knew they had to stay. They had to try to get the townspeople to understand. Over the next several days, they approached every family member, every friend, every person they could, but the result was always the same. People didn't want to hear what they had to say and didn't want to see what they had to show them.

Billy and Beth finally gave up. Sitting down on a door stoop, they began to make plans to leave. Then they noticed someone coming toward them. It was Old Joe. He had lived out just beyond the high end of town for as long as they could remember. They watched as Old Joe came closer, and then they saw him slowly reach behind his head and lift aside his old, tattered, dull black cloak. He slowly spread a pair of wings that looked as dull and tattered as his cloak, and began to rise into the air!

Beth and Billy sprang to their feet. Throwing aside their cloaks, they leaped into the air and soared around Old Joe. Their questions flew at Old Joe even faster than they did. "How long have you known?" "Have you done this before?" "Are you the only one?"

Old Joe waited for them to calm down a little, and then explained that he had discovered many years earlier what could happen when you pulled your cloak aside. He had been as excited then as they were now. But when he had tried to share it with others, they had all turned their backs on him, cloaks firmly in place. In the end, he had just given up trying and given up flying.

But now there were three! As they hovered, wondering what to do next, they heard a giggle. Looking down, they saw a group of children looking up at them from the alley entrance. All of a sudden one of the little children reached back, pulled her little black cloak aside, spread her little wings, and ... *bruuuuuuup* ... flew into the air! In an instant, the other children had reached behind their backs to their cloaks. *Bruuuuuup ... bruuuuuuup ... bruuuuuuup!* The sky above the town was filled with flying children darting left and right, up and down.

Shouting with joy, Billy, Beth, and Old Joe joined them. What an incredible sight it was for the townspeople as they looked up to see what was happening.

One group said, "Why, I thought it was so dangerous, but look, even a little child can do it." And they reached behind their backs, lifted their cloaks aside, spread their wings, and flew into the air.

Another group looked up and said, "Well, I thought it was a trick, but there is not enough rope or wire in the whole town to explain this." They reached behind their backs, lifted their cloaks aside, spread their wings, and flew into the air.

And there was that third group. "Now, I've always said that if walking was good enough for my parents and my grandparents, it was good enough for me. But I'm telling you, if Gertrude up there can do it, I can do it!" Reaching behind their backs, they lifted their cloaks aside and joined the rest of the town in the air.

"Where should we go?" someone asked.

"Let's go find the village of the legend!" another answered.

So they all flew together out past the town and away from their mountain, high above that deep, overgrown valley. As they approached the other mountain, they saw the other village. Soaring above it, they looked down and saw people who looked a lot like them.

"Come on!" the people of Walkertown called out. "You can do it, too." Looking up, those people in the village below began to pull their cloaks aside, spread their wings, and rise into the sky.

A few people in that village discovered, after moving their cloaks, that their wings were stunted and crippled. They couldn't fly on their own. But others from both villages began to swoop down. Gripping the ones who could not fly under their arms, they lifted them into the air with the others, and soon, everyone from both villages was flying together in one tremendous cloud of wonder, wings, and laughter.

"Where should we go now?" someone asked.

"Let's go find the lake of the legend!" others shouted.

They rose high on the wind currents, back over the valley, and up, up to the peak of Walkertown's mountain. There it was, just as the legend described. No one from either village had ever seen or dreamed of anything more beautiful than this deep blue lake bordered by meadows and forests of so many shades of green.

But then, as they flew directly over the lake, the people saw a reflection in the lake far more beautiful than even the lake itself. It was the reflection of a place higher than that highest of mountains, and with one voice, they all said, "Oh! Let's go there."

Upward they flew in a long spiral, higher and higher. As they rose, those being carried saw that their wings were changing. They were no longer crippled! Shouting for joy, they cast out from those carrying them and flew on their own.

Still higher they all climbed, and then several saw a shining figure with an enormous wingspan soaring far above them. Beth and Billy cried out, "It's Him! It's Him! That's the One who showed us how to fly!"

All the people saw Him, and as they rose to meet and follow Him, they began to shine as He shined. Higher and higher He led them until they came to the glorious place they had seen reflected in the lake, a place beyond our ability to imagine.

They're still there.

Susie and Angelique

This is a story neither long ago nor far away. It is the story of Susie and Angelique.

Susie was an adorable baby who became a beautiful little girl and a wonderful young woman. She was a loving, obedient daughter, a terrific student, and a loyal friend.

What made her even more amazing was that she was a loyal friend to so many people. Susie truly cared for everyone she met. She accepted people as they were, seeing value in them as they were and treating each of them as special. If there had been an award in high school or college for the person most likely to go to heaven, Susie would have won it hands down. And so it came as a surprise to no one when, upon graduation from college, this young Catholic woman announced her intention to become a nun.

Susie passed through the training and rites to become a nun with the same grace and ease that defined everything she had done before. When Sister Susie arrived at her first parish appointment in the suburbs outside a major city and met the priest in charge, he asked her what type of outreach ministry she would like to make part of her parish service. Susie did not hesitate in responding. "Prison ministry," she said.

The very next day, Susie drove the parish Volkswagen around the bypass loop encircling the city. From there she took an old rural road to the state prison at the edge of the county. When she arrived at the prison, the very first person she visited was Angelique.

Angelique was, like Susie, an adorable baby and a beautiful little girl. But her life had taken a very different turn. You see, Angelique was raised in the inner part of that nearby city. She had never known her father. She saw her mother die from a drug overdose. Angelique had taken drugs herself. She had committed several what we for some reason call "petty" crimes, and now she was in prison for what was anything but a "petty" crime. She was on death row, scheduled for execution in two weeks for killing a police officer.

Angelique had testified that she had killed out of self-defense, and tried to explain how this particular policeman was corrupt and brutal, but with a track record like Angelique's, who was going to believe her?

Not that any of this made a difference to Susie. Susie looked at Angelique just as she had looked at everyone else all of her life, seeing value in her just as she was. She reached out to Angelique in compassion, as she always had. But this time the response was not the same.

"Where do you get off, girl!" Angelique said. "You don't know anything about me, who I am or where I've been, what I've done or what's been done to me. Unless you've walked in my shoes, sister, you've got no right to tell me nothing." And just like that, the visit was over.

The story, however, was not over.

When Susie left the prison that day, she didn't get back on the bypass loop to her suburban parish. Instead, she drove into the heart of the city. Leaving the car in long-term parking, she went into a hole-in-the-wall clothing store and bought an outfit almost identical to one she had seen in a picture in Angelique's cell: a short, tight leather skirt; a sequined tank top; and black lace hose. She then went to a nearby hole-in-the-wall beauty parlor, where she had her hair teased and colored like she had seen in the same picture, and put on more makeup than she had worn in all the rest of her life put together. Finally she went into a little shoe store where she bought a pair of four-inch spiked heels. It was comical to see her come wobbling out onto the sidewalk.

But you can learn a lot about walking in heels in twenty blocks, and that's how far she had to go to get to the inner part of the city where Angelique had spent her life. On the way, there were several catcalls, some dirty and some just mean.

When Susie got to Angelique's neighborhood, she first arranged for a place to stay: a one-room basement flat, no windows and cash in advance. Because the rent took all her cash, she next went to the welfare office and stood in that long line of shame so she could get enough money for some groceries.

Then she went job hunting. But there weren't many jobs available in that neighborhood. Even where there were a few openings, they were not interested in someone who looked like Susie now looked. And her vows kept her from the one profession in this neighborhood that was ready to use her. Instead Susie stopped looking for a job and started trying to meet people, to see how she might be their friend.

This neighborhood wasn't used to someone like Susie. Time after time, day after day, her offers of kindness were rejected. There was a drive-by shooting one afternoon and a small child was hit. As the mother rushed her wounded child into their tenement, Susie followed, hoping to use her nurse's training to help. But the woman locked the door and wouldn't open it for anyone.

At the end of the week, still jobless and friendless, Susie went back to the welfare office for more grocery money, but this time they told her, "Honey ... no babies, no money."

Susie was on the way back to her flat that day when the gang got her. The city sanitation workers found her unconscious in an alley several hours later. They took her to the indigent ward of the old hospital that served this neighborhood, where they began treating her injuries—injuries so serious, she was still not approved for discharge six days later when she sneaked out of the hospital. She had to go, you see, because Angelique was scheduled for execution the next morning.

When Susie arrived at the prison, it took a while to convince the prison guards that she was who she said she was. And when she finally made it to Angelique's cell, it took a while to convince Angelique. But when she did, what a difference! You see, now Angelique could look at Susie and say, "You've walked in my shoes! You've been where I've been, done what I've done, had done to you what's been done to me."

They began to talk together. It wasn't long before they began to cry together, and then laugh together, and then pray together. All night long, they talked, cried, laughed, and prayed.

When the warden and guard came for Angelique the next morning, she actually had the strength to go with them on that long walk down that short hallway. Susie was beside her every step of the way.

Then, when they arrived at the end of the hallway and the guard began to remove Angelique's handcuffs so she could be strapped into the electric chair, what had been an amazing story became incredible.

Susie stepped forward ahead of Angelique and sat down in that chair. The guard looked at the warden, who looked at Susie and then slowly nodded. The guard strapped Susie down, reached over and pulled the switch, and Susie died. They led Angelique outside the prison gate and told her she was free to go.

Angelique stood outside the prison gate for a long time, trying to come to some understanding of what had just happened. When she did finally leave, it wasn't to go back to the inner city. She went around that bypass loop to the suburbs, to Susie's parish and the office of Susie's chief priest, where she promptly announced her decision to become a nun.

Just imagine how that priest must have reacted to such a request from such a woman. It wasn't just her criminal record. She had had virtually no education from the standpoint of school or church. She wasn't even baptized!

But Angelique was not to be denied. It took years to get her GED and college training, and to become acquainted with Scripture and church traditions. It took more years to complete the training and rites to become a nun and receive all the approvals necessary to enter Sister Susie's order. But she did it, and she was baptized very early in the process. Oh, what a baptism!

And, oh, what a ministry! When Angelique became Sister Angelique, she went straight back to the prison and the inner city. Everywhere she reached out, people would look at her and say, "Hey, you've walked in my shoes! You've been where I've been, done what I've done, had done to you what's been done to me." Countless lives were transformed!

After many wonderful years of blessed ministry changing the lives of precious people, an eighty-five-year-old Angelique left her worn-out body behind and went to heaven. When she got there, who do you think was waiting for her? Susie! And the hug they shared was the hug of two people who knew each other's hearts because they had walked in each other's shoes.

As they began to walk together on this new journey, clad in robes of light and shoes of glory, they could see with unveiled eyes the One walking with them who had always walked with them—the One who is glory Himself! He is the One who walks not just in their shoes, but in your shoes and my shoes—our Lord and Savior Jesus Christ.

Enoch

Imagine a little boy. It is thousands of years ago, thousands of years even before Jesus is born. This little boy would get up every morning, and he would play with the other little girls and boys, laugh, and do his chores.

Every now and then something very special would happen for this little boy. He would see this old, old man come slowly out of his hut and take a seat on a large rock in the sun. And the little boy would run up to him crying, "Great-grandfather, Great-grandfather!"

The old man would grab the little boy up and hug him, and say, "What do you want, little Enoch?"

And little Enoch would say, "Tell me a story, Great-grandfather. Tell me a story!"

"What story do you want to hear?" the old man would ask.

"Tell me about the garden, Great-grandfather," the little boy would answer. "Tell me about the garden."

"Ah ... the garden," said the old man, smiling. "It was so beautiful. There were plants and trees everywhere, and flowers all year-round. You see, there were four seasons—spring and summer, fall and winter, just like here, but it was never too hot or too cold. You didn't even have to wear clothes to keep warm or protect your skin from the sun."

"People went naked?" asked little Enoch with a giggle.

"Yes, but it didn't bother anyone then. It was just Great-grandmother and me, so it was all right." He paused. "It was just right."

"Tell me about the animals, Great-grandfather."

"Well," answered the old man. "There was every kind of animal you can imagine in the garden—sheep and cattle, lions and tigers, elephants and hippopotamuses." The old man reached over and mussed the boy's hair. "Animals like horses, only with longer legs and long, long necks, and

332

spots. We called them giraffes, and they were so tall, they could eat the tops of trees."

"Did the lions and tigers eat the giraffes, like they do our sheep, Great-grandfather?"

"No, Enoch. None of the animals ate other animals. Everyone and everything was at peace. Wolves and lambs, lions and cattle would lie down together to sleep. Great-grandmother and I would run and play with them all. We would rub their bellies and, when needed, take thorns out of their paws, because we were supposed to take care of the animals. And we all could eat all the food we wanted because of the fruits and vegetables that came from the plants and trees."

"What did they taste like, Great-grandfather?"

"Oh, Enoch, they all tasted different and all tasted wonderful. What's your favorite food?"

"Pizza!" shouted out the little boy.

"Oh, there were all kinds of pizza plants—cheese flavored, pepperoni, even anchovy." The boy made a silly grimace. "What other food do you like, Enoch?"

"Beefsteak," said the boy with a slightly guilty look.

The old man laughed, "Well, there were huge tomatoes in the garden that tasted just like the best beefsteak you ever ate! Then for dessert, there was one tree we called the Tree of Life, which had twelve different kinds of fruit on it, and when you ate that fruit, it gave you such energy! You never got sick, and you never got tired, and you never got old, like I am."

"And while you ate," the old man added, "or played, or just sat back in the sun like we are doing now, the birds would sing. Birds were everywhere, thousands upon thousands of them, in every color and size, and they would all sing their beautiful songs in an incredible harmony, praising the Lord."

"Was that the best part, Great-grandfather?"

"No, little Enoch. As wondrous as the singing of the birds was, it wasn't the best part. The best part was walking with the Lord. Sometimes the Lord would come in the morning, at sunrise, and sometimes He would come with the evening breeze. We would walk, and we would talk, and He would tell us we were His very own."

"What did the Lord look like, Great-grandfather?"

The old man thought a moment. "I'm afraid I don't exactly remember, little Enoch. It seems like at times the Lord would be there walking and look like you or me or someone in the village—a human being. And at other times I remember not really seeing Him at all. I just knew He was there—a Spirit that you can't see with your eyes or touch with your hand. But either way, you feel and see and experience everything different just because the Lord is there with you. There's nothing like it, nothing more wonderful—nothing more real."

"I want to go to the garden, Great-grandfather!" shouted little Enoch. "Right now!"

A sad look crept into the old man's eyes. "I'm sorry, Enoch. You can't go to the garden right now. Great-grandmother and I made a terrible mistake, and nobody can go right now."

"But I want to walk with the Lord!" replied the boy.

A smile returned to the old man's face. "Ah … now, that you can do, little Enoch." The old man laughed and repeated, "That you can do."

"How?" Enoch asked, jumping on the old man's lap and climbing up right next to his face.

"Believe, little Enoch. Believe in the Lord. Believe that He is with you and that He loves you more than anyone else can. And He will walk with you, and talk with you, and tell you you're His very own.

"Then one day, little precious Enoch, if you walk with the Lord, He will take you to that garden you so much want to see. You will live there together with Him and all the other people who have walked with Him, forever."

The old man kissed the boy, and the boy kissed him back. Together they sat on the rock in the sun while they listened to the birds … and praised the Lord.

[Read Genesis 5:18-24, and then "count the years" in Genesis 5:1-24]

A Christmas Diary

I love Christmas! Yes, we have commercialized and trivialized it, often giving Santa and Rudolph center stage instead of our Lord. And we Christians will often schedule so many activities at Christmastime that we are challenged to believe there can be a silent, holy night.

Nevertheless, during the Christmas season, everyone has to spend at least a little time thinking about Jesus Christ, because all of us, believers and not-yet-believers, know Christmas is His birthday. Even for not-yet-believers, Christmas is the birthday of a man whose life forever changed the course of history. For believers, it is the birthday of the man whose life, death, and resurrection changed their everlasting lives and the face and future of all creation. Oh, I love Christmas!

Just a few years after the Lord drew me to a life of faith in Him, I spent some time imagining how God felt about Christmas. Please let me share with you what I wrote: "A Christmas Diary."

"Today is the day! I realize many people think God doesn't get excited, but I am perfectly excited! I am eternally Father, but today I get to experience my fatherhood in a new way. Today I get to experience birth in a new way. Today I become a man.

I will live among the people I love for a while as Emmanuel. I will teach them as Wonderful Counselor. I will show them signs and wonders as the Son of Mighty God. And then as Prince of Peace, I will bring peace between my people and me by embracing the new name I give myself: "Jesus." "God saves"!

I will die for them as their Savior. I will rise for them as the resurrection. I will come live within them as the life everlasting!

Whom shall I invite to this, my birthday? Who will best bring comfort to my mother, Mary, the woman who will bear me, nurse me, raise me, and watch me be crucified? Who will encourage Joseph, my obedient stepfather, the man who will teach me his work during the time I prepare to begin my work?

I will invite the angels to my birthday, because there must be music (I love music!) and because those who hear of this birthday must know it is divine.

I will invite shepherds to my birthday, because I have come for the poor and the simple, and because I am the Great Shepherd.

I will invite wise men to my birthday, because I come not just for the poor and simple, nor just for the Jew, and because I desire not just men's hearts but their minds. The magi gifts will help my people understand the gift of giving. The angels and shepherds will help them understand joy.

Finally, as my most special guests, I will invite the children to my birthday—those young of mind and body and those just young of heart. They will see me lying in a manger, a food trough, because I am the Bread of Life. They will see my star because I am the Light of the World.

And as they hold my infant body so carefully in the arms of their imagination, they will see that out of God's love for them, God becomes vulnerable to them. All powerful and all knowing, never ending: because I choose to love them, I choose to feel the pain when they don't love me back.

Dear diary, it will be a very merry Christmas! For in being born as a child, I will give birth to my children, and we will love each other forever!

The Color of Church

Written as a puppet skit, with a black girl puppet (MR) and a white boy puppet (JP), this can also be performed as a live skit with actors or read like a story. As we begin, it is Sunday morning. Our young boy is sitting on the front porch of his new home when our young girl walks by.

MR: Hello.

JP: Hello.

MR: I've never seen you in this neighborhood before.

JP: I just moved here.

MR: Oh ... well, my name is Mary Ruth Campbell.

JP: Hi! My name is James Phillip Hamilton the Third. My Mama Cheryl calls me Jimmy, but everybody else calls me JP.

MR: Well, hello JP! [*Pauses.*] You know today is Sunday. Do you go to church?

JP: Yeah, when someone will take me.

MR: Do you want to go to Sunday school and church with me? I go to St. Mark House of Prayer right down the street.

JP: Well, uh ... I've never been to a black church before.

337

MR: Oh, we're not a black church.

JP: You go to a white church?

MR: No.

JP: I don't understand. I mean, I know I'm new around here, but all I see in this neighborhood are black people and white people.

MR: Uh, uh … that's not what my great-uncle Samuel says. He says we're all brown. Some of us are light brown and some of us are dark brown, but we're all brown … just like the dirt God made us from.

JP: So you go to a brown church!

MR: No!

JP: But you said you were all brown.

MR: We were, but now as Christians we've been washed in the blood of Jesus!

JP: So you go to a red church.

MR: No!

JP: But blood is red, isn't it?

MR: Yes … and Jesus' blood flowed red when He died on the cross. But He isn't there anymore. He's the King of Kings and Lord of Lords and sits at the right hand of God Almighty in a big purple robe!

JP: Oh, so you go to a purple church.

MR: No, JP! Jesus is the King! He wears the purple. We get His Holy Spirit.

JP: What color is that?

MR: The Holy Spirit doesn't have a color, silly. The Holy Spirit is invisible.

JP: So you go to an invisible church.

MR: No!

JP: But I thought you said …

MR: My great-uncle Samuel says that some churches act like they're invisible, but that we aren't supposed to be invisible … because if the church is invisible, no one will know how to find Jesus.

JP: Well, if your church isn't black and it isn't white and it isn't brown and it isn't red and it isn't purple and it isn't invisible, then just what color is your church?

MR: My great-uncle Samuel says that our church is love colored!

JP: Love colored?

MR: That's right. He says that when you look at our church, all you are supposed to see is love.

JP: Wow!

MR: So … do you want to come to church with me?

JP: You bet. Your church sounds cool!

MR: No.

JP: No? What do you mean, no, this time?

MR: Our church isn't cool. We don't have air-conditioning yet.

JP: Oh.

MR: But my great-uncle Samuel says air-conditioning isn't so important when you're love colored. Amen?

JP: Amen!

Both: [*To congregation.*] Amen?

God Bless You

Doug Tweed

Printed in the United States
By Bookmasters